IRISH WRITERS

in the

IRISH AMERICAN PRESS,

1882–1964

Stephen G. Butler

University of Massachusetts Press
Amherst and Boston

ISBN 978-1-62534-367-3 (paper); 366-6 (hardcover)

Designed by Sally Nichols
Set in Adobe Caslon Pro
Printed and bound by Maple Press, Inc.

Cover design by Patricia Duque Campos
Cover art by John Rooney, pen and ink *Portraits of Irish
Writers Brendan Behan, Oscar Wilde, and James Joyce.*
Copyright © 2017, johnrooneyillustration.com/impressum.

Library of Congress Cataloging-in-Publication Data

Names: Butler, Stephen G., author.
Title: Irish writers in the Irish American press, 1882–1964 / Stephen G.
Butler.
Description: Amherst and Boston : University of Massachusetts Press,
2018. |Includes bibliographical references and index. |
Identifiers: LCCN 2018019135 (print) | LCCN 2018042820 (ebook) | ISBN
9781613766125 (e-book) | ISBN 9781613766132 (e-book) | ISBN
9781625343673 (pbk.) | ISBN 9781625343666 (hardcover)
Subjects: LCSH: English literature—Irish authors—Public opinion. |
Authors, Irish—19th century—Public opinion. | Authors, Irish—20th
century—Public opinion. | Public opinion—United States. | Irish
American journalists—Attitudes. | Irish Americans—Attitudes. | Irish
Americans—Ethnic identity—History.
Classification: LCC PR8752 (ebook) | LCC PR8752 .B88 2018 (print) | DDC
820.9/9415—dc23
LC record available at https://lccn.loc.gov/2018019135

British Library Cataloguing-in-Publication Data
A catalog record for this book is available from the British Library.

of Whom shall we say?
while kinderwardens minded their twinsbed, therenow
theystood, the sycomores, all four of them
—Finnegans Wake, 555.6–8

This book is dedicated
to the four women in my life
who have made it round and full and whole:
my wife Erin, my twins Brigid and
Lily, and my baby Adare.

Contents

Acknowledgments

THEY SAY IT takes a village to raise a child. The same could be said of publishing a book.

My first word of appreciation must go to my parents, Matthew and Anne, immigrants from de Valera's Ireland who met and married in John Lindsay's New York City. It is to them I owe my Irish American identity and my abiding interest in Irish culture.

Throughout my formal education, I'm very lucky to have been encouraged to pursue my interests in reading and writing, literature and history, by the following teachers and mentors: at Cathedral Prep, Father Joseph Gibino, Dan O'Keefe, Joe Russo, Brian Payne, and Monsignor Richard Marchese; at Iona College, Brother Robert Durning (r.i.p.), Cedric Winslow, Hugh Short, George Bournoutian, Deborah Williams, John Mahon, and Brother Charles Quinn (r.i.p.); at CCNY, Bill Herman (r.i.p.); at Drew University, C. Wyatt Evans.

But of all the teachers and mentors I've had the good fortune to meet, none have been so unfailingly helpful as the members of my dissertation committee at Drew University, Jonathan E. Rose and Christine Kinealy. Jonathan's invaluable counsel has helped guide the project that became this book from its conception to its publication. And Christine's tireless example and continuous encouragement motivated me to keep on working and keep on writing.

I also owe a word of thanks to Frank Naughton, editor of *New York Irish History*, who has provided me numerous opportunities to share my work in print. And it was Frank who introduced me, fortuitously, to Mary McGlynn and Terry Byrne, co-chairs of the Columbia University Seminar on Irish Studies. The ideas articulated in this book have benefited from discussions in that seminar. I am much obliged to Mary and Terry for offering a forum to present, discuss, and refine my insights. I want to express my appreciation as well to the Schoff Fund at the University Seminars at Columbia University for its help in publication.

I would also like to thank Pat Hoy and Denice Martone for giving a disheveled, sleep-deprived new father a chance to teach in the Expository Writing Program at New York University. Knowing that my career did not hinge on the publication of this study has made finishing it that much more enjoyable.

At University of Massachusetts Press, Brian Halley deserves my special acknowledgment. Brian believed in this project from the outset, and advised and assisted me through every stage of the publication process with both patience and wisdom.

Last and certainly not least, I owe a deep debt gratitude to my wife, Erin, who, down all the years, down all the days, has never stood in the way of my dreams, as troublesome as they must often have seemed.

IRISH WRITERS
in the
IRISH AMERICAN
PRESS,
1882–1964

An Audience of Some Importance

T HIS PROJECT HAD its genesis in my first semester of graduate
school at Drew University when, during an Intro to Historiography course, I had my initial, disorienting encounter with Daniel Patrick Moynihan's seminal 1963 essay "The Irish." Contemporary readers
are perhaps more familiar with Moynihan because of the problematic legacy of his 1965 report *The Negro Family: The Case for National
Action,* a legacy that Ta-Nehisi Coates explored in his provocative
think piece "The Black Family in the Age of Mass Incarceration."[1] Yet
the negative consequences of what's often simply called the Moynihan
Report should not obscure the importance of the book that contains
his essay on the American Irish, *Beyond the Melting Pot: The Negroes,
Puerto Ricans, Jews, Italians, and Irish of New York City.* Moynihan co-
authored *Beyond the Melting Pot* with Nathan Glazer, and the two are
often credited with helping to establish the field of ethnic studies as
we know it today.[2] Despite appearing more than half a century ago,
Moynihan's essay is still read and anthologized, no doubt in large part
because of the dearth of historiography focusing on twentieth-century
Irish America.[3] In *The American Irish: A History,* Kevin Kenny notes

that "twentieth-century Irish-American political history has been studied in depth, but the social, cultural and even religious history of this period are still in their infancy compared to the rich body of historical literature that has been produced on the nineteenth century."[4]

When, as a novice scholar, I first read Moynihan's essay on the Irish, I could not help marveling at a work so full of intelligent divination, however inaccurate. Moynihan was not a historian but a sociologist, and thus his critical viewpoint was Janus-faced, issuing seer-like claims about the past as well as the future. Moynihan's observations about the then current state of the Irish in New York were shrewd and insightful, but his forecasts about the future of Irish America were fascinatingly wrong. What the future Democratic senator from New York correctly and wistfully observed in the early 1960s were large numbers of Irish Americans assimilating into the lower middle class and leaving for the suburbs, no doubt buying lawnmowers and registering Republican on the way out. But in a addition to a diluting of urban-proletarian essence and a severing of ties with the Democratic Party, Moynihan identified three other major trends that he believed would contribute to the disappearance of a recognizable Irish identity in New York City in particular, and America more generally: "the decline of immigration, the fading of Irish nationalism, and the relative absence of Irish cultural influence from abroad on the majority of American Irish."[5] Moynihan's prescience in identifying these three factors should be applauded since, in fact, they certainly did have a major impact on Irish American identity—just in reverse of what he anticipated. Put another way, most of Moynihan's prognostications about the death of the American Irish might have come to pass if a funny thing had not happened: as in the famous song about Tim Finnegan, the corpse arose in the middle of the wake.[6]

First, in the late 1960s, sectarian violence reignited in the six counties of Northern Ireland, fomenting Irish American political activism and reawakening a passionate, if sometimes simplistic, Irish Catholic nationalism.[7] Then, during the 1980s, unemployment in Ireland rose to unprecedented modern levels, resulting in a huge influx of young undocumented Irish immigrants into traditional Irish American strongholds such as New York, Boston, Chicago, and San Francisco.[8]

And finally, Irish cultural products as diverse as U2, *The Crying Game*, and *Riverdance* began being consumed in huge numbers, not just by Irish Americans but by all Americans.[9]

Having come of age during this resurrection of Irish American identity and this flowering of Irish culture in America, I was shocked to learn from Moynihan about a time not very long ago when Irish Americans existed in willful ignorance of, exhibited ambivalence toward, or at times even exulted in an adversarial relationship with the creators of culture in Ireland. As a prime illustration of this antagonistic relationship, Moynihan referred to the infamous reaction to John Millington Synge's *Playboy of the Western World*.[10] But Moynihan also noted that, much more recently, Brendan Behan had been banned by Judge James Comerford from marching in the 1961 Saint Patrick's Day parade. Even more puzzling than the treatment of Behan was Moynihan's observation that "ironically, it is precisely those persons who were most attached to the Irish cause and Irish culture of the nineteenth century who are having the most difficulty maintaining such attachments in the present time" and that "those who would most value their Irishness seem least able to respond" to the literary achievements of "Shaw, Wilde, Yeats, O'Casey, Joyce, and the like." Moynihan explained that these "Protestants, agnostics, atheists, socialists, communists, homosexuals, drunkards, and mockers . . . have had but few traits that commend themselves to the Catholic middle class."[11]

This last observation was particularly puzzling because, on the wall of my own lower-middle-class Catholic bedroom in Woodside, Queens, these degenerate Protestants, agnostics, atheists, socialists, communists, homosexuals, drunkards, and mockers were celebrated and proudly displayed in a posterized pantheon purchased upstate in an East Durham gift shop during the annual Irish Festival. Puzzling because that same posterized pantheon, titled simply "Irish Writers," was plastered on the walls of barrooms named after the literary creations of these very degenerates, bars such as the late, lamented Bloom's on Queens Boulevard in Sunnyside, bars wherein many lower-middle-class Irish Americans like me did their drinking. And besides Bloom's, my youthful ramblings around the metropolitan area had also brought me to watering holes such as Yeats' Tavern on Bell Boulevard in Bayside,

Behan's Pub on Katonah Avenue in Woodlawn, Ulysses Folk House on Stone Street in the financial district, and most absurdly, given the playwright's socioeconomic views, Sean O'Casey's Authentic Irish Pub inside the Marriott Hotel in Park Ridge, New Jersey.[12]

Reading Moynihan, then, made me puzzled about the actual reception histories of Oscar Wilde and William Butler Yeats and J. M. Synge and George Bernard Shaw and Sean O'Casey and James Joyce and Brendan Behan—the specific Irish writers he mentioned who were also enshrined in the well-known poster.[13] Consequently, I set out to discover to what degree these particular men and their poems and plays and novels really had been ignored or shunned or condemned and suppressed by Irish Catholic communities in America over the years. This focus on the writers mentioned by Moynihan and included on the poster may seem more gimmicky than scholarly, but clearly, the poster, as well as related products like Irish Writers tea towels and Irish Writers coasters and Irish Writers calendars that fill the shelves of Irish gift shops, souvenir stores, and heritage-hawking websites, are all material objects that bear some important relationship to conceptions of ethnic identity. In the 2013 anthology *Extended Family: Essays on Being Irish American from New Hibernia Review*, the editor, James Silas Rogers, writes:

> The awareness that Ireland has produced an astounding number of fine writers is very much a marker of Irishness. No other group invokes its literary tradition with the same élan. One would not expect to walk into a bar in the American South, for instance, and be greeted by a picture of Faulkner or Welty, whereas images of Yeats and Joyce are all but compulsory in an Irish joint. Admittedly, the decorations of an Irish pub may be a dubious window on Irish-American cultural values. But popular culture does emerge from deeper sources; a felt connection to a literary tradition is more than ornamental in Irish life.[14]

Exploring the curious nature of these "cultural values" and this "felt connection to a literary tradition" was the primary goal of this book when I began writing it.

No doubt the parameters of such a project present a couple of inherent problems, the first being the much commented-upon phallocentrism of the Irish Writers poster itself and, indeed, of Irish literary scholarship more generally. In just the few weeks while I was trying to compose this introduction, I saw one newspaper article about the Irish Writers merchandizing phenomenon with the provocative headline "Twelve Irish Writers, Supposedly Our Greatest, and Not a Vagina between Them."[15] And I read another about the controversy surrounding the recently published *Cambridge Companion to Irish Poets,* reporting that "Irish women poets are rising up en masse against their repeated exclusion from literary history, signing a pledge of refusal to participate in anthologies, conferences and festivals in which the gender balance is skewed."[16] The post on the ACIS (American Conference for Irish Studies) Facebook group that linked to the latter article opined that the lesson of inclusion should have been learned after the debacle following the publication of *The Field Day Anthology* in 1991. And indeed it should have been. Books and products whose raison d'être is to present to consumers and/or students a comprehensive or at least representative sample of Irish Writers or Irish Writing or Irish Poets or Irish Poetry should strive for inclusivity.

But this book is neither an anthology nor an attempt to study a characteristic cross-section of writers who wrote in an Irish context. Rather, the book's invocation of "Irish Writers" in its title refers quite literally to a group of writers whose image has been impressed onto a set of cultural products emblazoned with that motto. The focus of this book is thus on Irish writers who happen to be men, because it is male writers whose image has been commodified. Furthermore, it is those same men who were named by Moynihan as the influential mid-century Irish writers who had supposedly been rejected by middle-class Irish Catholic Americans.

Because of the overt exclusivity of the work I have undertaken, I add here something modeled on what Seamus Deane, the chastened editor of *The Field Day Anthology,* wrote in the opening pages of one of his earlier books. In fact, both Deane and Hugh Kenner begin important books about modern Irish literature by trying, preemptively, to defend their work against criticism concerning the writers they excluded. In the introduction to *Celtic Revivals: Essays in Modern Irish Literature, 1880–1980,* Deane writes: "[These essays'] miscellaneous nature is not entirely countered by the presence within them of recurrent concerns. There are obvious omissions . . . Their exclusion is not a silent judgement. But their inclusion would have meant a very different book."[17] Similarly, in the author's note at the start of *A Colder Eye: The Modern Irish Writers,* Kenner writes: "This book tries, within the limits of space, to tell a coherent story . . . It is not true that what I do not discuss I dismiss . . . [Excluded writers] are part of a different story, or perhaps a different way to tell this one."[18] And so, though I make no pretense to possessing the brilliance of either Kenner or Deane, let me also articulate a hope that the recurrent concerns of this book create a coherent if not a complete account of the way a handful of celebrated Irish writers were read and reviewed and written about by an Irish American audience who represent a segment of Irish America passionately engaged with Irish culture.

Limited Knowledge and Fuzzy Feeling?

On the one hand, Moynihan suggests that by the middle of the twentieth century, middle-class Catholic Americans who were self-consciously Irish had become divorced from the politics and culture of the Irish Republic and were at best stuck in the rut of nineteenth-century Young Ireland–style cultural nationalism. Reading Moynihan, one imagines Judge Comerford's lace-curtained parlor: walls decorated by ornately framed portraits of Thomas Davis and William Smith O'Brien, bookshelves lined solely with Duffy's Library of Ireland series, a record of John McCormack singing one of Thomas Moore's airs playing on the antique phonograph. On the other hand, in their memoirs, essays, and articles about growing up Irish in postwar America, prominent and popular writers like Peter Quinn and Maureen Dezell recall a culturally oblivious youth in which Irish American identity was equated with religion and/or American politics and/or social drinking. In *Looking for Jimmy: A Search for Irish America,* Quinn, the son of a judge who briefly represented the east Bronx in Congress, writes: "Our Irishness was largely synonymous with Catholicism and the Democratic Party. It didn't involve much, if any, awareness of Irish history or literature. I never heard my parents mention Yeats or Synge or Joyce. As far as I knew, Brian Boru was a bar on Kingsbridge Road."[19] In *Irish America: Coming into Clover; The Evolution of a People and a Culture,* Dezell, the daughter of an insurance executive, writes: "Like many Americans who trace their ancestry to Eire, I grew up with limited knowledge and some fuzzy feeling about my heritage . . . I recall thinking it had to do with being Catholic but not Italian or Polish; that it involved a lot of joking, singing, and drinking." Dezell also adds to this list "an affinity for what was called Anglo-Irish literature," though she doesn't specify whether this literature was the novels of Goldsmith, Swift, and Edgeworth and/or the poetry and plays of Yeats, Synge, and Lady Gregory.[20]

While Moynihan, Quinn, and Dezell certainly provide a wealth of persuasive anecdotal and experiential evidence to support their claims about the impoverished nature of mid-twentieth-century Irish American identity and culture, the potential universality of these claims is complicated and sometimes contradicted when one encounters the rich trove of Irish American print culture that has been preserved on microfilm and is just starting to be put online. The archival evidence presented in this book suggests that while the typical editor or reader of an Irish American newspaper certainly did view the world through the frame of Roman Catholicism and surely did see the situation in Ireland through the lens of nineteenth-century-style nationalism (in its various forms as cultural nationalism, constitutional nationalism, or physical force nationalism), many Irish American journalists and Irish American citizens enthusiastically and vigorously participated in a transatlantic engagement with contemporary Irish culture, Irish literary movements, and Irish literary figures in ways that have not been adequately recognized or analyzed by scholars of the Irish in America.

Perhaps this gap in knowledge about what these Irish Americans read, and how they read it, has something to do with the fact that the editors and readers of this ethnic press tended to be immigrants from Ireland rather than their children, grandchildren, or great-grandchildren born in the United States. In *The Columbia Guide to Irish American History,* Timothy Meagher makes the striking claim that these immigrants were "irrelevant" to Irish America. Meagher explains that "increasingly after 1930, Irish immigrants seemed a quaint oddity amid so many more American-born Irish Americans. Irish immigrants became almost an ethnic community within an ethnic community with traces of a brogue, differing tastes in music, and tight connections with family members setting them apart from native-born Irish Americans."[21] While this ethnic community within an ethnic community may not have been especially relevant to the larger Irish American culture described and defined by countless influential commentators, I argue in this book that this small but significant group of Irish Americans was an important and relevant transmitter and supporter of Irish culture and Irish litera-ture.[22] These seemingly irrelevant immigrants created the institutional frameworks that provided the intricate networks of communication between Ireland and America that allowed for the continual transmis-sion of cultural and political developments. Such institutions included organizations as radically varied in their aims as the Clan na Gael and the Thomas Davis Irish Players, to name just two. They also helped cre-ate the foremost institutional framework used in this book: a vigorous Irish American and American Irish Catholic periodical press.

Complex and Contradictory Artifacts

As noted earlier, in this book I set out to explore specific historical situations in which a limited sample of Irish writers and/or their texts intersected with those members of the Irish American public who, in Moynihan's phrase, "would most value their Irishness."[23] I defined these intersections broadly, including diverse events in which audienc-es may have encountered the personality and ideas of the writer (as in the lecture tours of Wilde and Yeats), or occasions when audiences may have encountered writers' works on the stage (as in the case of Behan's *Hostage* on Broadway and the Abbey Theatre's American tours, which included plays by Yeats and Shaw and O'Casey and of course J. M. Synge). Additionally, I included indirect instances in which readers may have encountered a discourse surrounding a writer's life and/or his work on the page (that is, in newspapers, magazines, or journals) with-out actually encountering the author or the text (as in the case of Synge, who was notorious for writing *The Playboy of the Western World* before that play ever graced the stage in America, and James Joyce, whose nov-el *Ulysses* was of course banned in the United States until 1934). With such an expansive understanding of intersection, I was able to include both the cases when Irish writers were physically present in America for extended periods (for instance, Wilde, Yeats, Behan), as well as the cases when it was only their poems or articles or plays or novels or infamy that had crossed the ocean (for instance, Synge and Joyce). In all these cases, what most interested me was not the formal intricacies of various kinds of texts or literary modes but rather the response of Irish Americans to the writers and/or to their work.

Through this attention to the response of readers and viewers, I hoped to remedy what Jonathan Rose, in "A Preface to a History of Audiences," has called "the receptive fallacy"—the flawed process by which literary critics "try to discern the messages a text transmits to an audience by examining the text rather than the audience."[24] With an awareness of the receptive fallacy as a kind of guiding light, I sought to discover the response of real readers and playgoers and lecture attendees so as to justify and illustrate my conclusions about the meanings particular audience members created out of these literary productions and performances. Such readers were found primarily through extensive research within the wide array of Irish American newspapers and Catholic periodicals that were published during the broad time period under consideration. The views of these audience members as reviewers and letter-to-the-editor writers were resurrected, given voice, and analyzed. Confronting the actual words of long-forgotten men and women who contributed their commentary to the public sphere of print culture allowed me to discover and analyze the nature of specific moral, political, and, yes, literary grievances leveled against the writers and their works. As a result, the book is in no way a hagiography of Irish writers chronicling their heroic virtue in battling what, it turns out, has too often been presented by literary critics, biographers, historians, and the writers themselves as nothing more than the philistine prejudices of middle-class Catholic reactionaries and/or oversensitive, jingoistic Irish American nationalists in the face of true literary art.

In both topic and methodological approach, then, my work resembles John P. Harrington's study *The Irish Play on the New York Stage, 1874–1966*. Harrington, who is concerned with the complex interplay between drama and audience expectations, examines the opening nights of seven specific plays written by Irish playwrights. He takes into account the time and place of production, but also various factors related to the business of theater in order to "set a record of exemplary transactions between art and society." But the society and the audience he discusses is a New York one, not a specifically Irish American one, or as he explains, "The Irish American theater audience in New York is part of the audience for Irish plays, not the whole of that audience."[25] Therefore, while Harrington's study is supremely valuable as a contribution to the history of Irish theater in general, and New York theater in particular, my work attempts to chronicle a history of a particularly Irish American audience.

In addition to Harrington's book, Lawrence Rainey's *Institutions of Modernism: Literary Elites and Public Culture* provided an especially inspiring model for my work. I was guided in large part by Rainey's subversive proposal that instead of the "scholastic scrutiny of linguistic minutiae . . . the best reading of a work may, on some occasions, be one that does not read it at all."[26] Instead of analyzing the literary texts themselves, Rainey extracts meaning from the complex, surprising ways that modernist literature became entwined with various institutional structures such as patrons, deluxe editions, and little magazines. Readers should know and understand in advance that in following Rainey's example, much of my work avoids closely reading the texts themselves. Instead, I try to analyze the response of actual Irish American men and women to these authors and their literary works.

In the introduction to *Institutions of Modernism*, Rainey admits that "for many academic literary critics the presence of any story at all has become an object of suspicion. Narrative is thought to be a linear and monologic form that offers factitious coherence at the cost of analytic complexity." But Rainey reminds literary critics that "stories are complex and contradictory artifacts. The apparent ease with which they may be recounted should not be confused with a resistance to analysis. Stories *are* analysis—by other means."[27] The story told in this book and the analysis performed in it is divided into seven chapters, followed by a conclusion. Each chapter focuses on a specific juncture when Irish writers and/or their work crossed paths with an Irish American public. These intersections are arranged chronologically and span more than eight decades. This method of organization allows for detailed accounts of each particular intersection, while also providing the necessary perspective for the larger analysis of the persistent attitudes and subtle changes in the approach of the Irish American press toward literature, changes that reflect both a durable form of Irish American identity and a slowly evolving conception of Irishness.

Chapter 1 concentrates on the lecture tour of North America Oscar Wilde made in 1882. It recounts how the Irish American press at first welcomed Wilde because of the reputation of his rebel-poet mother, Speranza. But in a year filled with the political and agrarian unrest of the Land War that would transform the economic and social structure of Ireland, the chapter illustrates how most Irish American journalists soon came to mock or ignore the young aesthete because of his lack of nationalist conviction.

Chapter 2 contrasts Wilde with William Butler Yeats, who, it is shown, began his relationship with Irish America in the pages of the *Boston Pilot* as an impassioned propagandist for Irish cultural nationalism in general and a new kind of Irish theater in particular. The chapter attests that despite developments in Ireland, specifically clerical suspicion about Yeats's religious views and nationalist circumspection about his devotion to the cause, Yeats enjoyed a warm welcome from Irish Americans when he first visited the United States in the months spanning 1903 and 1904.

Chapter 3 focuses on the interval between Yeats's lecture tour and the infamous visit of the Abbey Theatre's Irish Players. This chapter illustrates how Yeats's efforts in Ireland as well as in Irish America were complicated by the growing transatlantic controversy around the work of J. M. Synge.

Chapter 4 chronicles how Yeats's reputation among Irish Americans was subsequently damaged by his insistence on presenting Synge's *Playboy of the Western World* as part of the repertoire for the Abbey Theatre's first American tour in 1911–12. Here I seek to complicate many previous accounts of the reception afforded the Abbey by showing that Irish American opinion was not homogeneous, uninformed, or unsophisticated. Furthermore, I attempt to demonstrate that Yeats managed to muddy the waters of the debate by insisting that *The Playboy* was a realistic work and that the National Theatre was presenting authentic reflections of contemporary Irish life onstage.

Chapter 5 describes the financially successful American tours undertaken by the Abbey Theatre in the 1930s. This chapter reveals that despite Yeats's best intentions to create a new poetic drama, and despite the provocative and powerful work of Sean O'Casey, the Abbey became a theater that was acclaimed by Irish Americans mostly for its light social comedy, exemplified by George Shiels's play *The New Gossoon.*

Chapter 6 examines the reception of James Joyce's work in Irish America in light of the lessons learned from the *Playboy* fiasco. Beginning in 1917, when reviews of Joyce's fiction first appeared in American journals, including reviews written for cosmopolitan audiences that insisted on the fundamental importance to his art of his Irish background and his Catholic upbringing, the chapter reveals that Joyce's achievements, and the legal battles fought in the name of those achievements, were for the most part ignored by editors, reviewers, and bibliographers who served an American Irish Catholic readership. But the chapter also details how, despite this de facto boycott, Joyce was granted his rightful place in the Irish Catholic literary tradition by scholars during the 1950s.

Chapter 7 focuses on Brendan Behan's sojourn in New York during the run of *The Hostage* on Broadway in 1960. While cataloguing the numerous objections Irish Americans expressed in print about Behan and his work, I argue that Behan was quickly absolved and canonized after his death because he had forged meaningful connections with the local Irish American community in New York.

The conclusion briefly reiterates the book's evidence and main idea, surveys the shifting cultural landscape of 1964 Irish America, and advocates for both a broader conception of Irish studies as well as for writing that embraces rather than erases the complex and contradictory stories that make up Irish American history.

Taken as a whole, these chapters chronicle the diverse ways in which a specific, significant subset of Irish Americans have engaged with literature written by Irish authors about Ireland. The evidence shows that these Irish writers were not judged on literary merit alone. Rigid religious and political standards were applied with remarkable consistency to Wilde, Yeats, Synge, Shaw, O'Casey, Joyce, and Behan. And yet, while I was doing research on each intersection of Irish writer and the Irish American public, it was revealing to discover the amount of literature and culture that filled the pages of Irish American newspapers each week. Of course, on the whole, patriotic, social, and religious subject matter dwarfed the content related to poetry, drama, or creative prose. But this book shows that those men and women most concerned with their Irishness were not illiterate or anti-literature. When they criticized Oscar Wilde in 1882, they did so via poems that praised his mother's verse; when they cheered Yeats in 1904, they did so because they believed he was continuing the mission of Young Ireland and working with Douglas Hyde to revive Gaelic culture and the Irish language; while they protested *The Playboy,* they wondered why the National Theatre couldn't produce more plays like *Cathleen ni Houlihan;* while they took issue with the drama of Shaw and Synge and O'Casey, they embraced the comedy of George Shiels; while their newspapers avoided any talk of James Joyce and his dirty books, those same newspapers often included items concerning Joyce's contemporaries Padraic Column and Oliver St. John Gogarty; while they condemned Behan's *The Hostage* on Broadway, they supported a production of John Murphy's *The Country Boy* in the Bronx.

Clearly, then, the Irish American audiences I present to you in this book were not indifferent to modern Ireland and its contemporary literature. On the contrary, many Irish American editors and readers were deeply, passionately, and often knowledgeably engaged with the culture of the land they'd left behind. They may have been just a fraction of the population of a larger Irish America, and they may not have created the Irish American culture we typically read about in memoirs, monographs, and surveys, but these Irish American audiences were neither ignorant nor irrelevant. Rather they were a vital part of Irish American and, sometimes, Irish history.

CHAPTER I

"Speranza's Son"

IRISH AMERICA DISMISSES OSCAR WILDE, 1882

Tᴏ THE YEAR 1882 was a remarkable one in the Atlantic world, a year immortalized by Thomas Beer in the enigmatic opening lines of his book *The Mauve Decade:* "They laid Jesse James in his grave and Dante Gabriel Rossetti died immediately. Then Charles Darwin was deplored and then, on April 27th, 1882, Louisa May Alcott hurried to write in her journal: 'Mr. Emerson died at 9 p.m. suddenly. Our best and greatest American gone.'"[1] Other notable literary deaths that year included Henry Wadsworth Longfellow and Anthony Trollope, who both expired naturally. Less well remembered, perhaps, are Charles Guiteau and Myles Joyce, who were both punished capitally—the former when his defense, that sloppy doctors had actually killed President Garfield after he had merely shot him, was rejected by a jury of his peers; and the latter when his denial about participating in a Ribbon Society murder of a rival family of Maamtrasna farmers, a denial delivered in the Irish language, fell on the ears of an English-speaking high court.

Throughout Ireland, violence of the kind represented by the Maamtrasna trial and depicted in Trollope's final, unfinished novel, *The*

Land-leaguers, was rampant. The centennial of Grattan's parliament had begun with Michael Davitt and Charles Parnell both locked up under the Coercion Act—the one-armed agitator in Portland prison and the uncrowned king in Kilmainham jail. Upon their arrest in October 1881, the Land League leaders, in their last official act before the organization was suppressed, had issued the No Rent Manifesto. Reporting on these events for the *Irish World and American Industrial Liberator,* the newspaper that had been most responsible for raising the cash needed to fund the Land War, was Henry George, whose influential books *Progress and Poverty,* published in 1879, and the *Irish Land Question,* published in 1881, had fueled the agitation by proposing that land nationalization, not legislative independence, was the cure-all for Ireland's ills. In May 1882, Parnell and Gladstone had secretly negotiated the Kilmainham Treaty, effectively ending the Land War, which had indeed done much to ensure the eventual fall of feudalism in Ireland. Parnell was set free on May 2, and Davitt was released four days later, the same day Ireland's chief secretary and undersecretary were knifed to death in Phoenix Park by a shadowy group of republicans called the Invincibles, the assassination demonstrating yet again, depending on one's point of view, the depraved savagery of unrepentant Fenians or that Ireland unfree would never be at peace.

In February 1882, not very far from Phoenix Park and environs, a prodigal son of Cork and his Dublin-born wife had welcomed a son who, twenty years later, would fly through the nets of religion and nationalism, fleeing into exile on the Continent, where he would go to form in the smithy of his soul the uncreated conscience of the Irish race. Meanwhile, in October, thousands of miles away at the New York Nursery and Child Hospital, a Limerick girl who may or may not have been married to a sculptor, or a music teacher, of Cuban, or perhaps Spanish, nationality, delivered a baby boy whose indisputable American citizenship would, thirty-four years later, save him from a British firing squad and allow him a political career that more than any other would determine the shape of the emergent Irish nation-state.

The year 1882 was also when Father Michael McGivney, an Irish American priest in Waterbury, Connecticut, established a mutual benefit society for Catholic men that would grow to become the largest organization of lay Catholics in the world. This organization was named not after Saint Patrick, Ireland's patron, nor after Saint Columcille, the great dove of the Celtic church, nor after Saint Brendan the Navigator, who had, according to legend, sailed across the Atlantic waves on a crude curragh in the sixth century, but rather after the Italian explorer credited with discovering the New World for the Spanish. Why? No doubt to remind American nativists that Catholics were not just a recently arrived nuisance. Another reminder, not of the Roman Catholic past but of the Irish Catholic present, must have been Cork-born Patrick Collins's election in November to the U.S. House of Representatives—the first Irishman to represent Boston in the capital. Earlier in the year, another proud Irish Catholic son of the Puritan City, John L. Sullivan, the Boston Strongboy, had challenged Paddy Ryan, the Trojan Giant from Troy, New York, for the heavyweight boxing title. And according to at least one source, among the Gilded Age glitterati there in Mississippi City, Mississippi, to witness Sullivan's ninth-round knockout was Oscar Wilde, a young dandy recently arrived from London who was covering the fight for a British magazine.[2]

At that point in time, the decadent novel and four comedies on which rest Wilde's literary fame were not yet written; by 1882 he had merely self-published one melodrama and one collection of lyric poems. And so rather than being famous for his writing, he was actually recognized for being mostly, well, recognizable. His persona had been thoroughly lampooned by George du Maurier in the pages of *Punch* and by Gilbert and Sullivan onstage in their popular comic opera *Patience.* Caricature may well be the tribute mediocrity pays to genius, as Wilde alleged, but Wilde had come to America to trade handsomely on those caricatures, not on the genius which he claimed, famously and probably apocryphally, was the only thing he had to declare to U.S. Customs. When Wilde disembarked in New York, this self-described genius was welcomed by the *New York World* as "the great English exponent of aestheticism."[3] But in fact the tour had less to do with promoting a school of art or a way of life than it did with promoting a play that satirized that school of art and way of life. Specifically, as Richard Ellmann explains in his magisterial biography *Oscar Wilde,* the young aesthete had come to America to lecture and pique interest in towns where *Patience* would be playing, an early and brilliant example of cross-promotion dreamed up by the promoter Richard D'Oyly Carte.[4]

Whether Wilde was an earnest English exponent of art for art's sake or a brash British con artist in aesthetic guise was not of much concern to the *Irish Nation,* a ferociously republican newspaper published in New York by John Devoy, a Fenian exile who was the architect of the New Departure in Irish politics, which had merged Davitt's agrarian protest and Parnell's parliamentary maneuvering. The *Irish Nation* greeted Wilde with the headline "Oscar's Arrival: What Speranza's Son Proposes to Do in America; His 'Philosophy' and His Play."[5] To the likes of Devoy, then, Wilde was not English at all but one of Ireland's own, namely, "Speranza's Son." And the expectations for such a son must have been considerable, for Wilde's mother was a rebel poetess, one of the celebrated women of the *Nation* who had contributed so much to the cultural nationalism of the Young Ireland movement and the aborted revolution of 1848. And Speranza—née Jane Elgee, later known as Lady Wilde—hoping, one supposes, that the apples would not fall far from the tree of liberty, had later dedicated a volume of verse to her two boys with the words: "I made them indeed / Speak plain the word country. I taught them no doubt / That a country's a thing men should die for at need."[6] Irish Americans must have been disappointed, then, to learn that Speranza's son planned to speak not of the country of his birth but of "The English Renaissance," "The House Beautiful," and "The Decorative Arts." Not surprisingly, the *Irish Nation* protested with this headline:

SPERANZA'S SON
Oscar Wilde Lectures on What He
Calls "The English Renaissance."
THE UTTERNESS OF AESTHETICISM
Phrasing about Beauty while a Hideous
Tyranny Overshadows His Native Land
TALENT SADLY MISAPPLIED

Beneath the disapproving title, though, was a fairly innocuous introductory paragraph about Wilde, calling him "the youthful Irish poet and clever aesthetic *poseur*" and describing his address as a "maudlin art sermon."[7] This lead-in was followed by a reproduction of the text of the lecture in its entirety.

Devoy's paper was not the only Irish American publication to take note of Wilde's presence while making an issue of his politics, nor was it the only voice of Irish American opinion prominent during this period. In fact the robust press in America dedicated to Irish Catholic readers represented a wide range of views on Irish nationalism and on its relationship to both Catholicism and socioeconomic philosophy. In chapter 7 of his influential study *Irish-American Nationalism, 1870–1890*, Thomas N. Brown provides an extremely helpful discussion of these divisions in the context of the events of 1881–82. He describes the conflicts and crises of this brief but important period as being dominated by "Parnell, who stood for nationalism; [Henry] George who stood for humanitarian social reform; and Davitt, who tried to stand for both."[8] Brown shows how in the Irish American press John Boyle O'Reilly's *Boston Pilot* embraced Parnell's move toward a Home Rule agenda, Patrick Ford's *Irish World and American Industrial Liberator* aligned itself with George and Davitt, and Devoy's *Irish Nation* lashed out at all of the above, each of whom was daring to prematurely abandon the plan Devoy had formulated in the New Departure. In addition to the three papers mentioned by Brown, this chapter considers two other Irish Catholic publications: Patrick Meehan's *Irish-American* and James O'Brien's *Sunday Union*.

The *Irish-American* had been founded in 1849 by Patrick Lynch, a Young Irelander who had fled to New York after the disastrous rebellion of 1848. Since 1857 the paper had been edited by Lynch's stepson Patrick Meehan. Meehan had been a prominent member of the American branch of the Fenians, but after being shot in the head by a member of a rival faction within the organization in 1870, he had distanced himself from the group. With the formation of the Land League, however, he had reentered the contentious fray of nationalist politics.[9] In 1882 Meehan's periodical was firmly established as a journal for "men from the growing Irish Catholic middle class," and as such it followed "a conservative course both in American politics and in the politics of Irish nationalism."[10]

After Wilde's first public appearance before a large audience at Chickering Hall in New York, the *Irish-American* ran an article discussing the event. Although it paid special attention to his outfit—"He was attired in an evening dress coat, white waistcoat, knee breeches, black silk stockings and pumps"—the rest of the notice was quite positive and respectful, reporting that he was "well received" and bestowed with "frequent and liberal" applause. It went on to comment that "the lecture was a frank and bold presentation of the extreme tenets of the modern English worshippers of the beautiful." Following this praise, the article suddenly digressed into an unexpected criticism of Lady Wilde, who had, it appeared to the author, "gone over to the enemy ranks" by joining the " Committee for Relief of Distressed Irish Ladies." Attempting to be clever, the author called such behavior the "concentrated essence of sublimated inconsistency."[11]

After this initial report on Wilde and the attack on his mother, the *Irish-American's* coverage of the lecture tour basically consisted of brief, bantering items related to Oscar. In the same issue as the article on the lecture, the *Irish-American* reprinted some silly fluff from the *Norristown Herald* which noted that Wilde was a big, strong man who might not appreciate the way the paper had been covering him.[12] Two weeks later, the beginning of the "Personal" column noted facetiously, "Wilde—The Singer of the Simple Sunflower is mentioned in the Oxford University Calendar as 'Oscar Fingall O'Flahertie Willis Wilde.'"[13] Next, the *Irish-American* reprinted this attempt at humor from the *Courier-Journal:* "The editor of the New York *Times* says Oscar Wilde's rhymes are fit only for the reading of ecstatic milliners. The milliners will endeavor to get even by selling the editor's wife a new bonnet."[14] And finally, a "Fireside Sparks" column reported, "O'Wilde, according to the *Republican,* is coming to O'Maha."[15] Obviously, all of these trite examples demonstrate that Wilde was, for the most part, being taken less than seriously.

Dr. James W. O'Brien's *Sunday Union* was the self-described "Irish Citizens and Catholic Family Sunday Newspaper." Like the *Irish Nation* and the *Irish-American,* it both criticized and ridiculed Wilde. At the beginning of his visit, the paper published the poem "To Oscar Wilde" by a J. Ryan, who chastised Wilde for his lack of commitment to the republican cause his mother had espoused while also alluding to the vapidity of the aesthetic credo. Here is a representative verse:

It ill becomes Speranza's son,
In Ireland's hour of grief and dole,
To stand aside and calm look on,
With cold, unsympathetic soul!
It ill becomes you Oscar Wilde,
To shun the path your mother trod,
She braved the foe—degenerate child—
You kiss the hands that wield the rod.[16]

Later in his tour the *Sunday Union* published one of Wilde's own poems, "Rome Unvisited," under the erroneous title "O, Roma, Roma!" The poem included the stanza:

When, bright with purple and with gold
Come priest and holy cardinal,
And borne above the heads of all
The gentle shepherd of the fold.
O joy to see before I die
The only God-anointed king,
And hear the silver trumpets ring
A triumph as he passes by![17]

Having chided Wilde for his slowness in embracing nationalism, perhaps the editor wanted to remind him that his conversion to the true faith, a conversion he had been flirting with since his Oxford days, was also belated. Soon enough, yet another poem concerning Wilde appeared in the *Sunday Union*, this one, unsigned and titled "Quite," parodied the witty, satiric tone of *Patience*.[18] And two weeks later, in the "Incident and Anecdote" column, one last piece of anonymous wit regarding Wilde graced the pages of the *Sunday Union*, some of the rhetoric once again borrowed from *Patience*.[19]

It should be noted that not all Irish Americans or Irish American publications were so quick to ridicule or to chastise Oscar, and in fact, a kind of hereditary benefit of the doubt seems to have been extended his way by many. Richard Ellmann recounts how, on Saint Patrick's Day 1882, a Father Shanley of St. Paul, Minnesota, introduced Wilde as "the son of one of Ireland's noblest daughters—a daughter who in the troublous times of 1848 by the works of her pen and her noble example did much to keep the fire of patriotism burning brightly."[20] And in his study *Oscar Wilde in Canada,* Kevin O'Brien describes a scene in which Patrick Boyle, editor of the *Irish Canadian,* welcomed Wilde to Toronto on behalf of its Irish citizens. O'Brien explains that this welcome was due in large part to the legacy of Speranza.[21]

The friendliest of all the Irish American newspapermen, though, was the *Boston Pilot*'s John Boyle O'Reilly. O'Reilly, like John Devoy, was a convicted Fenian conspirator. In fact, it was Devoy who had recruited and enlisted O'Reilly into the Republican Brotherhood while O'Reilly was ostensibly serving in the Tenth Hussars of the British army, stationed just outside Dublin. The two men were arrested within days of each other when the conspiracy unraveled in February 1866, and both did hard time in the British penal system, the list of their various places of incarceration providing a familiar litany for Irish nationalists: Kilmainham, Mountjoy, Millbank, Portland, Chatham, Dartmoor.[22] But unlike Devoy, who was eventually released from Chatham in 1871 when Gladstone commuted the sentences of many Fenians on condition that they never again reside in Ireland, O'Reilly had already been transported to faraway Western Australia after an attempted escape from Dartmoor.[23] O'Reilly arrived in Australia in January 1868, but little more than a year later he succeeded in escaping from the penal colony onboard a whaling ship. He arrived in America in November 1869.[24]

O'Reilly settled in Boston and quickly rose from reporter to editor and proprietor of the *Pilot,* his co-owner being Boston's Archbishop John J. Williams. O'Reilly was not just an influential newspaperman; he was also a successful novelist and an acclaimed poet. In an undated pamphlet titled *The American Irish,* Lady Wilde described the *Pilot* as "one of the best of these [Irish American] journals" and O'Reilly as "the distinguished author of *Songs from the South Seas,* a series of wild, fierce tales of adventure, remarkable for startling originality of conception, nervous language, and a full flow of sonorous harmonies of versification."[25] By 1882, O'Reilly had even become a kind of token Irish Catholic amid the literary salons of Boston: "A wit, poet, editor, story-teller, O'Reilly was a . . . favorite of the literary Brahmins, the liberals, almost everybody"; he was also "a host, indeed, to any newcomer, and especially one from Ireland."[26]

It was appropriate, then, that O'Reilly served as Wilde's host in Boston. But O'Reilly was not exactly hosting a stranger. In fact, he was already somewhat familiar with Wilde's oeuvre before he met the young poet in person. He had previously done Speranza the favor of giving Wilde his first American exposure by publishing Oscar's poem "Graffitti D'Italia (Arona, Lago Maggiore)" in the September 23, 1876, *Pilot*.[27] Wilde had revised this poem for his published collection and renamed it "Rome Unvisited"—the very same previously mentioned quasi-Catholic-sounding poem that the *Sunday Union* had printed. Now that Wilde was in town, O'Reilly ran the poem again, under the new title, on the front page of the *Pilot*.[28] Adjacent to Wilde's poem was an article his mother had originally written for London's high-society journal *The Queen*, titled "The Future Opportunities for Woman."[29] Later in the tour, Oscar would seek O'Reilly's assistance with the publication of a volume of Speranza's poems, which Wilde self-deprecatingly claimed were "so unlike the work of her degenerate artist son."[30] Then, on the eve of his departure, Wilde even sought O'Reilly's direct financial aid after being hoodwinked by a gambling scam, writing: "I have fallen into a den of thieves, who are unscrupulous and lying: they owe me money which they won't pay me and I want to get back to England . . . I want you to send me 250 dollars till I get home, to pay my lawyer, etc."[31]

Whether because of his personal relationship with the Wildes or because of his own decorum in editing the *Pilot*, O'Reilly's treatment of Oscar certainly contrasts rather conspicuously with what is found in the other Irish American papers. Before Wilde arrived in Boston, the *Pilot* had published both a candid literary introduction to his poetry and a defense of his character against spurious caricatures in the press. Each piece is worth examining at length. The first piece, under the headline "Oscar Wilde: Something about His Parents and His Poems," begins with a brief family history that mentions the Irish bona fides of both father ("an enthusiastic antiquarian") and mother ("a lady of taste and culture, and of considerable literary reputation").[32] This was followed by an editorial discussing Oscar's verse that is notable for its prescient analysis of Wilde's obvious talent, his derivative style, his sensuous subject matter, and his lack of genuine political or religious conviction. The second piece, the editorial, sought to present a more accurate image of the young visitor than readers would have been used to seeing and reading about: "He is more manly, and a great deal less silly than the Bunthornes and Postlethwaites for whom he is supposed to have stood as a model," and "the talent that 'Speranza's' son undoubtedly possesses will show itself with more credit than it has yet done, though the volume of his poems recently published gave a very favorable illustration of it."[33]

In the next week's *Pilot*, excerpts from Wilde's lecture appeared on the front page under the headline "Oscar Wilde on the School of Aesthetics."[34] But surprisingly, given the favorable notices O'Reilly had been providing Wilde, this issue also included a terse editorial chastising the aesthete for his disengagement, especially in comparison to Lady Wilde: "Oscar's mother was a brave-souled patriot, who preferred Liberty to Oppression, who nobly sang the cause of her own country. He has no country, or rather he is weak enough to glorify England as 'my country' and to speak of 'we Englishmen.' We fear that Oscar has a strong head and a weak heart."[35]

Whether because of the earnest pleadings of a patriotic penman like John Boyle O'Reilly or some other calculation, there can be no doubt that in America, Wilde did start to trumpet his Irish connections more loudly while at the same time beginning to make public comments on the political situation in Ireland. Some of his literary biographers have gone so far as to locate a seminal point in Wilde's sense of his own nationality and/or ethnicity during this period. Davis Coakley, for example, claims, "It was his lecture tour in North America in 1882 that brought Wilde face to face with his Irishness."[36] Ellmann probably informs Coakley's opinion, for he wrote, "An unexpected result of his tour was that [Oscar] rediscovered himself as an Irishman."[37]

And sure enough, as the tour progressed, Wilde did indeed begin to espouse publicly a more advanced, pro-nationalist philosophy. This can be evinced from a March issue of the *Irish Nation*, which published an interview with Wilde that it picked up from the *St. Louis Globe-Democrat*, adding the sardonic headline "Oscar's Opinions: The Land League, Emigration, Home Rule and Separation Discussed from an

Aesthetic Standpoint." In the interview Wilde stated, "I am entirely at one with the position held by the Land League." Yet he called the Absolute No-Rent Policy "the one foolish thing that the Land League have done" and said that the total secession of Ireland from the United Kingdom "is another folly." At the end of the exchange, Wilde agreed to be categorized as a "Home Ruler."[38]

Then, nearly four months into the tour, on the last night of an extended engagement in the San Francisco Bay area, Wilde unveiled a lecture titled "The Irish Poets and Poetry." The talk began with a general discussion of the role of poetry in Celtic culture, as well as Celtic poetry's colossal influence on modern thought. Wilde then accused the Irish poets before Thomas Moore, poets such as Goldsmith, of being, despite their "very beautiful, refined and charming" work, "entirely wanting in national feeling." To such poets Wilde contrasted the Young Irelanders, whom, he admitted, he had been trained by his mother "to love and reverence . . . as a Catholic child is the saints of the calendar." Not surprisingly, then, Wilde praised the poets of '48 extravagantly: Thomas Davis ("I know of no poet whose passionate utterance, whose width of vision were greater, or who could combine sweetness and strength in such perfection"); James Clarence Mangan ("none was so wonderful in his genius . . . the Edgar Allan Poe of our country, whose romantic life and wretched death are among the many tragedies of literature"); Charles Gavan Duffy ("who . . . is quite as valuable to art as he is to democracy"); Thomas Darcy McGee ("one of the most remarkable leaders of Irish-American journalism"); and his own mother ("a young girl who had been brought up in an atmosphere of alien English thought, among people in bench and senate, and far removed from any love or knowledge of those wrongs of the people to which she afterwards gave such passionate expression"). Wilde also praised poets of a more recent and local vintage, mentioning the work of his Boston host, John Boyle O'Reilly, and Daniel O'Connell, grandnephew of the Liberator and resident of San Francisco, whose recent publication *Lyrics* Wilde described as a "charming little volume"; Wilde even recited O'Connell's "Feelings of an Irish Exile," which he said had "a simplicity and sweetness quite its own." The gist of Wilde's lecture can be summarized with these words: "But indeed the poetic genius of the Celtic race never flags or wearies. It is as sweet by the groves of California as by the groves of Ireland, as strong in foreign lands as in the land which gave it birth. And indeed I do not know anything more wonderful, or more characteristic of the Celtic genius, than the quick artistic spirit in which we adapted ourselves to the English tongue. The Saxon took our lands from us and left them desolate. We took their language and added new beauties to it."[39] Whether Wilde was merely pandering to his audience or expressing genuine artistic admiration for Celtic genius it is difficult to say. But the ability of a son of the Protestant Ascendancy, whose own genealogy was, by all measures, much more Saxon than Celt, to identify with the dispossessed Catholic peasantry was certainly a neat rhetorical trick.

In a very instructive introduction to the lecture, which he edited and reconstructed from Wilde's fragmentary manuscript and contemporary newspaper accounts, Robert D. Pepper raises a number of issues that further complicate any straightforward reading of the text. First of all, he notes that the subject matter for the lecture was not even Wilde's own idea. Rather, this particular talk was requested via a petition signed by prominent local Irishmen.[40] Second, he suggests an interesting reason why Wilde might have agreed to give the new lecture, one that had nothing to do with patriotism: Wilde's lecture on the English Renaissance had been pirated, and Wilde was convinced that people were not coming to hear him speak because they had already encountered his words in print. Oscar complained to the press about this pirating and even related an incident in which he had reprimanded, to no avail, newsboys who had tried to sell him his own work in a railcar.[41]

But Pepper implies that Wilde may have been guilty of something resembling an intellectual property theft of his own, noting that "nearly all of Oscar's generalizations about Celtic culture and Celtic poetry are taken from [Matthew] Arnold's . . . *On the Study of Celtic Literature.*" Pepper claims that Oscar borrowed from that text's final section Arnold's "comments on style, rhyme, and the beauties of Ossian"; he also notes that the passage Oscar recited from Ossian "is given verbatim as Arnold quotes it" and that the entirety of another passage in the lecture "is also taken from Arnold"; he even guesses that Wilde's advocacy, at the close of the lecture, for the establishment of an Irish library and museum in

San Francisco "probably owes something to Arnold."[42] In addition to the serious implication of plagiarism, perhaps Pepper's most contentious conjecture concerns why the existing manuscript, which was never published in Wilde's lifetime, is missing so much material found in the contemporary press accounts. He concludes that the "fervently pro-Irish and anti-English" material spoken from the platform "is the sort of thing that might have embarrassed the more mature, apolitical Oscar, making his living as journalist and author in London."[43]

Ultimately, it is impossible to gauge the sincerity of this lecture in particular or the evolution of Wilde's political consciousness in general. Wilde was, after all, a man who would one day celebrate "The Truth of Masks," and so his sudden discovery of his inner Irishman in America certainly can be clouded by the suspicion of performance, or perhaps even opportunism. In their book *Oscar Wilde's Profession,* Josephine Guy and Ian Small suggest that "we must be prepared to see Wilde's politics in partly cynical terms—that he was commodifying a form (or brand) of Irishness and Aestheticism that he knew would sell to his American audience."[44] And even Coakley, who argues for the authenticity of Wilde's authentically self-conscious Irishness, nonetheless writes that Wilde "realized that many Americans would be interested in him not for his advocacy of the beautiful but because of his links with Ireland," and consequently Oscar "rose to the occasion and was soon . . . only too happy to dilate on 'Anglo-Saxon stupidity' in his lectures and to give nationalist answers to the many reporters who interviewed him about relations between England and Ireland."[45]

"Rising to the occasion" may well be Coakley's euphemism for Wilde's habit of either telling people what they wanted to hear or talking out of both sides of his mouth, two talents Oscar seems to have cultivated in America. An example of the former talent is noted by Pepper, who reveals that during his lecture titled "Art Decoration," Wilde had made "an oblique bow" to the followers of the popular San Francisco populist demagogue Dennis Kearney, "Irish-born sandlot orator" and "implacable foe of Chinese immigration." According to Pepper, "Oscar advised his audience: 'don't borrow any Chinese art, for you have no need of it any more than you have need of Chinese labor.'" Wilde's advice, wrote a contemporary reporter quoted by Pepper, "was hailed by the anti-coolie esthetes near the door with loud applause." In Pepper's estimation, "the theatrical Wilde was clearly playing to the gallery."[46] Another example of clearly playing to the gallery and telling them what they wished to hear took place when, after visiting with Jefferson Davis, Wilde informed the *Atlanta Constitution,* "We in Ireland are fighting for the principle of autonomy against empire, for independence against centralization, for the principles for which the south fought."[47] The second talent, the one for speaking out of both sides of one's mouth, appeared when news of the assassination of Lord Cavendish reached the States and Wilde was asked to comment by a reporter in Philadelphia; he managed simultaneously to criticize and justify the murders: "When liberty comes with hands dabbled in blood it is hard to shake hands with her . . . We forget how much England is to blame. She is reaping the fruit of seven centuries of injustice."[48]

Unlike Wilde's literary biographers, who have paid great attention to Wilde's engagement with Irish issues during his American tour, historians of the Irish in America have largely overlooked Wilde's visit and refrained from analyzing what it might reveal about Irish America during this period. So what does it reveal?

The examples of lampooning and/or criticism directed at Wilde from the pages of the *Irish Nation,* the *Irish-American,* the *Sunday Union,* and even the *Boston Pilot* demonstrate that Irish American nationalists, when not impugning Wilde for his lack of activity on behalf of the cause of Ireland's liberty, were often simply mocking Oscar's aesthetic poses. And this treatment of Wilde suggests that the kind of cultural nationalism championed by the Young Ireland movement remained, as late as 1882, the standard for the kind of literature the Irish American press would publish and promote. And the truth is that in 1882, Wilde was an Irish writer who had never written a nationalist poem or ballad in his life, and as a matter of fact, he was an Irish writer who never would write one.[49] Not surprisingly, then, the evidence clearly shows that during Wilde's time in America, it is his mother's rhetorical presence, not his own, that is palpable in the pages of these journals. Once his arrival had been duly noted, his attitudes and attire mocked, and his lack of Irish nationalism criticized, Oscar fades from the attention of the editors and publishers of these newspapers; but Speranza remains.

Recall that after Wilde's first lecture, the *Irish-American* was uncon-
cerned with his aesthetic theories but expressed outrage at his mother's
perceived desertion from the nationalist ranks. The *Sunday Union* likewise attacked Lady Wilde, this time for writing in an English magazine
that "Ireland's only hope is to get rid of her children" by emigration; the
criticism was presented as a kind of mock obituary, under the heading
"In Memoriam Speranza."[50] Months later, the *Irish Nation* reprinted a
poem from the *Boston Pilot,* "The War of Nations," under the name of
Lady Wilde, not Speranza. But despite the aristocratic title of its author,
the poem certainly would have pleased nationalists, as it concludes with
the rousing republican stanza "Beware, O Kings! / The People yet may
know their power, and then / The cry of suffering humanity / For retri-
bution of their ancient wrongs / Will startle earth, and reach the ear of
God."[51] A similarly themed piece of verse, "The Shorn Sheep," credited
to Speranza, not Lady Wilde, can be found in the *Irish World* during this
time period. The concluding lines are "And patiently through sorrow, toil
and tears / The poor must bear the bitter yoke of want / Until the rending
of the thunder cloud / Flashes the light of freedom on the world, / And
the dread vengeance of the Lord comes down / On those who left them
naked to the blast."[52] Given that the *Irish Nation*'s ultimate goal was the
establishment of an Irish Republic and that the *Irish World*'s primary
concern in 1882 was the land question, it is not surprising that the first
poem prophesies the overthrow of monarchy, while the second imagines
divine justice for the economically oppressed.

In 1882 the *Irish World* was actually the most popular of all the Irish
American weeklies, with a circulation of sixty thousand.[53] The paper's
editor was Patrick Ford, a Galway-born famine refugee whose family
settled in Boston. As a young man, Ford worked as a printer's apprentice at *The Liberator,* William Lloyd Garrison's abolitionist newspaper.
After serving in the Union Army during the Civil War, he founded
the *Irish World* in 1870. Ford advocated social and economic reform
in America as well as political revolution in Ireland. To reflect this,
in 1878 he had actually changed the official title of the journal to the
Irish World and American Industrial Liberator. Ford's concern for the
working class resembled the progressive-minded interests of John
Boyle O'Reilly, although Ford's often contentious relationship with

the Catholic hierarchy and his unblinking advocacy of physical force nationalism—his paper collected donations for the infamous Skirmishing Fund—made him much more radical than the editor of the *Pilot*. Ford's influence was described anecdotally, if not entirely factually, by Hamil Grant in his book *Two Sides of the Atlantic: Notes of an Anglo-American Newspaperman:*

> Another great political force in his time was the late Patrick Ford, the Dynamiter, as he was commonly called. Ford ran a paper . . . which held the record, during many years, for one single issue—namely sixteen hundred thousand numbers—somewhere back in the eighties. This Irishman was described in the House of Commons by Sir George Trevelyan as "the greatest editor of all time," and if the size of an editor's audience be a sure criterion of editorial capacity, then Trevelyan was right; for the Galway Irishman's paper had a circulation of over a quarter of a million weekly, and that too in an age when one-fifth of so large a patronage was accounted colossal.[54]

And none other than Lady Wilde provided this telling description of Ford's controversial newspaper: "*The Irish World,* the favorite organ of the ultra-democratic party . . . openly advocates an armed invasion of Ireland, and the redistribution of all confiscated estates. This journal is indeed so violently anti-English, and the illustrations are so bitterly sarcastic on the English Court . . . that recently it has been stopped at the Irish post office, and the priesthood discourage its circulation among the people. It is, however, extremely popular with the extreme section of the American Irish, and is held to be a true exponent of their views."[55]

Obviously, Lady Wilde's ambivalent judgment of his publication did not stop Ford from publishing Speranza. And in fact, right below the poem written by Speranza, readers would have found a poem dedicated "To Speranza." It begins with the apostrophe "Speranza! O, Speranza! / Thy Voice! I hear it still, / Coming with force of lightning / From the throne of God!" and reads in part:

> Chiding for our childish animosities
> Demanding why we do not all
> At once uprise and with a single blow

Dispose the robbing, brutal idlers
Who waste, each one, the substance that
Should feed ten thousand toiling,
Starving children of the most High God![56]

The publication date of these two poems, December 30, 1882, coincides
with the end of Wilde's tour, but his imminent departure is never mentioned in the columns of the *Irish World*. This was consistent with how it
had covered the entire tour: the most popular and influential Irish American paper of the day paid no attention whatsoever to Speranza's son.

The archival record shows, therefore, that in 1882, in the midst of
bloody agitations and assassinations in their homeland, the members
of the Irish American press did not care at all about lilies or sunflowers,
beauty or style, and they certainly had no interest in learning about the
decorative arts or any English Renaissance. Irish American newspapermen were interested in nationalism, not aestheticism, and so they
published writers who were unmitigated in their Irishness and unapol-
ogetic about their militancy, even if they were dead, like the ubiquitous
John Mitchel, or dying, like the popular Charles Kickham. It is surely
a striking irony to discover that among the Irish American press, Jane
Elgee's poetry, whether it was published under the name Speranza or
Lady Wilde, was much more popular and taken much more seriously
than Oscar's, and furthermore, that brief lecture tours by Parnellite MPs
T. M. Healy and T. P. O'Connor in the first months of the year, and by
Michael Davitt in the early summer following his release, sparked more
debate and discussion in the pages of these journals than a year's worth
of Wilde's sermons.[57] Ultimately, then, Wilde's celebrity—if it was
noticed at all in these undoubtedly philistine, admittedly parochial, yet
indisputably patriotic publications—amounted to not much more than
a source of censure for the nationalist weeklies and of satire for a Catholic Sunday paper. When Wilde was about to leave, the *Irish Nation*,
unlike the *Irish World*, did mention it. The December 30 issue featured
a column under the headline "Oscar Going Home."[58] Implicit was the
knowledge that Oscar's home was of course England, not Ireland.

Coda

On March 1, 1895, twelve years and two months after his departure from America, Wilde helped catalyze his own tragic downfall by suing the Marquess of Queensberry for libel after the brutish father of Wilde's lover Lord Alfred Douglas, or "Bosie," had left a card at the Albemarle Club publicly dubbing Speranza's son a "posing Somdomite [*sic*]."[59]

By the time Wilde's scandal was splashed across the pages of the Anglosphere press, the Atlantic world was a very changed place from what it had been in 1882. In Ireland, Parnell was already dead, his career and health, as Wilde's would be, ruined by a scandal largely of his own reckless making. Parnell's old partner, Michael Davitt, was still very much alive and serving as MP for South Mayo. While Parnell and Davitt had won the Land War decisively, leading to almost total peasant proprietorship, Gladstone's Home Rule bills had been failures, the first defeated in Commons, the second rejected by the Lords. These failures delayed Ireland's political independence for another generation. And so, in the intervening years, Ireland's young nationalists would seek independence, both political and cultural, through means other than parliamentary legislation. Among the members of this rising generation were a promising young scholar named James Joyce, who in 1895 made his Jesuit teachers at Belvedere College, Dublin, proud by placing among the winners in the national Intermediate Examinations, as well as a tall young lad named Eamon de Valera, who was at the head of his class in the national school at Bruree and about to move on to the Christian Brothers school in Charleville.

Across the waves in America, the Venerable Father McGivney had gone to his eternal reward, whereas Patrick Collins had gone to his temporal one, serving as Grover Cleveland's consul general in London. And John L. Sullivan had lost his heavyweight title to Gentleman Jim Corbett in a prizefight fought under the civilizing rules codified by Wilde's ungentlemanly nemesis, the Marquess of Queensberry.

The Irish American press had changed in the intervening years too. John Devoy's *Irish Nation* had gone bankrupt in 1885, and the great Fenian would not return to the newspaper business until launching the *Gaelic American* in 1903. In 1890 John Boyle O'Reilly had succumbed to exhaustion, one scholar blaming his premature passing on the psychic toll inflicted by so many years writing "with the Brahmins looking over one shoulder and the Irish looking over the other."[60] O'Reilly died, as Parnell had, and Wilde would, a young man of just forty-six years.

Patrick Ford's *Irish World* remained influential, but Ford's nationalist militancy and social radicalism had softened with age.[61] During 1882, Ford's paper was seemingly too preoccupied with the political machinations involving Parnell, Davitt, and Henry George to pay any attention to Wilde; but in the comparatively calmer times of 1895, it ran what amounts to Wilde's Irish American obituary under the headline "Wilde as We Knew Him."[62] Beneath this headline was a lifelike drawing of Wilde, not one of the grotesque caricatures so often used to represent him. The article began, "Oscar Wilde, about whom so much is now being said, first achieved notoriety as the leader of the then infantile aesthetic craze." The anonymous author went on to provide a kind of truncated, selective biography, refusing even to hint at, let alone elaborate, the charges against Wilde that brought him so much notoriety.

Surprisingly, the article quoted a source, a "London critic," who expressed an opinion that must have been in the extreme minority during the days of the scandal: "Mr. Oscar Wilde has a very wholesome influence upon the contemporary thought, though there are people who think otherwise. It is not that he is original or even absurd. He is never entirely either. But he sticks his pen into the somewhat torpid consciousness of the average Englishman, and he digs up the clods of truth which have caked and hardened therein. He turns upside down the proverbial wisdom which most of us regard as eternal verity, and shows us that it looks as well one way as the other." To this same unnamed "London critic" these curious statements were also attributed: "Oscar Wilde dropped all his eccentricities of dress when he left America, which he visited fifteen years ago. He also dropped the O'Flaherty [*sic*] from his name. The Oscar Wilde who returned to England was the conventional nineteenth century gentleman, quiet in dress and reserved in manner." This observation almost gives one the sense that Irish eccentricity is somehow being balanced against British conformity on some kind of homosexual-heterosexual scale in Wilde's personality, and that by removing the former, he tipped toward the latter.

Another dichotomy suggested by the *Irish World* article is Roman Catholicism versus Hellenism, and after detailing Oscar's consideration of a conversion to Catholicism during his time at Oxford, it implied that Wilde again chose the wrong side: "Paganism triumphed over Christian Catholicism." The author then went on to talk about Wilde's poetry and called "Hélas!" Wilde's "most sincere and genuine" creation, praising it as "full of sad, vain longing and regret." Before printing the text of the sonnet, however, he admitted, "It casts a curious light upon a curious personality."

After the poem, which includes what the writer and at least some readers may have understood as prophetic lines ("Lo! with a little rod / I did but touch the honey of romance— / And must I lose a soul's inheritance?"), the thoughtful, measured tone of the article abruptly shifts to one of condemnation as if between the lines of verse lay all the secrets of Wilde's vice and perfidy:

> He has fallen so deep that no hand can raise him without being be-smirched with his own infamy. But in the gutter where he lies we can, without offence, do him such justice, at least, as he deserved. He was certainly a good son, patient, loving, devoted. He appeared to be a kind husband and a fond father, and his work had much in it that was useful. It is a pity that his hatred of conventionality and traditional shams had so much in it that was itself a sham, and worse . . .
>
> In the fall of Oscar Wilde art and literature have innocently suffered. But better no art and literature than the acceptance of Wilde.

The phrase that rudely greeted Wilde during his journey in Irish America—"talent sadly misapplied"—seems to echo here, lingering, as Wilde is cast into hell.

One last feature of this article that should be noted is that it never calls Wilde either Irish or an Irishman. Yet "Oscar Wilde's mother" is described as "perhaps the most famous woman poet of Ireland." And the reader is told how "her patriotic poems and lyrics, produced under the pseudonym 'Speranza,' endeared her to the hearts of her countrymen." Speranza was certainly Oscar Wilde's mother, but as far as the Irish American press was concerned, this article makes it painfully obvious that Oscar never lived up to the promise of being "Speranza's Son."

CHAPTER 2

The Celt in Irish America

WILLIAM BUTLER YEATS'S MISSION
TO THE NEW ISLAND, 1887–1904

IN JULY 1889, Oscar Wilde published a brief but laudatory review of a book of verse filled with the kind of poems he would not deign to write himself but would only recite and lecture about when pandering to Irish American audiences. The poems embodied the dreamy spirit of a Celtic literature that Matthew Arnold had conceptualized and that Wilde had all but plagiarized for his "Irish Poets and Poetry" lecture. In the review, Wilde described the verse and the poet, William Butler Yeats, in terms that again echoed Arnold: "nobility of treatment and nobility of subject matter, delicacy of poetic instinct, and richness of imaginative resource . . . naive and very primitive."[1]

The book was called *The Wanderings of Oisin,* and the poet was a thin, solitary young man given to a disheveled style that included dressing all in black and wearing both a floppy tie and a flowing cape. George Moore famously described Yeats as looking like a "great umbrella left behind by some picnic party."[2] To George Bernard Shaw, Yeats played the part of aesthete even better than Wilde: "Bunthorne was not a bit like Wilde; but he presently came to life in the person of W.B.Y., who out Bunthorned him enough to make him seem commonplace."[3]

Like Wilde, Yeats had spent his adolescence amid both provincial Dublin and metropolitan London. But Yeats did not have the privilege, or misfortune, of attending either Trinity or Oxford. Instead, his great place of education had been Sligo, a port town on the rugged northwest coastline of Ireland. Yeats spent significant parts of his youth with his maternal relations the Pollexfens, local shipping and milling magnates. His father's family had Sligo roots as well, his father's grandfather having been rector at nearby Drumcliff parish. Yeats began the autobiography of his early years, *Reveries over Childhood and Youth,* by cataloguing these older generations of relatives, all of whom were of solid, unremarkable Ascendancy stock: mercantilists and Anglican clergyman, British army officers and Irish civil servants.[4] By these relatives Yeats was taught to reverence British tradition; from their servants he learned to countenance Irish superstition.[5] It is also striking to read that unlike the young Wilde, who was taught by Speranza to venerate the saintly poet-martyrs of 1848, the young Yeats was inspired by "a book of Orange rhymes" to fantasize about fighting the Fenians to the death.[6]

Remarkable as it is in light of these mundane Ascendancy roots, W. B. Yeats's vital role as a self-consciously Irish artist leading a self-consciously Irish revival cannot be questioned or doubted. The example of Yeats stands in striking contrast to the debatable part assigned to Wilde by Declan Kiberd: "The story of the Irish *risorgimento* begins with Oscar Wilde . . . the first intellectual from Ireland who proceeded to London with the aim of dismantling its imperial mythology from within its own structures."[7] It was Yeats after all, not Wilde, who, in Kiberd's own words, "busied himself with the invention of a literary movement and the shaping of a post-Parnellite culture."[8] But as a means of advancing this movement and shaping that culture, Yeats did follow the example of Wilde in journeying across the Atlantic waves, an apostle for a very specific kind of art, bent on spreading his gospel with evangelical zeal to the new world. And Yeats, like any good evangelist, first prepared his way by writing a series of epistles.

"The Celt in London"

Amazingly, Yeats's first published verse in America appeared, like Wilde's, neither in a fashionable New York journal, nor in any earnest organ of the Brahmins, but in John Boyle O'Reilly's unmistakably Catholic and decidedly Irish *Pilot*. Yeats's mentor John O'Leary was on friendly terms with his fellow former Fenian, and that helps explain why the front page of the August 6, 1887, edition published a curious poem "written for The Pilot" about a Hungarian rebel with the exotic title "How Ferencz Renyi Kept Silent."[9] But despite this less than auspicious poetic debut, Yeats's main connection with the *Pilot* would be a series of fourteen prose articles that were typically headlined "The Celt in London." In addition to the *Pilot* articles, Yeats wrote seven pieces that appeared in the *Providence Sunday Journal,* a newspaper that was edited by a man named Alfred Williams, "whose interest in Irish letters was keen and early" and who was introduced to Yeats through Katherine Tynan.[10] When Williams retired in 1891, the new editor ceased taking an interest in things Irish, ending Yeats's connection with the paper.[11] Yeats's column appeared in the *Pilot* for two years after the unfortunate death of O'Reilly, so it is not clear what exactly severed his connection to the journal.

In total, then, there are twenty-one articles that were published between September 1888 and November 1892. These articles were collected and saved from obscurity by Horace M. Reynolds, a Brown University professor who published them with Yeats's consent, and a Yeats preface, in a volume under the title *Letters to the New Island,* which was originally published in 1934 and later reissued as part of Yeats's *Collected Works.* In his introduction to the collection, Reynolds described the importance, as well as the essentially transatlantic nature, of these letters: "Brought forth by an unknown young Irish poet in London and printed in New England, they are part of a nation's awakening to intellectual and imaginative energy."[12] The letters are extremely repetitious, dealing with many of the same authors and issues: Irish writers like Samuel Lever, Samuel Lover, T. W. Rolleston, and especially William Allingham were consistently denounced for their cosmopolitanism and their lack of national feeling, while Irish writers like Thomas Davis,

Samuel Ferguson, John and Ellen O'Leary, Standish O'Grady, and especially Douglas Hyde were continually celebrated for their patriotism and for mining the rich vein of Irish folklore and Celtic mythology; English literary culture was presented as dying a slow, creeping death, while Irish literary culture was described as in embryonic form, full of potential for the growth and development of national artists and a national audience.

A somewhat ambiguous but very important figure Yeats discussed in these letters was Dr. John Todhunter. The front page of the May 17, 1890, *Pilot* featured the "Celt in London" discussing the impending production of Dr. Todhunter's verse drama *A Sicilian Idyll*. Yeats praised Todhunter for bringing poetry back to the stage but castigated him for his Greco-Roman subject matter. Yeats presented Todhunter as another Irishman affected by the national literary vice, cosmopolitanism: "We are not content to dig our own potato patch in peace. We peer over the wall at our neighbor's instead of making our own garden green and beautiful . . . Dr. Todhunter could easily have found some pastoral incident among its stories more new and not less beautiful."[13] When Todhunter's play was actually performed, however, Yeats's comments became much more positive. In a letter to the *Pilot* published on June 14, 1890, the young romantic poet and future avant-garde dramatist began decrying melodrama and farce in favor of the poetic drama of Dr. Todhunter. Unlike in his previous letter to the *Pilot*, Yeats refrained from any criticism of Todhunter for utilizing non-Irish subject matter. It might be possible, therefore, to locate in Yeats's praise for Todhunter's method the beginnings of an amalgamation of ideas about national literature and poetic drama, an amalgamation that would take definite form in the years ahead.

Yeats's final article written for the *Providence Sunday Journal* was published on July 26, 1891. In it Yeats once again discussed Dr. Todhunter, who had produced another verse drama, this one called *The Poison Flower*, and whose play *A Sicilian Idyll* had moved from a small community theater in Bedford Park, west London, to the Vaudeville, one of the large theaters on the Strand. Yeats used the occasion to congratulate Todhunter and to criticize contemporary theater audiences: "Dr. Todhunter has heroically attempted to bring back our listless and

conventional public to something of the high thinking and high feeling of the playgoers of the time of Elizabeth." Yeats imagined an ideal
Elizabethan audience possessed of an admirable poetic culture: "The
knowledge and love of poetry were then a necessary part of good breed-
ing, for commercialism and Puritanism had not yet set their brand on
England."[14] And he credited Todhunter with trying to cultivate just
such an audience among modern playgoers: "He has gone near enough
to success to make it probable that we shall have a genuine public, however small, for poetic drama, and that we may see once more the work
of our poets put upon the stage as a matter of regular business, and
have plays of heroic passion and lofty diction, instead of commonplace
sentiments uttered in words which have at the very best no merit but
successful mimicry of the trivial and unbeautiful phraseology of the
streets and tea table."[15] The role Yeats ascribed to Todhunter bears an
uncanny resemblance to the role in which Yeats would eventually cast
himself: the poet-playwright whose dramatization of "heroic passion"
and implementation of "lofty diction" purges the modern stage of its
banal "tea table" realism, challenging his audience to confront the beautiful, the poetic, the Celtic.

On July 30, 1892, Yeats contributed to the *Pilot* not his typical letter from the Celt in London but a front-page article headlined "The
New 'Speranza.'" Yeats was in fact madly in love with his subject, Maud
Gonne, and had been obsessed with her for the better part of the three
years since they had first met.[16] When Yeats wrote about her for the
Pilot, Gonne was in the midst of a successful lecture tour through
France. In the article, Yeats quoted extensively from one of Gonne's
speeches, particularly a passage that describes the horrors of the famine of '48. He then praised the passionate magnificence of her oratory
as having "the serene beauty of good writing."[17] Yeats's comparison of
Gonne's oratory with the kind of literary drama he wished to create was
certainly no coincidence. Since at least 1889, Yeats had planned to write
a play based on a folktale he had collected about a Countess Cathleen
O'Shea, who supposedly sold her soul to save her starving peasantry.[18]
And Roy Foster claims that Yeats's introduction to Gonne had "helped
inspire the image of an aristocratic beauty sacrificing herself for the
love of her people."[19] The horrific famine imagery employed by Gonne

during her French lectures also overlaps with the setting of the play, titled *The Countess Cathleen,* which was published, and for copyright reasons performed privately, on May 6, 1892—just two months before this article appeared in the *Pilot.* Yeats's letter also included a line about a "voice calling upon the mountain at evening,"[20] which suggests the germ of the idea for *Cathleen ni Houlihan,* an allegorical play he would write during the summer of 1901 in collaboration with another aristocratic lady, Augusta Gregory, a political play whose theatrical debut featured none other than Maud Gonne in the starring role as the very embodiment of Ireland.

"The Celt in Ireland"

In July 1892, when he wrote his dispatch about Gonne, Irish Americans readers would have had little reason to guess that their Celt in London had begun to merge his enthusiasm for Irish literature with his ideas about poetic drama. But in his final letter to the *Pilot,* printed on the front page of the November 19, 1892, issue, Yeats did begin to reveal his grand project, a project that eventually resulted in the rise of a theater group of self-consciously Irish playwrights whose drama would attempt to bring poetic language and heroic action to the stage, a theater group whose work would try to aid in a process that Yeats's favorite folklorist and Gaelic scholar, Douglas Hyde, would soon dub de-Anglicization, a theater group whose representations of Irishness would one day cause tremors on both sides of the Atlantic. This final epistle appeared under the headline "The Celt in Ireland," and from the beginning Yeats made it clear that he had moved to Ireland permanently; he also made it clear that he had serious plans for his native land. The letter is worth quoting at length for the fascinating insights it provides about Yeats's ideas relating to the nation whose literary culture he hoped to invent:

> Your Celt has written the greater bulk of his letters from the capital of the enemy, but he is now among his own people and no longer "The Celt in London," but "The Celt in Ireland." At this moment he is sitting writing, or trying to write, in the big, florid new National Library . . . He is sitting dreaming much, and writing a little from time to time, watching the people come and go, and wondering what shall be born

of the new generation that is now so very busy reading endless scholas-
ticisms along the five rows of oak tables . . . At my left hand is a man
reading some registers of civil service or other examinations; opposite
me an ungainly young man with a puzzled face is turning over the pages of a trigonometry work; and a little beyond him a medical student
is deep in anatomical diagrams. On all sides men are studying things
that are to get them bodily food, but no man among them is searching
for the imaginative and spiritual food to be got out of great literature.
Nobody, with the exception of a few ladies, perhaps, ever seems to do
any disinterested reading in this library, or indeed anywhere else in Ireland. Everyman here is grinding at the mill wherein he grinds all things
into pounds and shillings, and but few of them will he get when all
is done . . . Can we find a remedy? Can we not unite literature to the
great passion of patriotism and ennoble both thereby? This question has
occupied us a great deal this spring. We think that a national literary
society and a series of national books like Duffy's library of Ireland
may do something, and have accordingly founded such a society and
planned out, with the help of a number of well known men of letters,
such a national series.[21]

Yeats went on to highlight how the committee members of this organization represent "all parties and opinions which have any claim to be
considered national," including several of the names that he had been
writing about in the *Pilot:* John O'Leary, Douglas Hyde, and Maud
Gonne. Yeats concluded the letter by admitting that "apart from our
literary society, things are not looking so bad for the future of our literature." Not surprisingly, he singled out for approbation the work of
Hyde and Standish O'Grady. Yeats also managed to include one final
swipe at Ireland's enemy as he promoted the work he so ardently championed in his letters to the New Island: "In England, I sometimes hear
men complain that the old themes of verse and prose are used up. Here
in Ireland the marble block is waiting for us almost untouched, and the
statues will come as soon as we have learned to use the chisel."[22]

Thirty years after these lines were printed, Yeats published his second autobiography, *The Trembling of the Veil,* book 2 of which is titled
"Ireland after Parnell." In this work, Yeats cast his cold eye back on the
period in which he was writing for the *Pilot* and famously described

"the sudden certainty that Ireland was to be like soft wax for years to come" as "a moment of supernatural insight" that guided all his activities during the subsequent years.[23] But perhaps the more accurate insight and the more appropriate metaphor was the one used by the youthful Yeats in his final letter to the *Pilot*. For the culture of Ireland, and by proxy the culture of Irish America, the culture that Yeats was so desirous of shaping, proved to be much less like the supple soft wax of his later imagination and much more like the marble he observed in the National Library—stubbornly calcified and not so easily formed. For the young men whom Yeats saw studying, that new generation of middle-class Catholic university students who aspired to be civil servants or professionals, those everymen who endeavored to grind everything into pounds and shillings to be put into savings accounts and greasy tills, were not so interested in the kind of imaginative and spiritual food Yeats would continually offer them.

Even among the group of potentially willing converts in the National Literary Society, Yeats had to confront the continuing influence of Young Ireland, the last great movement for Irish cultural nationalism. In "Ireland after Parnell," Yeats chronicled the challenges and difficulties this legacy posed to his efforts to organize a literary movement during these years: "No philosophic speculation, no economic question of the day disturbed an orthodoxy which, unlike that of religion, had no philosophic history, and the religious bigot was glad that it should be so."[24] Yeats blamed the conflicts that ensued from his efforts to do other than what Young Ireland would have done as the primary reason his plans were frustrated and postponed.[25]

Not surprisingly, the mature Yeats contrasted his young self staunchly with those who expressed such uncritical sentiments regarding Young Ireland, claiming, "I, upon the other hand, being in the intemperance of my youth, denied, as publicly as possible, merit to all but a few ballads translated from Gaelic writers, or written out of personal and generally tragic experience."[26] A cynic familiar only with Yeats's writings in the *Sunday Journal* and the *Pilot* might say that in the temperance of middle age, Yeats significantly minimized his adolescent zeal for Thomas Davis and the other poets of '48. But the truth of the matter is that the Yeats who had praised Davis as the epitome of a national writer in his initial American article in September 1888 had significantly evolved in the intervening five years.

And it would take another five years before such evolutions would become apparent to American readers. Specifically, in the December 1899 *North American Review,* Yeats published "The Literary Movement in Ireland," an article that outlined much of the work he had been doing since his letters to the *Pilot* and his career as a literary correspondent for American publications had ceased. The article opened by announcing that Yeats's movement had not merely arrived but was thriving:

> I have just come to a quiet Connaught house from seeing a movement of thought, which may do much to fashion the dreams of the next generation in Ireland, grow to a sudden maturity. Certain plays, which are an expression of the most characteristic ideals of what is sometimes called "the Celtic movement," have been acted in Dublin before audiences drawn from all classes and all political sections, and described at such length in every Nationalist newspaper, that the people in the cottages here in this quiet place are talking about them over the fire. Whatever be the merit of these plays, and that must be left to the judgment of time, their success means, as I think, that the "Celtic movement" which has hitherto interested but a few cultivated people, is about to become part of the thought of Ireland.[27]

The first part of the essay went on to describe how this transcendent cultural movement rose from the dust and debris of the political wreckage left in the wake of Parnell. Given the typical effusiveness of his praise for Young Ireland in his *Pilot* columns, what came next should have surprised Yeats's Irish American readers and provided evidence of his changing literary tastes: he contrasted the purely partisan ballads produced by the middle-class patriot-poets of 1848 with the much more sophisticated literature that was being produced at present, literature inspired by the mythology of the old Gaelic sagas and the folklore of the quasi-pagan peasantry, literature that was able to awaken "Irish affections among many from whom the old rhetoric could never have got a hearing."[28]

Yeats then listed all the organizations contributing to the cultural renewal, including those he had founded or helped organize—the Irish Literary Society in London, the National Literary Society in Dublin, the Irish Literary Theatre—as well as those he championed, such as the Feis Ceoil Committee and the Gaelic League. All these groups, Yeats noted approvingly, were "busy in preserving, or in moulding anew, and without any thought of the politics of the hour, some utterance of the national life, and in opposing the vulgar books and the music hall songs, that keep pouring in from England."[29] Yeats also proudly contended, "More books about Irish subjects have been published in these last eight years than in the thirty years that went before them, and these books have the care for scholarship and the precision of speech which had been notoriously lacking in books on Irish subjects."[30]

One thing Yeats did not discuss or even hint at is that one of the plays alluded to in the article's first paragraph, one of the plays inspired by the Celtic movement, one of the plays Yeats claimed had brought together an audience "drawn from all classes and all political sections," one of the plays whose fame Yeats insisted had already spread to the cottages of Connaught, had in fact been vociferously protested and denounced by certain factions in Dublin. Specifically, *The Countess Cathleen* had been performed five times during May 1899 under the auspices of the new Irish Literary Theatre Yeats had founded along with Lady Gregory, Edward Martyn, and George Moore. *The Countess Cathleen* was the verse drama Yeats had first written on the model of a folktale and which he later revised after being inspired by the vision of Maud Gonne's noblesse oblige. Recall that the plot depicted an aristocrat's selfless sale of her own soul to two merchant-devils who had been doing a brisk business among her starving subjects; the play ends with a just God recognizing the countess's motivation rather than judging her actual deed.

The production of *The Countess Cathleen* had been preceded by a pamphlet written by a formerly friendly acquaintance of Yeats who had more recently become a bitter adversary. The man's name was Frank Hugh O'Donnell, and years later Yeats would describe him as "half genius half sewer rat."[31] During the previous year, 1898, Yeats had denounced O'Donnell for printing a slanderous attack on Michael Davitt. Now, in 1899, O'Donnell responded with two letters to the editor of a Dublin paper, the *Freeman's Journal,* that were later combined into the pamphlet *Souls for Gold! A Pseudo-Celtic Drama in Dublin.*

O'Donnell's objection to the play is stated succinctly at the beginning
of his letter: "Out of all the mass of our national traditions it is precisely
the baseness which is utterly alien to all our national traditions, the bar-
ter of Faith for Gold, which Mr. W. B. Yeats selects as the fundamental
idea of his Celtic drama!"[32]

O'Donnell's pamphlet is sometimes dismissed as pure invective, but
as the editors of Yeats's *Collected Letters* point out, "although florid and
course, it reveals a close reading of the play and a knowledge of WBY's
career as a whole" that plays "skillfully on nationalist and Catholic
suspicions of WBY's attitudes to Thomas Davis, mysticism, sexuality,
Protestant proselytism, and pagan Celticism."[33] The editors also admit
the inaccuracy of Yeats's allegation that O'Donnell's pamphlet created
a reputation for anti-Catholicism that would dog Yeats for the rest of
his career; they argue instead that "it in fact crystallized . . . doubts that
had long gnawed at his Irish-Catholic readers." And these doubts were
further exacerbated by the public performance of the text: "Heterodoxy
in books of comparatively small Irish circulation held no immediate
danger to faith and fatherland, but the same ideas spoken from a public
stage to a popular audience rendered them far more disturbing and
disruptive."[34] The pamphlet outlined a multitude of orthodox theological reservations that could be raised against the themes of the play,
and in effect served as the opening volley in a series of battles between
the aspiring National Theatre and the Catholic-nationalist audience it
needed for both survival and validation.

When Yeats's play debuted, a group of students from Dublin's
Catholic university protested the production. James Joyce, who was
a classmate of the protesters and was in attendance that first night,
would memorably depict the rowdy scene in *A Portrait of the Artist as a
Young Man*.[35] The day after the performance, the earnest young Catholic nationalists composed a letter expressing their opposition, which
Joyce, displaying the stubborn iconoclasm for which he would become
renowned, refused to sign. Printed in the *Freeman's Journal* on May 10,
1899, it reads in part "We feel it our duty, in the name and for the honor
of Dublin Catholic students of the Royal University, to protest against
an art, even a dispassionate art, which offers as a type of our people a
loathsome brood of apostate."[36]

In his critical biography of Yeats, Terence Brown does an excellent job of contextualizing the debate inaugurated by O'Donnell and taken up by the Catholic students; he situates the row over *The Countess Cathleen* clearly within the Irish Ireland movement, which advocated "a version of Irish identity which was increasingly to appeal to the Irish middle classes in general, in which a commitment to Irish revival and to Catholicism were joined in a newly vibrant nationalism." According to Brown, because of the rise of Irish Ireland, "whatever degree of opportunity the post-Parnellite period had in fact offered to *déraciné* Irish Protestants like Yeats, to assume a leading role in national life, was now swiftly diminishing."[37] While this conflict was slowly but clearly developing in Ireland during the years between Yeats's letters to the *Pilot* and his article in the *North American Review,* in Irish America the hegemony of Irish Catholics made such tensions less obvious. As we shall see in the rest of this chapter, Anglo-Irishmen like Yeats and Douglas Hyde were not viewed as threatening to nationalist leadership in Irish America; instead, they were viewed as cultural champions of whom all Irishmen could be proud.

The Celt in America

To become personally acquainted with such accomplished cultural figures was one of the primary goals of John Quinn, a first-generation Irish American from Fostoria, Ohio, who had made himself an extremely successful corporate lawyer and man-about-town in New York City. In the summer of 1902, when Quinn paid his first visit to the land of his parents' birth, he was already a budding patron of writers and artists, whose manuscripts and paintings he had begun to procure with relish. Upon arriving in Dublin, Quinn set out "to collect images of his heroes in the cultural and political life of Ireland"; this entailed buying portraits of O'Leary, Hyde, and George Russell from John B. Yeats, the poet's father, and Jack B. Yeats, the poet's brother.[38] By the end of his month on the other side of the Atlantic, Quinn "had met and affected virtually everybody who was anybody in contemporary Irish letters."[39] The easy acceptance granted to Quinn by these accomplished Irish revivalists would be repaid handsomely in the years to come, for no other

Irish American had ever offered so much emotional, moral, financial, and legal support to Irish artists and writers.

When he sailed home, Quinn was definitely touched with the zeal of an acolyte and immediately set about organizing a New York branch of the Irish Literary Society. He decided that a performance of Yeats's drama would make an outstanding debut for the club. Quinn made all the arrangements and, eventually, notice of the plays as well as an exhortation to support genuine Irish literature was given in the May 29, 1903, *Irish-American*. The notice described the plays as "racy of the soil, and the work of one of the leaders in the Gaelic revival, the poet W. B. Yeats." The notice also presented the plays as an opportunity to demonstrate "patronage that will be accorded dramatic productions of which none of us need be ashamed."[40]

The three Yeats plays, *The Land of Heart's Desire*, *The Pot of Broth*, and *Cathleen ni Hoolihan*, were performed on the evenings of the third and fourth of June at the Carnegie Lyceum. Subsequently, the June 6, 1903, *Irish-American* included a rueful report on the performances, noting small, disapproving audiences.[41] In a letter to Yeats, Quinn told him, "The plays came off very successfully . . . the performances were excellent," and "one thing these plays have done is to make your name much more widely known here."[42] But in his next letter Quinn had to report, no doubt with embarrassment: "We took in upwards of $500 the two nights of the plays, but I am sorry to say that we have no profits . . . I am very sorry that I cannot send you some royalties." On a positive note, though, Quinn assured him, "You are known now to a great many who before the Irish Literary Society of New York was started and the plays given did not know what you stood for."[43]

Despite the promise of this debut, the New York Irish Literary Society was almost immediately confronted, or one could say doomed, by the same issue that had much more publicly greeted Yeats's Irish Literary Theatre in Dublin, namely, the accusation of heresy directed at Yeats. Almost as soon as the society had formed, Quinn ominously reported that a motion to make Yeats an honorary vice president had "aroused some opposition" on the grounds that the poet was "anticlerical"; ultimately, one of the other honorary vice presidents, Archbishop John Farley of New York, had withdrawn his name for the sake of propriety.[44] Yeats responded to Quinn's report with this rather oblivious reply: "I wonder why the Archbishop resigned. Was it 'where there is Nothing' or the old Countess Cathleen row? I have never attacked the Church as far as I know, but one must be able to express oneself freely, and that is precisely what no party of Irishmen Nationalist or Unionist, Protestant or Catholic, is anxious to permit one."[45] Not surprisingly, perhaps, the performance of Yeats's three plays was the first and last dramatic event sponsored by the New York Irish Literary Society under Quinn's directorship. Once the scheme had, for all intents and purposes, collapsed, Quinn turned his attention to another project, lining up a lucrative lecture tour for Yeats.

In his article "Yeats in America," Declan Kiely has suggested that the lecture tour was arranged by Quinn and Lady Gregory partly as a means of distracting Yeats from his heartbreak over Maud Gonne's sudden marriage to John MacBride.[46] But Quinn was no doubt just as concerned with burnishing Yeats's reputation in America, and to do so, he realized he would have to counteract the charges of anti-Catholicism. As a result, Quinn instructed Lady Gregory to contact a friend of hers, a Father Donovan, who Quinn hoped would promote Yeats among other American priests of a literary inclination; Quinn explained that "the point of this request is that in case any narrow-minded priest objects to the theology of Yeats' writing there may be some priests here who can be relied upon to defend him or whose friendship for him could be pointed to as an evidence of the fact that he is not a Presbyterian in disguise."[47]

While clerical support may have been difficult to obtain, Quinn had no trouble getting Yeats favorable press in the nationalist weeklies. Just as his plays had been, Yeats's tour was respectfully and enthusiastically advertised by the *Irish-American* and the *Irish World* as well as by John Devoy's new publication the *Gaelic American,* which had debuted in September 1903. The *Irish-American* was the first to report on the visit, which it described as a lecture tour "under the auspices of the Irish Literary Society of New York." The announcement noted that Yeats planned to visit Harvard, Yale, the University of Pennsylvania, Amherst, the College of the City of New York, Columbia, Stanford, and the University of California, where he would discuss "The Intellectual Revival

in Ireland," "The Theatre and What It Might Be," "The Heroic Literature of Ireland," and "Poetry in the Old Time and the New."[48]

A week later, the *Gaelic American* included a similar report but added
that "to educate the Irish people by means of a theatre thoroughly Irish in
spirit and character is his aim, and he comes to the United States to enlist
the sympathy of Irish-Americans." The article also quoted an interview
Yeats had granted to a New York reporter in which he noted: "The plays
that we produce are not in Gaelic but English. Nevertheless, a movement
has sprung up, which is due to the Gaelic League as well as to our efforts,
to produce Irish plays in the ancient Irish language."[49] This last claim by
Yeats is provocative, given the fact that the primary aim of the literary
revival he instigated was of course to produce a beautiful and uniquely
Irish literature written in *English*. Yeats's claim that a secondary effort of
his movement was "to produce Irish plays in the ancient Irish language"
can certainly be viewed as not entirely forthright.

Yet in a fascinating introduction to Yeats published in the "Gaelic
Notes" column of the *Irish World,* he was presented as a true Gaeilgeoir.
Here it is in full:

> Mr. W. B. Yeats is at present on a lecture tour in America. His lectures
> are mainly devoted to Irish literature. As between a school of Celtic note
> literature in English, to which some suppose Mr. Yeats to belong, and
> the only possible national literature, i.e., that in the national language of
> the country, we have heretofore clearly expressed ourselves. A national
> literature in English would be a false goal to set up. But there is no
> question of that kind involved now. Mr. Yeats is as sound on that point
> as the most advanced Gaelic Leaguer. His lectures are devoted toward
> spreading a knowledge of the beauties of ancient Irish literature, and
> toward turning attention alike to the ancient civilization of Ireland and
> the national revival of that civilization which is now taking place. There
> is certainly no one better fitted to do this in America than Mr. Yeats.
> A recent critic—an English one, if we remember correctly—placed Mr.
> Yeats among the first of living poets in the English tongue. His genius,
> his inspirations, his themes, are Irish of the Irish. His too few lyrics, his
> fairy songs, his prose works have that peculiar, indefinable quality about
> them which reveals genius, and which cause them to haunt the memory.
> He is a true artist. He does not prostitute his art by rhymed prose on
> the most prosaic and often ignoble themes, like Kipling and others of

the Saxon cult. Above all, he is a true Irishman. He is intensely devoted to his country, and is an earnest Gaelic Leaguer. We have reason to be proud of him, and we trust his countrymen and women everywhere he lectures will not fail to hear him and give him a cead mile failte.[50]

While the *Irish World* columnist demonstrated an impressive knowledge of Yeats's oeuvre as well as an acute awareness of his burgeoning critical reputation, that columnist also clearly misrepresented Yeats's aims to readers by taking Yeats at his word about the secondary goals of his movement. In a later "Gaelic Notes" column, the *Irish World* blamed uninformed American journalists, not the poet himself, for any confusion on this point:

> All of these writers in American papers and magazines fail absolutely to discriminate between these two movements. The Gaelic movement is to restore Gaelic and restore Irish nationality in literary, intellectual and social independence of England; the movement which these American writers confound with that is a movement in English literature, sharing some of the marks of several other such movements, as that of Keats for instance . . . We repeat that those who have by blood, tradition or racial sympathy imbibed some of the instincts of the Gael, but have been irreparably cut off from a complete enjoyment of Gaelic literature and a full inheritance of Gaelic thought in its own tongue, necessarily find an apostle in Mr. Yeats and a feasting place in his school. But even that school could not long exist without the Gaelic movement.[51]

In spite of the obvious ambiguity surrounding the incongruent goals of the non-Gaelic-speaking and-non-Gaelic-reading Yeats and those of the Gaelic League, Yeats's tour was unambiguously and enthusiastically covered by the American Irish press during late 1903 and early 1904.

The *Irish-American* printed a front-page notice on November 28 announcing: "William Butler Yeats, poet, dramatist and author, who is at present visiting America, gave his first lecture on last Wednesday evening . . . [A] large and enthusiastic audience was present to hear Mr. Yeats."[52] On December 5, the *Irish World* was thrilled to inform its readers in the "Gaelic Notes" column that Yeats had publicly zinged Rudyard Kipling during a question-and-answer session.[53] The following week, the *Irish World* reported, with similar approval, that Yeats had quipped during a lecture at the Long Island Historical Society, "The reason English novels and English poets are popular with their audiences is that their audiences are not interested in anything." The report also described an exchange between Yeats and a Sidney V. Lowell, who asked the poet "if it would not be better for Irishmen to take pride in the fact that they helped build up the British Empire, rather than to persist in cherishing their ancient traditions." Yeats replied with a wonky retort about England's unfair overtaxation of Ireland, offered as proof that there was nothing to be proud of in the empire.[54] In the same issue, on the editorial page, Yeats was complimented for his response to Mr. Lowell's question, and the editor expressed hoped "that his own kindred will avail themselves of every opportunity of hearing him" since Yeats was "one of their race of whom they may well be proud."[55]

On December 19, 1903, all three newspapers published nearly identical notices about Yeats's upcoming lecture at Carnegie Hall. The *Irish-American* again told its readers that Yeats was well worth hearing.[56] The *Irish World* added: "A better and more sincere Irishman than Mr. Yeats does not live. He is the chief standard-bearer of the intellectual and literary revival in Ireland."[57] In the same issue, the *Irish World* also reprinted an article about Yeats from the *New York Tribune* under the headline "Yeats' Patriotic Mission: Using the Irish Theatre as a Means to Help Along the National Revival Movement."[58] The *Gaelic American* notice for the Carnegie Hall lecture included the subheading "His Splendid Record as a Nationalist." The article highlighted Yeats's "great patriotism and intense national spirit" by recounting two past incidents proving Yeats's republican bona fides. The first incident involved a dinner the London group had organized in honor of Conan Doyle, a dinner whose menu included a toast to the queen's health. The article described how Yeats tore up the menus, preventing any Irishman from drinking to the monarchy. The second incident involved a lecture in Dublin to which the viceroyalty had been invited; someone from the Dublin society had rolled out the red carpet for the visit of such distinguished guests, but Yeats had them immediately rolled up when he arrived. The article also reprinted a letter Yeats had written rebuking the queen at the time of her visit to Dublin in 1900 during the Boer

War. Finally, the article closed with this enthusiastic exhortation: "Mr. Yeats has all the imagination and emotion, the passion and the inspiration that are and must always be the main source of poetry, and the Irishmen of New York should turn out in large numbers to welcome this creator of beautiful things, as beautiful as anything that is being done in our time."[59]

A week later, the *Irish World* ran a story with the headline "W. B. Yeats Honored: County Sligo Men Give a Dinner to the Irish Poet and Dramatist." Yeats's quoted remarks display the kind of anti-English and pro-nationalist sentiments that would have appealed to such a patriotic and benevolent society. Yeats was also quoted addressing the specific role his theater could have in its relation to the lives of those who live well beyond the pale of Dublin in country places like Sligo:

> All that we have had with which to do this work has been a handful of dreams. But it is dreams that set the imagination afire and nothing is so necessary to well-directed patriotism as an imagination aflame. Only the other day I received a letter from home telling me that a new play had been produced in my little theatre in Dublin and that production had been a great success. Yet the author of that play was a not very lettered son of an unlettered farmer. That is a sample of the work we are doing at home for the dear old land and her people.[60]

The playwright to whom Yeats was referring is not at all clear in the article, but R. F. Foster posits that Yeats may have been inaccurately describing Padraic Colum, whose father was a workhouse master and whose play *Broken Soil* had been staged late in 1903.[61] A letter from Yeats to his sister Lily also supports such an interpretation.[62]

But one wonders if Yeats could have been referring to Seumas MacManus, the son of a Donegal farmer, whose one-act play *Townland of Tamney* was produced by the Irish National Theatre Society just a few weeks later, in January 1904. Interestingly enough, soon after Yeats's arrival in America, MacManus began his own lecture tour of the United States. During February 1904, the *Gaelic American* actually printed advertisements for both speakers adjacent to each other, describing MacManus as an "Irish Story Writer and Poet" whose lecture would provide "Irish wit and humor"; Yeats was hailed as "The Renowned

Irish Poet and Dramatist" who would be delivering an address on Robert Emmett at the annual celebration sponsored by the Clan na Gael.

The intriguing possibility that Yeats was praising MacManus's aflamed imagination and well-directed patriotism in 1903 is undermined, however, by a letter Yeats wrote to John Quinn in February 1904 in which he says, "MacManus' play is rubbish & I was furious at its acceptance."[63] In August 1907, Quinn would add to the scorn directed at MacManus by writing to Yeats: "I was very much incensed . . . over an article by 'Shame-us' MacManus on 'Sinn Fein: Its Genesis and Purposes' . . . I have underscored in red and blue ink the parts in which, in the way of a cunning peasant, he works in things which the Gaelic League has accomplished as having been done by Sinn Fein."[64] When Yeats made his second lecture tour of America during the fall of 1911, MacManus was once again speaking to American audiences contemporaneously; MacManus's unfavorable public comments about Yeats at that time must have caused the poet to second-guess his championing of the cunningly imaginative peasants and unlettered farmers' sons who had begun to denounce him not just in Ireland but on the other side of the Atlantic as well.

In 1903 and 1904, however, Yeats had no need to defend himself against any accusations, since, as has been shown, the press coverage was full of approbation and, by all accounts, his audiences were respectful and receptive. The *Gaelic American* of January 9, 1904, for instance, claimed, "No Irishman who has spoken on a New York platform for very many years received a warmer welcome or more hearty applause than Mr. Yeats, and none deserved it better."[65] This kind of adulation followed Yeats as he journeyed from the Northeast to the Midwest. Both the *Irish World* and the *Gaelic American* reported on the welcome he received in Indianapolis. The *Gaelic American* described a function in Yeats's honor organized by "prominent members of the Emmet Club, Ancient Order of Hibernians, and other well-known Irish-American Societies."[66] A similar account ran in the *Irish World* under the headline "Indiana Irishmen Enthusiastically Welcome the Irish Poet and Dramatist."[67] In the same issue, the *Irish World* also reprinted a poem from the *Indianapolis Sentinel* written by a J. P. O'Mahony and dedicated to Yeats. Though brimming with nostalgic and patriotic sentiment, it is also full of the kind of schoolboy thoughts and clichéd rhetoric Yeats despised as the legacy of Young Ireland, a legacy that was obviously still very much in vogue among Irish American nationalists. Here is the first verse:

"TO ERIN'S BARD"

How fares it with the distant land—
Oh, Bard of Erin, say?
Are men as brave as to take their stand
As those who passed away?
Oh, sing to us the tidings glad
From that wild-wave-washed shore;
"Her sons are true
To dare and do—
As were the men of yore."[68]

While in the Midwest, Yeats also experienced the positive reception of two extremely Catholic audiences. After he lectured at the University of Notre Dame, Yeats told Quinn, "The Fathers were a delight, big merry Irish priests who told me fairy stories & listened to mine & drank punch with me."[69] Yeats also wrote to Lady Gregory describing his astonishment at "the general lack of religious prejudice" he found on all sides at Notre Dame.[70] From there Yeats traveled to Chicago, then to St. Paul, where he was invited to speak by Archbishop John Ireland. Yeats described that audience to Quinn "as one of the easiest to stir"— surprising in light of the fact that Yeats claimed "a great part of it" was composed of "priests to be."[71]

From Minnesota, Yeats continued west, all the way to the Pacific coast, where he was greeted in San Francisco with yet more praise from the Irish American press. In its February 13 issue, the *Gaelic American* ran an article effusively headlined "Yeats Captures California: The Great Irish Poet Addresses Immense Audience in San Francisco." The article quoted a report from the *San Francisco Leader*, a paper founded in 1902 by a Father Peter Yorke, a labor activist and militant Irish nationalist who also happened to be a cousin of John MacBride, Maud Gonne's drunken, vainglorious lout of a new husband. That report stated: "In one week [Yeats] has done more for the Irish name and the

Irish cause in the centres of culture than could be done in years. And he has inspired his own people with enthusiasm, with pride, with fresh courage." The article also mentioned that in addition to speaking before academic audiences at Berkeley, Stanford, and Santa Clara, Yeats had spoken "under the auspices of the League of the Cross" to an audience made up of "all manner of people—men and women interested in the cause of Ireland, clergy, professional men, litterateurs."[72] On that occasion, according to the *Gaelic American,* Yeats had been introduced warmly by a Father Philip O'Ryan, whose remarks once again suggest that the clerical circumspection that dogged Yeats in Ireland and New York was not present in this part of America:

> Cradled in the West, which the barbarism of modern civilization ne'er has spoiled, and where the traditions of the Gaelic race have remained pure, there arose a young enthusiast with the vision of the prophet and the soul of the poet. He gathered up the traditions and legends, the folk-lore and the heroic literature which are the very elements of Gaelic literature. He inspired other gifted children of song and clasped hands with the brave men who went forth to revive the old tongue. Mother Erin, who had been for a generation without a voice, is justly proud of her favorite son.[73]

The absolute apogee of American Irish adoration for Yeats, however, would come a month later, when he returned to New York and delivered the speech that had been advertised in the *Gaelic American* for weeks: the address on "Robert Emmet, the Apostle of Irish Liberty" at the annual celebration held under the auspices of the Clan na Gael. The Clan na Gael was of course the American wing of the Irish Republican Brotherhood; John Devoy, the editor of the *Gaelic American,* had long been the leading member of this organization, and 1903 was the centenary of the rising led by Emmet. According to Declan Kiely, "this was [Yeats's] only overtly political lecture subject, one he had been reluctant to deliver until persuaded by Quinn."[74] Perhaps the increased fee of $250 Yeats earned for the night aided Quinn's considerable powers of persuasion. But days before he delivered the lecture, Yeats wrote in a tone of frustration to Lady Gregory: "I am dreadfully busy over my Emmet lecture, which is a frightful nuisance. It is indeed as you say, a sword dance and I must give to it every moment. I had no idea until I started on it how completely I have thought myself out of the whole stream of traditional Irish feeling on such subjects. I am just as strenuous a Nationalist as ever, but I have got to express these things all differently."[75] But the four thousand patriots who turned out to hear Yeats speak, the largest audience he addressed while in America by far, were in no way disappointed with what the newest apostle of Irish liberty had to say. The *Gaelic American* reported that Yeats "received a welcome that will tingle pleasantly in his ears as long as he lives" and that his address was "fully appreciated by the audience and will long be remembered."[76]

In some ways, Yeats's speech on Emmet can be compared to the address on Irish poetry Wilde had delivered in San Francisco more than twenty years earlier: in both cases, the topic was chosen by the audience rather than by the speaker, and ultimately the speaker "was giving an audience what he assumed it wanted, in terms that bear little relation to his private opinions as recorded at this time."[77] But in contrast to those of Wilde, Yeats's general cultural concerns were, to be fair, much closer in content to the themes addressed in the mercenary lecture. And it should be noted that John Quinn's motives in arranging the tour were obviously not as purely profit driven as D'Oyly Carte's had been in promoting Wilde. Furthermore, it must be stressed that unlike the aesthetic precepts his fellow Dubliner had elucidated two decades earlier, Yeats's ideas about Irish literature were taken seriously and listened to enthusiastically by many Irish Americans. Terence Brown elucidates some of these striking points of contrast as well as other differences between the two tours:

> [Yeats] was further advanced in a literary career [than Wilde] . . . Yeats . . . was more obviously Irish than Wilde; he was traveling under distinctly Irish-American auspices and was offering lectures on Irish topics . . . Quinn's achievement was to gain him a hearing . . . in the American universities . . . such as Yale, Smith, Amherst, Mount Holyoke, Wellesley, Bryn Mawr and Vassar, where Irish-America could not have been assured of a welcome, as well as at the lesser known or distinctively Irish schools such as Trinity College . . . and Notre Dame.[78]

Or in other words, it was shrewd of Quinn to get the professors on Yeats's side, never mind the priests.

But for Patrick McCartan, a Sinn Fein operative who served as envoy to the United States during the revolutionary Irish Republic and who later developed a close friendship with Yeats during the poet's last tour of America in 1932, Yeats's engagement with America's elite universities implied something very different. In an encomium written for the *Ireland American Review* after the poet's death, McCartan implied that Yeats's reputation had been undermined by Irish Americans:

> As a poet of genius . . . Yeats has been appreciated much more in the colleges and universities, and hence by the people of America, than in the colleges and universities or by the people of his own country. One might justly assume that this was due to the influence of Irish-Americans. It is strange, however, that in some of our colleges and universities where Irish influence predominates he was as much neglected as at home. Would not one naturally think that in America an Irishman of genius would be first recognized by these institutions? . . . It was in purely American institutions such as Harvard, where Irish influences were for long negligible, that this outstanding Irishman first received the tribute due to genius. It was in these centres of learning that Yeats' aims were fully grasped and their realization watched with sympathetic and increasing interest.[79]

What McCartan seems to suggest, then, is that Yeats was not so much shrewdly guided toward the Ivy League by Quinn as he was relegated there when the doors to Irish Catholic colleges and universities were unexpectedly closed to him.

But the evidence displayed in this chapter demonstrates that while the majority of the conservative Irish Catholic clergy who controlled Catholic academia in America did not embrace Yeats, a minority of the clergy and a preponderance of Irish American organizations did so eagerly and enthusiastically. This evidence, then, clearly supports yet another interpretation of the tour, this one provided by R. F. Foster: "The emigrant Irish, basking in the reflected glory of his fame, suspended their reservations about the depth of his nationalism . . . WBY's sophisticated

Celticism, and high claims for Irish culture above English materialism, struck a satisfying chord."[80]

This relationship between Yeats and Irish America—aloof circumspection by conservative clergy and the institutions they controlled but zealous acceptance by the patriotic societies and the nationalist press; polite apathy for his abstruse literary theorizing and his unconventional poetic dramas but unqualified admiration for the man because of his tireless efforts on behalf of Ireland—would have perhaps continued for the remainder of the Great Organizer's long, distinguished career if Yeats had not been instrumental in introducing to the Western world another talented Anglo-Irish littérateur whom Yeats had first met floundering in Paris in 1896. Advocating the course of action he had spelled out in so many of his early dispatches to America, Yeats advised this young artist named John Millington Synge to forsake the cosmopolitan and to embrace the local, to forgo imitation of current literary trends and to develop his own style based on the national traditions of Ireland. Forget Paris and go to Aran, Yeats had told him, and go he did. The eventual result of Synge's pilgrimage to those primitive isles was a slim oeuvre of just six plays that would forever alter the course of modern Irish literature. But in terms of Yeats's reputation among the American Irish, the result of his championing of Synge was that the "Celt in London" who had so zealously spread the good news about the revival of Irish literature from the capital of the enemy, the "Celt in Ireland" who had returned heroically to his native land in order to direct and channel the energies of that revival into a national theater, the "Celt in America" who had so impressed audiences with his preaching about the Irish revival would be transformed, suddenly and shockingly, into a "British government pensioner" who peddled lies and blasphemies about the Irish Catholic peasantry to American theater audiences eager to have their stage Irish stereotypes reinforced.

CHAPTER 3

"No End of a Row"

THE NATIONAL THEATRE IN THE SHADOW
OF SYNGE, 1903–1909

O N OCTOBER 14, 1903, just weeks before William Butler Yeats
embarked on his first, triumphant lecture tour of America, the
poet wrote to his chief American promoter and patron, New York lawyer
John Quinn, to report on the Irish National Theatre Society's production
of John Millington Synge's *In the Shadow of the Glen,* the first of the
playwright's works to be performed in public. The play, set in a Wicklow
cottage, depicts a suspicious old farmer named Dan Burke who fakes his
death to test the intentions of his young wife, Nora. When a neighbor
named Michael Dara immediately proposes to Nora, Dan reveals his
plot and kicks his young wife out of their home. At the end of the drama,
a defiant Nora decides to run off with the tramp who has been witness
to these events. Yeats told Quinn: "Synge's play played beautifully, but
has stirred up no end of a row by its morals. After the attacks which will
come in the weekly papers we expect a row on Saturday."[1]

As it turned out, there was no disturbance at the theater, but Yeats
was right to predict a campaign in the press against the play. The *Inde-*

pendent, the *Leader, An Claidheamh Soluis,* and the *United Irishman* all denounced *In the Shadow of the Glen.*[2] Yeats located the center of the opposition in the last of these publications, Arthur Griffith's newspaper, which he deemed "the organ" of "the extreme national party."[3] On October 17, the *United Irishman* had claimed that the play was "no more Irish than the Decameron. It is a staging of that old-world libel on womankind—the Widow of Ephesus."[4] The *United Irishman* not only questioned the authenticity of the plot but also denounced the decision of the National Theatre to perform such a play. On November 8, the *United Irishman* summed up its argument by claiming that Synge was "as utterly a stranger to the Irish character as any Englishman who has yet dissected us for the enlightenment of his countrymen."[5] These charges—that neither the decadent playwright nor his immoral subject matter was in any way authentically Irish, and therefore that his work was not suitable for the National Theatre—would dog Synge for the rest of his brief but consequential career.

Yeats responded to the charge that the play was a libel on the women of Ireland by writing a highly ironical letter to the *Dublin Daily Express* signed with a pseudonym that incorporates the subject of his climactic speech in New York: "Robert Emmet MacGowan." The letter writer made the point that Synge's play was an insult to Ireland just as *Antony and Cleopatra* was an insult to the people of Egypt, and *Macbeth* an insult to the humanity of Scotland, and *Romeo and Juliet* an insult to Catholic Italy. The letter closed with an invitation to organized protest followed by an adjournment to a pub, and the writer explained how he could be identified: "They will know me by my Gaelic League button and the pike which I shall carry in my right hand."[6] The letter is no doubt humorous, but its analogy is obviously faulty in that the Bard was neither an Egyptian nor a Scotsman nor a Catholic Italian, nor was he part of a dramatic project that claimed to represent the ancient idealism of a specific nationality for a specifically national audience. That was the rub Yeats ignored in this piece, but one he would continually try to address as he defended Synge.

Yeats replied to the charges of the *United Irishman* directly, in a letter published in the October 10 edition of that paper. He began by arguing for the merits of an Ibsenite realism devoid of mere patriotic propaganda:

"If we think that a national play must be as near as possible a page out of *The Spirit of the Nation* put into dramatic form, and mean to go on thinking it to the end, then we may be sure that this generation will not see the rise in Ireland of a theatre that will reflect the life of Ireland as the Scandinavian theatre reflects the Scandinavian life."[7] But later in the letter he suggested that in addition to realism, audiences must be open to Aristophanic satire. Finally, he made an appeal for artistic freedom based purely on the totally subjective nature of art: "Literature is always personal, always one man's vision of the world, one man's experience, and it can only be popular when men are ready to welcome the vision of others."[8] Surprisingly, what Yeats left out of his defense of Synge was any discussion of the play's "lofty diction," a diction that was, no doubt, opposed to the "unbeautiful phraseology of the streets and tea table"; these were traits even Synge's detractors may have acknowledged in the play, and this was the primary quality Yeats had advocated in his letters to the New Island when he first became interested in the theater as a young man.[9]

The quarrel about *In the Shadow of the Glen* never did become an issue of any consequence while Yeats was lecturing in America during 1903–4, but that was not because his impassioned but inconsistent defense of Synge had decided the matter. In fact, the quarrel about *In the Shadow of the Glen* was just a prelude to the mighty row that another Synge play would cause. By the time *The Playboy of the Western World* premiered in Dublin on January 26, 1907, Joseph Holloway, Dublin diarist, Abbey insider, and theater observer par excellence, could describe Synge as "the evil genius of the Abbey" whose dark masterpiece about the power of a young liar to charm an entire Mayo village was "the outpouring of a morbid, unhealthy mind ever seeking on the dunghill of life for the nastiness that lies concealed there."[10] And legend has it that the janitress of the Abbey concurred with Holloway, pondering rhetorically, "Isn't Mr. Synge a bloody old snot to write such a play?"[11] One Abbey playwright, William Boyle, even withdrew his three plays, *The Building Fund*, *The Eloquent Dempsey*, and *The Mineral Workers*, from the theater's repertoire "as a protest against . . . attempting to force a play—at risk of a riot—upon the Dublin public contrary to their protests of its being a gross misrepresentation of the character of our Western peasantry."[12]

Not surprisingly, the play had its defenders, who attacked its detractors with equal intensity. One unnamed young doctor who attended the second performance, but whose wit is suggestive of Oliver St. John Gogarty, commented to Synge, "I wish medical etiquette permitted me to go down & stand in front of that pit & point out among the protesters in the name of Irish virtue the patients I am treating for venereal disease."[13] And in a public debate Yeats sponsored following the disturbances, John Butler Yeats, William's father, chastised the hostile crowd, a scene Yeats would depict years later in his poem "Beautiful Lofty Things": "My father upon the Abbey stage, before him a raging crowd: / 'This Land of Saints,' and then as the applause died out, / 'Of plaster Saints'; his beautiful mischievous head thrown back."[14]

On February 18, Yeats wrote to John Quinn to discuss the row and its aftermath. Yeats told Quinn that the riots had led to a clear break in the alliance between advanced nationalists and the revivalists, an alliance that in Ireland had been showing signs of strain for the better part of a decade: "It has been for some time inevitable that the intellectual element here in Dublin should fall out with the more brainless patriotic element, and come into existence as a conscious force by doing so."[15] In a public debate held at the Abbey after the disturbances, Yeats again saw his enemy clearly: "They were followers of Arthur Griffith and obscure members of the Gaelic League, come down to serve their country, by attacking the culture that they fear."[16] While dismissive of the hostile Dublin audience, Yeats expressed concern to Quinn about potential reactions to the play in Irish America: "I am rather anxious about the presentation of the Play to America . . . The 'Playboy' if taken up wrongly, by Irish Americans might upset things."[17] To combat any misinterpretations proactively, Yeats proposed an introduction to an American edition "explaining that the Play means that if Ireland goes on, loosing [*sic*] her strong men by emigration at the present rate, and submitting her will to every kind of political and religious dominion, the young men will grow so tame that the young girls will prefer any man of spirit, even though he has killed his father, to any one of them."[18] This fanciful interpretation of the play as a piece of anti-emigration propaganda never materialized. But unfortunately for Yeats, another of his insights did prove to be an astute prognostication: "I should think that [Irish Americans] will resent even more than here, any harsh picture of the country, which they see through clouds of tenderness."[19]

Quinn was, of course, sympathetic to Synge, and when he wrote back to Yeats, he described all the public relations work he was busy doing on Synge's behalf, using his many contacts in the worlds of publishing and journalism:

> I gave a copy of Synge's book on Aran to Gregg of the *Evening Sun* and he gave it a fine review . . . I also gave Gregg a copy of *The Playboy* and he gave it a good notice . . . I am writing Roberts about an offer of the Baker & Taylor Company to become Synge's publishers here. Young Hackett is now reading all the plays, loaned by me, and will submit terms in a few days . . . I gave a copy to my friend Townsend Walsh and he wrote me two letters about it . . . I have sent copies to Synge, together with the favorable newspaper notices—as I said to Synge, the good with the bad.[20]

But Quinn was also typically forthright about the negativity surrounding the playwright and his work : "I fought fight after fight over *The Playboy*. All the Irish or Catholic Irish-American newspapers republished . . . attacks and it would be false to say that damage was not done by it. Damage was done. I argued the matter out with John Devoy . . . and gave him a copy of the play. I tried to *make* him see the humor of it. He laughed at some of the scenes. Then he took the book home, read it and in a few days said he was madder than ever, that it was an 'outrage.'"[21]

Quinn then explained how he was trying to counteract the damage that had been done. Primarily, he was aiming to undermine the authority of the play's opponents:

> At the time of the first performance young [Bulmer] Hobson was here. He was dining with Judge Keogh, D. F. Cohalan, John Devoy and myself. Hobson said the play was "rightly hooted down." I ventured to inquire upon whose authority he said that. He said Arthur Griffith had condemned it. I replied: "Is Arthur Griffith a dramatic critic too? I knew he was a statesman, but I didn't know he was a critic. Do you think if he applied to *The Times* in London or to the New York *Herald* or *World* for the position of dramatic critic and they asked him to show his qualifications, that his membership of the National Council and his begetting of the

Sinn Fein programme would secure him the job? Wouldn't they inquire
about his knowledge of the drama; his knowledge of its history, its tech-
nique, his knowledge of contemporary continental drama, of the ancient
classical Greek and Latin drama, and so on?" Hobson had to admit that
he didn't think Griffith would get the job. Then I said: "He may be a great
statesman; you undoubtedly believe he is, but as a dramatic critic he is an
ass—a joke—an amusing donkey; he's not worth discussing."[22]

Quinn seems to have been unaware, or at least unwilling to admit, that
Griffith had been at one time vice president of the National Theatre
Society. And the irony of such a dismissive denunciation of amateur
criticism issuing from the lips of a lawyer who was basically an au-
todidact when it came to the fine arts was no doubt lost on the ever
self-assured Quinn.

Quinn concluded the letter by shrewdly advising Yeats, "You had better not come before this public more directly (I mean the Irish-American
papers) in defense of Synge than you have."[23] Quinn saw that the Irish
American nationalists, like their Dublin brethren, would not be swayed
by any kind of subtle reasoning in regard to *The Playboy*. Quinn's description of such men's critical prowess offers a fine example of his talent for
mixed metaphor and invective, as well as his keen insight:

> An Irishman can't ever be a sane critic. He can't criticize anything without
> thinking it fair to make it the basis of a personal attack. The true critic
> dissects a thing lovingly and carefully. The Irish critic goes at the subject
> of dissection like a drunken sailor and with a shillelagh and a sledge-
> hammer, batters the poor corpse all around the room, and when he has
> mashed the poor thing into an unrecognizable pulp, or thinks he has, he
> points to the poor mass and says it is only jelly or calls it poison, and then
> he thinks he has done something great. They are not critics; they are only
> scavengers. In *The Playboy* case you have, of course, a classic illustration of
> Irish criticism—unreasoning condemnation by the Irish "critics" on many
> grounds, among others that it is anti-national and holds the Irish people
> up to ridicule in the face of the world, and particularly of England; then
> the presentation of the play in England with praise from English critics;
> next the Irish scavengers pointing to the English praise of the work as
> conclusive proof of their charge, because whatever is praised in England
> is anti-Irish and anti-national, of course, so the play is a libel on Irish life.[24]

A good example of this kind of Irish-drunken-sailor-with-a-shillelagh-and-sledgehammer criticism—as applied to Synge, Yeats, and even Oscar Wilde, who had died eight years before—can be found in the February 8, 1908, *Irish-American Advocate,* a newspaper that had been founded in 1893 by John C. O'Connor.[25] Under the headline "The Neo-Celtic Drama," the unsigned piece laments that "the Irish National drama has fallen upon evil days." Yeats is described as a "poseur" who "has been for years working in the vain endeavor to establish a cult of decadence which is destined eventually to die of inanition." Yeats and Synge are then compared to "the sunflower and lily band who 'blossomed' some years ago under the lead of an Irish asthete [*sic*], who shall be nameless." The note concluded by championing the "well-deserved castigation" that was sure to meets Synge's new anticlerical play *The Tinker's Wedding.*[26]

A slightly less belligerent notice concerning Yeats and Synge appeared under the heading "Irish Plays for New York" in the following week's *Irish-American.* It announced that "under the directorship of William Butler Yeats, a company of Irish players" which included the Fay brothers were being brought to New York to put on "Mr. Yeats's play 'A Pot of Broth' . . . [and] other plays of their repertoire." This notice misrepresented Yeats's involvement in the production, it had the wrong article in the title of the peasant comedy (it's *The Pot of Broth*), and it didn't explain that the Fay brothers had resigned from the National Theatre after a dispute with the directors. The author of the notice, clearly oblivious to these errors and omissions, went on to praise a Mr. Charles Frohman, who organized the production, as "too shrewd" to allow "the offensive rot of the Synge tribe of decadents" onto the New York stage.[27] The following week's *Irish-American,* judging that its warnings had been heeded, offered a positive review of "*A Pot of Broth* [*sic*]" as played by W. G. Fay, F. J. Fay, and Bridget O'Dempsay. The reviewer concluded: "The whole manner of acting is daintily and thoroughly Irish, simple and natural. Its delicate reality is of course lost on the average New York audience but there certainly ought to be enough sober-minded Irish-Americans in this great community to give the venture the practical stamp of approval it so richly deserves." The reviewer also challenged his readers to support the production: "Now here is a real Irish presentation of a bit of real Irish peasant life done

in the most artistic dramatic manner. Let us see how much real enthusiasm there is for dramatic truth for the Irish character among the
shouters."[28] Taken together, the two *Irish-American* notices are remarkable in the way the former presents Synge, and by association Yeats, as
part of "the tribe of decadents" disseminating "offensive rot," whereas
the latter depicts the Fays and the National Theatre company as van-
guards of the Irish Ireland movement providing "a real presentation of a
bit of real Irish peasant life done in the most artistic dramatic manner."

In the column next to the second notice was printed another piece of
commentary suggesting the ambiguity the Yeats family name inspired
during this period:

"AN UNWISE ALLY"

John Butler Yeats, R.H.A., more familiarly known as "Jack" Yeats,
and father of the writer W. B. Yeats, has been in New York for several
weeks . . . "Jack" Yeats believes that "Art" with a big A, is the real thing,
and that "religion is but a side chapel in the temple which artists are
building up." He is also of the opinion that if the financial authorities
in Ireland would only endow the landscape painter, George Russell—
the "A.E." of poetic fame—"with money and leisure so that he might
pursue the art of landscape painting they would in my opinion do much
more for this country than by endowing a Catholic University." It is
hardly necessary to go much further to take Mr. Yeats' measure. One
very irreverent listener declared "He is talkin' through his caubeen."[29]

Besides the fact that this was printed parallel to praise for a production
of his son's play, what makes this interesting is not the predictable indignation inspired by the senior Yeats's suggestion that A.E.'s paintings
had more national value than a Catholic university. More interesting
is that six weeks earlier, when John B. Yeats first arrived, the *Irish-
American* had placed a prominent picture of him and his daughter Lily
alongside a front-page feature touting the Irish industrial movement.[30]
Clearly the Yeats family contained multitudes.

When John Quinn wrote W. B. Yeats to inform him about the
reception of the Fays, his report also suggests the variety of responses
the poet-dramatist's work could inspire during this period. On the positive side, he admitted, "the critics' notices . . . are quite frankly very

favorable—much more favorable than I thought they would be." In Quinn's own judgment, however, the performance was "not a success," the production compared unfavorably with the one he had staged in 1903, and the Fays were "really amateurs." Quinn explained that "New York audiences are much more cosmopolitan than you may imagine. There are not two per cent of them made up of Irish people." But among the Irish who were in attendance, Quinn ominously related that "several of them were complaining that the play was not 'representative' and that it made out the farmer and his wife to be half-fools."[31]

A few months after *The Pot of Broth* had been put on in New York, Yeats informed Quinn that Synge had become seriously ill. Quinn responded: "I wonder what the 'pathriots' will say about him now. It is the same old story, pearls before swine."[32] When Synge succumbed to his illness, Quinn wrote in shock to Yeats, full of lamentation for the death of a talent so young. Answering his own question about the "pathriotic" swine, Quinn informed Yeats that "John Devoy wrote a half-column in *The Gaelic American*, still talking philology and discussing questions of pronunciation in various counties and claiming that *The Playboy* misrepresented Irishmen. But it was written with a friendly intention."[33] Quinn actually downplayed the evenhanded ethos of the obituary, which acknowledged both sides of *The Playboy* controversy: "The attacks on it were resented by [Synge's] friends as unjust, dictated by narrowness and bigotry and resentment because it described faults of the Irish peasantry which cannot be denied"; "it was attacked by men who knew the Irish peasantry better than Synge, because it was claimed to be a true picture of everyday peasant life in the West of Ireland." While of course arguing for the latter position and pointing out the hypocrisy of Quinn and Yeats—"the resentment of Synge's friends was inconsistent on the part of men who claim the right to criticize and who justly claim that criticism is the very salt of the literature"—it nonetheless closed on a very positive, respectful note: "Synge had great dramatic talent, he was a good Irishman, had a good speaking knowledge of the Irish language, and his early death is a great loss to Ireland."[34]

After mentioning Devoy's obituary, Quinn told Yeats that a much more detestable one had been published in "a Jesuit paper called *America*, a weak imitation of the London *Tablet*." Quinn described the piece as containing "six sentences and as many lies or false insinuations about Synge. It is not worth while noticing but it shows the brutality and lack of feeling of the churchman mind."[35] The *America* article reads in part:

> A laudation of I. M. [*sic*] Synge is going around the secular press and there is an intimation that we are to have more of it. He belonged to a small set of literary "log-rollers" who posed as the only true artists in Ireland, and professing to represent the spiritual element of the Irish character of which they were ignorant, have imported Ibsen and Hegel to help them out. Mr. Synge became notorious for writing a play that was hissed off the Irish stage and broke up the National Theatre in Dublin . . . The play lacks literary merit, being a medley of incongruities dressed out in Ibsenized brogue. Now that the author is no more, the matter might be allowed to rest, had not the ill-advised propaganda of his friends tended to provoke a repetition of the scenes which the play originally excited.[36]

Two and a half years after Synge's death, Yeats's long-fermenting desire to bring the entire Abbey repertoire to America finally became a concrete reality, ensuring that the prediction made by the anonymous Jesuit who authored the mean-spirited obituary would come true.

CHAPTER 4
"Weary of Misrepresentation"

RECONSIDERING THE ABBEY PLAYWRIGHTS
IN IRISH AMERICA, 1911–1913

In her memoir *Our Irish Theatre,* Lady Gregory wistfully recalls the events leading to the Abbey Theatre's first American tour:

I think from the very first day Mr. Yeats and I had talked at Duras of an Irish Theatre, and certainly ever since there had been a company of Irish players, we had hoped and perhaps determined to go to *An t-Oilean ur* "the New Island," the greater Ireland beyond the Atlantic. But though as some Connacht girls said to me at Buffalo, "Since ever we were the height of the table, America it was always our dream," and though we had planned that if for any cause our Theatre should be nearing its end we would take our reserve fund and spend it mainly on that voyage and that venture, we did not ourselves make the opportunity at the last. After we had played in the summer of 1911 at the Court Theatre, as ever for a longer period and to a larger audience, we were made an offer by the theatrical managers, Liebler & Co., to play for three or four months in the United States, and the offer had been accepted. They mentioned certain plays as essential, among them *The Playboy of the Western World.*[1]

But this decision to journey beyond the Atlantic to the New Island, with the detested *Playboy* in tow, would sorely test the hopes and determination of Yeats and Lady Gregory. For it turned out that many of the newspapers the Connacht girls of Buffalo would have read, as well as the patriotic and cultural organizations to which they would have belonged, questioned and challenged the legitimacy of the Abbey's status as the national theater of Ireland.

The simple facts of the controversy are not in dispute: many Irish American organizations and publications did express the opinion that the national image of Ireland was smeared by the characterization of the peasantry presented in *The Playboy of the Western World*, a smear they argued would detract from both the hard-won status of Irish Americans as respectable American citizens and from the cause of Irish Home Rule, which was about to come before Parliament for the third time. A number of Irish American publications also presented *The Playboy* as the latest battle in a war against negative representations of the Irish on the American stage. In accordance with this view, these organizations and publications advocated strategies that had been successful during prior engagements with those who would propagate stereotypes. These strategies that were employed against *The Playboy* alternated between (1) organized protest, on the grounds that freedom of expression within the theater was balanced by the right of audiences to protest filth, falsehood, or blasphemy on the stage; (2) attempted suppression, on the grounds that *The Playboy* fit the legal definition of indecency or immorality; and eventually (3) boycott, on the grounds that the riotous protests were providing free publicity and perpetuating negative stereotypes (the very thing demonstrators were meant to be protesting onstage). Adele Dalsimer's neat summarization of the tour's reception in major American cities is accurate: "The Abbey's opposition attempted censorship in Boston, threw eggs and potatoes in New York, had the cast arrested in Philadelphia, and worked for its arrest in Chicago."[2]

Lady Gregory chronicled her battle against these forms of protest in "'The Playboy' in America," a chapter of *Our Irish Theatre*, which includes appendixes titled "In the Eyes of Our Enemies" and "In the Eyes of Our Friends." In these sections of her book, she presented a triumphant narrative in which art ultimately conquered all: "But works of imagination such as those of Synge could not be suppressed even if burned on the market place. [Irish American opponents] had not realized the tremendous support we had, that we were not fighting alone but with the intellect of America as well as Europe at our back."[3] In his book *The Irish Play on the New York Stage, 1874–1966*, John Harrington examines the controversy in an insightful chapter titled "Synge's *Playboy*, the Irish Players, and the Anti-Irish Irish Players." Harrington highlights how Lady Gregory's conquest "was the victory of artists over audience,"[4] the triumph of what Yeats would eventually describe as "an artist's arrogance—'Not what you want but what we want.'"[5] But unfortunately for those curious about the history of the Irish in America, this artistic arrogance of Yeats and Lady Gregory has gone unchecked by many of the scholars who have accepted Lady Gregory's Manichean account of the opposition to the Abbey's first American tour.[6] In fact, her account is a simplified version of an extremely complicated collision of artists and one of the audiences they were ostensibly trying to engage. Following Lady Gregory's lead, many commentators have offered similarly reductive interpretations of these events. Here is just one example of the many that could be mentioned: "This fight for artistic freedom is one which every generation must make against the shibboleths which society erects against the artist, his material and his medium."[7]

This banal assessment neither challenges nor complicates Lady Gregory's version of the conflict between Irish Americans and the "Irish Players"—a name coined by the directors of the Abbey Theatre "to distinguish it financially and so avoid the charge of diverting the resources of a national theatre for the entertainment of other nationals."[8] And by merely ratifying Lady Gregory's interpretation, many scholars have glossed over the volatile brew of issues this controversy fermented, thereby begging questions related to the rights of audiences to protest what they find offensive and the responsibilities of so-called national theaters to their audiences. But even more egregiously, many scholars have overlooked important issues that contributed to the confrontation, avoiding, for instance, a discussion of the supportive relationship Irish America had shared with the literary revival prior to the Abbey's tour, neglecting to mention the positive responses some Irish Americans experienced when viewing other plays in the repertoire, and refusing even to consider objections by Irish Americans to the supposed "realism" of the plays. It is these critical omissions that I seek to redress in this chapter.

Friendly Enemies?

If one were to read only Lady Gregory's *Our Irish Theatre,* one would assume that the sole official organ of Irish American opinion was John Devoy's *Gaelic American,* the most militantly republican of all the Irish American publications. But of course when the Irish Players arrived in 1911, Irish American weeklies served a readership that was not completely homogeneous in regard to the national question or to questions of American politics or economics. And as Terry Golway explains in his biography of Devoy, in many ways the *Gaelic American* was actually the most atypical of all the Irish American newspapers:

> The *Gaelic American* had all the trappings of the many other ethnic weeklies in the nation's immigrant cities, but its goal was quite different. Devoy's paper would not be an immigrant's guide to assimilation; it would not cover the tragedies, triumphs, and struggles that were a working-class Irish-American's lot. It would not crusade for better housing, safer working conditions, and an end to child labor. Instead of trying to turn the Irish into better Americans, the paper existed to propagate the gospel according to Clan na Gael. Its readership was not to be the great mass of Irish America. With its erudite analyses of European politics and dispatches from various lands struggling under Britain's yoke, the paper was written and edited for educated and highly literate leaders of Irish America. A solicitation for classified advertising noted that the paper circulated in "the homes of people who needed servants." Priced at five cents, with subscriptions available for $2.50 a year, it was distributed throughout the country, attaining an influence beyond its circulation of about thirty thousand.[9]

The kind of Irish American newspaper that Golway most obviously contrasts to the *Gaelic American* is the *Irish World and American Industrial Liberator.* In 1911 that paper was still being run by the elderly Patrick Ford, but it had evolved considerably over the years. Ford "had abandoned his earlier radicalism and now lined up consistently behind the Catholic Church he had once criticized"; furthermore, Ford now supported John Redmond's constitutional nationalist organization the United Irish League of America, which was "composed mostly of Irish Americans of high social standing and often considerable wealth" and which "outspokenly opposed socialism and other radical movements."[10] The *Boston Pilot* was another publication that had a long history of serving as a guide for Irish immigrants in their attempts to assimilate. The *Pilot* had become "the official organ" of the Boston diocese when the Donohoe family sold its controlling share of the paper to Bishop William O'Connell in 1908.[11] The paper still covered Irish issues, but its raison d'être was now religion and American patriotism, not Irish nationalism; in 1911 each issue of the *Pilot* was emblazoned with the motto "Be just and fear not. Let all ends thou aim'st at be thy God's, thy country's and truth's." Additionally, the *Irish-American* was one of the first, and for many years had been the most popular, of the American Irish journals; in 1911 it was still publishing, despite the passing of Patrick Meehan in 1906. Meehan's successor was Major Edward T. McCrystal, an Ancient Order of Hibernians man as well as a veteran of New York's fighting Sixty-ninth Regiment. And, finally, there was the *Advocate*. By 1911 the name of the *Irish-American Advocate* had been shortened to simply the *Advocate*, which billed itself as "a weekly paper of Irish news and miscellany, and devoted to the business, social, athletic and political doings of the Irish population of greater New York."

All these papers are mentioned to demonstrate the diversity of opinion and variety of interests represented by Irish American publications besides the *Gaelic American*. Yet Lady Gregory's chapter on *The Playboy* does not mention any of these other Irish American newspapers, a selective strategy that subsequent scholars have imitated.[12] The result of this limited evidence is, not surprisingly, a skewed presentation of Irish American reaction, resulting in generalities such as these: "The most vehemently expressed Irish-American reading . . . was less subtle still than the angriest Dublin letter writers";[13] "The Irish Americans lacked critical detachment. Their writing was emotionally charged and generally abusive";[14] "The campaign against the Abbey and its dread offspring *The Playboy* lasted for the duration of the first tour and was marked by vitriol and racial abuse";[15] or "The nature of their opposition can be understood when one reads this typical statement: 'The New York Irish will send the Anti-Irish Players back to Dublin like whipped curs with their tails between them.'"[16] An echo chamber of savage indignation did eventually develop, and such emotionally charged, vitriolic, and abusive statements are typical of the rhetoric that the *Gaelic American* eventually adopted. But such rhetoric was not typical of the *Gaelic American* initially, nor were all Irish American publications in lockstep agreement about the Abbey Theatre. Furthermore, to suggest that all criticism leveled against the tour was entirely abusive and in no way substantive is a claim not supported by the archival evidence.

Examining the microfilmed archives of the *Gaelic American* and looking at the issues preceding the arrival of the Irish Players reveals many surprising findings. In an August edition of the *Gaelic American,* one unearths this brief but approving note: "The members of the Irish National Theatre, who are shortly concluding a most successful season at the Court Theatre here, may probably pay a visit to the United States in late autumn."[17] In another August issue one stumbles upon an article about the Irish American poet Shaemas O'Sheel with this flattering and laudatory line: "Mr. O'Sheel acknowledges that he believes William Butler Yeats has carried English lyric poetry to its highest point of loveliness and subtlety, and that he (O'Sheel) is best pleased with those of his poems which are most in the manner of Yeats."[18] Then, in a September issue, one discovers an article applauding the publication of a volume of translation by the Celtic scholar Kuno Meyer, containing praise for the founder of the Abbey and his greatest protégé: "This volume, should take its place in the library of the booklover on the shelves besides Yates [*sic*], Singe [*sic*], Fiona MacLeod and George Russell."[19] In that same issue one also finds a reprint of this short blurb from the *New York Times Book Review* that praised another of the Abbey's founders: "Children and folklorists will enjoy the stories Lady Gregory has assembled in 'The Kiltartan Wonder Book.' They are Irish tales that have come down from generation to generation, and are published about as they were repeated to Lady Gregory by sundry aged Irishmen."[20]

As demonstrated in chapter 2, and as these brief quotations should make clear, many Irish Americans admired William Butler Yeats for his poetic genius and respected him for his advocacy on behalf of Irish literature. It also seems apparent in these few examples that a similar kind of respect was afforded to the work of Lady Gregory and the Abbey Theatre. Further evidence of such respect can be found in the collection of letters published as *Devoy's Post Bag,* where one discovers this polite and appreciative note from the aristocratic directress of the Abbey to the fire-breathing Fenian editor of the *Gaelic American,* who is never named in *Our Irish Theatre* but is referred to only as "the enemy":

> July 8, 1908
>
> Dear Mr. Devoy,
>
> I wonder if I may ask you again to do me a kindness, as you did before, through Mr. John Quinn's intercession, in the case of *The Gaol Gate*? The play I enclose, *Dervorgilla,* has been played several times at the Abbey Theatre, and with success. We want to print it this autumn in the little Annual connected with the theatre, *Samhain,* but as you know I cannot print here first without losing American copyright. It will be most kind if you will print and copyright it for me, if your space allows, and I shall be very grateful.
>
> Yours faithfully,
> Augusta Gregory
>
> If you print it, will you add to your kindness by sending me a copy?[21]

What this note makes clear is not only that Devoy had been on somewhat friendly terms with Lady Gregory but also, more important, that he had a history of aiding the Abbey directors in securing American copyright for their work. Yet such facts are never mentioned by Lady Gregory in *Our Irish Theatre,* and their discovery no doubt complicates the nature of the relationship between a ringleader of the protesters and those artists responsible for the performances of the Irish Players.

A close reading of the archival evidence also reveals that the initial opposition to the tour was based on Catholic, rather than nationalist, objections. So on September 2, 1911, for instance, the same day the *Gaelic American* ran the puff for the Kuno Meyer book that should have taken its place on the shelf next to Yeats and Synge, the *Irish World* published an article with the headline "So-Called Irish Players on the Wrong Track." While this article did unabashedly dismiss Yeats, Gregory, Shaw, and Synge for their politics—"they are not Irish Nationalists, and they do not represent Irish life or sentiment or history"—its main idea was that the goal of the tour was "to put their pagan poetry on the American stage as 'Irish' drama."[22] Paula M. Kane, in her perceptive article "Staging a Lie: Boston Irish-Catholicism and the New Irish Drama," has dubbed this idea "the pagan conspiracy theory" and shows how central it was to the attacks on *The Playboy* in particular and to the Abbey Theatre more generally.[23] To buttress the argument, the *Irish World* article quoted extensively from a piece written by "Rev. Dr. Hogan of Maynooth" that had appeared in *Ecclesiastical Review*. Father Hogan was of the opinion that Yeats and Lady Gregory were not attempting to de-Anglicize Ireland, as they claimed, but rather to de-Catholicize it, ushering in a "pagan renaissance." As evidence, Hogan noted, "It is owing to them that some few of our Catholic people are calling their children by the pagan names of Fin, Deirdre, and Ferdiad."[24] Kane points out that an article from the *Irish Ecclesiastic Record* making similar claims was used by another Irish American publication, the *National Hibernian*, to advance this conspiracy theory.[25]

The Jesuit periodical *America* also tried to foment antagonism toward the tour in a series of articles. The September 30 issue featured a piece titled "The 'Irish' Players and Playwrights" written by a Father M. Kenny. The article was chiefly concerned with refuting the impression encouraged by Yeats and Gregory that the Abbey Theatre and the Gaelic movement were one and the same: "Their claim to have initiated the Gaelic literary revival and be its chiefest flower is supported neither by the history of the movement nor by the intrinsic worth of their productions." While admitting the prominent role of Anglo-Irish Protestants like Samuel Ferguson, Aubrey de Vere, Standish O'Grady, and Douglas Hyde, Kenny constructed a history of the revival that was centered on the labors of Irish Catholics:

> Aided and blessed by bishops and clergy, Gaelic gradually forced its way into the primary and intermediate schools and the universities; a purely Gaelic magazine was founded at Maynooth, which is now the literary

outlet of its students, and the National Ecclesiastic College has become the chief centre of Gaelic propaganda. Meanwhile a long list of writers (among whom may be mentioned such priests as Canon O'Leary, Fathers Dineen, Henebry, Hogan, S.J., Mac Erlean, S.J., O'Kelly, Sheehan, O'Reilly and Hayden, S.J.) have been editing texts, preparing dictionaries, grammars and text-books, writing plays, poems, stories, essays and miscellaneous works and translating the classics into Gaelic, while Gaelic thought was gradually infusing the organs published in English, nearly all of which are vigorously supporting the movement. This is a summary of the Gaelic Revival; the story of what in it that is vigorous and genuine will not record the name of W. B. Yeats or of J. M. Synge.

In contrast to these noble toilers for the old tongue, Yeats was presented as an opportunist who had latched on to the Gaelic movement to further his own career. Kenny also reminded readers of Yeats's penchant for producing material with decidedly unorthodox and anti-Catholic plots, material such as his short story "The Crucifixion of the Outcast" and his plays *Countess Cathleen* and *Where There Is Nothing.* Not surprisingly, Father Kenny denounced Synge as Yeats's "pièce de résistance," a specimen of "Gallic decadence" foreign to the Gaelic movement and hostile to Catholic Ireland: "[Synge] is an alien studying curious specimens, and a superior person, to whom the natives are interesting savages and good material for his art; whether they are injured in the process is not of consequence."[26]

One also finds in Father Kenny's article, as well as in subsequent articles that appeared in *America,* many of the insinuations that were later propagated by the Irish American weeklies: first, the charge that the Irish Players "were received with noisy rapture by a certain class in England, not, however, on their dramatic merits, but because, at a time when the Irish question was the bone of political contention, their representation of Irish character suited the tastes of anti-Irish partisans";[27] and second, the revelation that Yeats, "after preaching extreme politics and lofty ideals, accepted a government pension."[28] In addition to the discovery that the Jesuits in many ways established the avenues of attack, the most remarkable thing found in *America* is an article in which the Jesuits actually took the likes of the *Gaelic American* to task for denouncing only *The Playboy* and not the entire repertoire presented by Yeats and Lady Gregory: "An advanced Gaelic organ exposed [*The Playboy's*] barbarities, but gave a clean bill of health to Mr. Yeats and the rest of his program. Doubtless they also had not read the plays they approved. Well, we have read them. We found several among them even more vile, more false, and far more dangerous than 'The Playboy,' the 'bestial depravity' of which carries its own condemnation; and we deliberately pronounce them the most malignant travesty of Irish character and of all that is sacred in Catholic life that has come out of Ireland."[29] With these vehemently argued Catholic objections to the entire repertoire of the Irish Players in mind, let us return to the coverage Devoy's paper afforded the tour—coverage, don't forget, that was lambasted by *America* as not critical enough.

The September 23 *Gaelic American* included this not very subtle headline:

AN UN-IRISH PLAY

"The Playboy of the Western World"
Is a Vile Caricature of the
Religious Nature of Irishmen and
Women, and the Abbey Theatre
Company Should Be Advised
Not to Reproduce It Here[30]

This headline was followed by a synopsis that Daniel Murphy has described as "biased and inaccurate."[31] The charge of purposeful misrepresentation is based on the *Gaelic American's* citation of the provocative line "Doesn't the world know you reared a black ram at your own breast, so that the Lord Bishop of Connacht felt the elements of a Christian and he eating it after in a kidney stew," even though that line had been cut for public performances of the play. But all the newspaper's quotations of the text are accurately transcribed from Synge's written version of the play. So even if one does concede that the representation of the play as performed, if not as written, was misleading, it is important to note again that the article does not object to any other plays in the Abbey's repertoire. This is why the *Gaelic American* was subsequently chastised in the pages of *America*. Furthermore, the article closed with a comment and rhetorical question that again revealed respect for the directors of the National Theatre and their mission: "The strangest feature in connection with this vile production is that Lady Gregory and W. B. Yeats are its sponsors. Are they interested in galvanizing into life in this country the corpse of the stage Irishman?"[32]

When Yeats's plays had first been performed in 1903 under the auspices of the Irish Literary Society of New York, they were, of course, presented by the Irish American press as a sophisticated antidote to the stage Irishman represented in plays like *McFadden's Row of Flats*. More than likely, the *Gaelic American* author, recalling the aid the paper had given Quinn and Yeats in *their* efforts to combat the stage Irishman, was alluding to the famous claims made in the original manifesto for the Irish Literary Theatre: "We will show that Ireland is not the home of buffoonery and of easy sentiment, as it has been represented, but the home of an ancient idealism. We are confident of all Irish people who are weary of misrepresentation, in carrying out a work that is outside all political questions that divide us."[33] If this possibility is admitted, the possibility that the *Gaelic American*'s editor John Devoy believed he still shared a mission with Lady Gregory and Yeats, then the full heading to one of the abbreviated headlines that Lady Gregory included in the appendix to *Our Irish Theatre* would help illustrate the controversy more fully and more clearly. I have added italics for emphasis:

> IRISHMEN WILL STAMP OUT THE PLAYBOY
> United Irish-American Societies, *Finding Friendly Pleadings Useless*,
>   Resolve
> To Suppress, At Any Cost, The Vile Libel On Irish Womanhood And
> Gross Misrepresentation of Their Religious Feelings—A Foul, Gross
> And Vulgar Attack *Lauded By William Butler Yeats As A True
> Picture Of The Mind Of Ireland*—Drastic Measures Will
> Be Taken If Found Necessary[34]

While Devoy has been charged with unethical citation, it is Professor Murphy and Lady Gregory who are guilty of the more egregious manipulation of text. Murphy elides the "friendly pleadings" part and "lauded by William Butler Yeats as a true picture of the mind of Ireland" in his quotation of the headline.[35] Lady Gregory omits the subheading entirely.[36] But the parts left out of the headline are keys to understanding the larger context that scholars have misconstrued. Such context helps show that this infamous headline is much more than simply the menacing ravings of an insecure ethnic mob. It is the protest of an ethnic group who wanted to continue aiding the cause of the Irish literary revival, fighting the good fight against the stage Irish buffoon, but who refused to accept a supposedly realistic representation being foisted upon them by a coterie of playwrights whose social class and religious background often alienated them from the subject matter they presented onstage. It was a protest against cultural appropriation before such a concept had gained critical currency.

The contradictory impulse to extend some kind of friendly greeting while simultaneously making demands and threats in response to issues of representation and appropriation can also be found in the *Gaelic American*'s September 30 issue, which is rarely mentioned in any scholar's reconstruction of the controversy. That edition's headline read:

IRISH PLAYERS WELL RECEIVED IN BOSTON
Sure Of A Cordial Welcome Everywhere If They Cut Out "The
    Playboy Of
The Western World," Which Is A Gross Misrepresentation Of Irish Life
—Irish in America Will Not Tolerate That—Based On The Insulting
Theory That Irish Men And Women Treat Murderers as Heroes,
Which Shows Grotesque Ignorance Of Their Feelings

The article beneath this headline began by noting that "the opening performance consisted of Synge's comedy, 'The Shadow of the Glen,' T. C. Murray's tragedy, 'The Birthright,' and Lady Gregory's amusing farce, 'Hyacinth Halvey.'" The article also highlighted that "the theatre was filled with an appreciative audience and all the plays were well-received." Furthermore, the article clearly stated that "Irish men and women in America will be glad to see [the troupe] succeed everywhere and to help them succeed," but it counseled that "management will make success possible by keeping on the lines on which such a good beginning was made in Boston." And that "good beginning" referred, of course, to the fact that *The Playboy* had not been performed. The article concluded by restating this advice: "The proper thing for Mr. Yeats to do is banish it from his programme. Then he will be received with open arms and given a hundred thousand welcomes."[37]

Evidence to support the *Gaelic American*'s claim that Irish Americans had in fact warmly welcomed the Irish Players during their first stop in Boston can be corroborated in the September 30 issue of the *Boston Pilot,* which went so far as to run a gushing notice that sounds as if it could have been written by Yeats or Lady Gregory.[38] The same issue of *America* that chastised an "advanced Gaelic organ" for not denouncing the entire repertoire of the Irish Players also scolded "several Catholic weeklies" for publishing "eulogies of the 'Irish Players" productions." The writer presumed that this happened "through want of acquaintance . . . with their contents and tendency" but reminded readers that "at least five of these plays . . . are more dangerous than plays openly immoral, inasmuch as, besides being immorally suggestive, they tend directly and indirectly to destroy all respect for Religion, Church, priesthood and sacraments, the foundations and safeguards of morality."[39] This notice demonstrates again that initially it was the Jesuits who were the fiercest enemies of the Irish Players. Meanwhile in the *Pilot,* Synge was described as "a master dramatist, the beauty of whose language is not surpassed by the masters of the Elizabethan period . . . a veritable 'lord of language' . . . [whose] stagecraft is as fine as his wordcraft." Besides praising Synge, whoever wrote the article shrewdly drew attention to the fact that the company was about to begin rehearsing a dramatic work written by Johanna Redmond, daughter of the popular and respected head of the Irish Party who was about to deliver the country to the doorstep of Home Rule.[40]

Another relative of a distinguished Irishman whose association with the Irish Players could only have helped their reputation in Boston was Mary Boyle O'Reilly, widow of John, who contributed a laudatory note to the *Boston Post.* Mrs. Boyle O'Reilly praised the company for enacting "brave and beautiful and touching memories which, through the ignorance of the second generation, have ceased to be cause for gratitude or pride" as well as for "deal[ing] a death blow to the coarse and stupid burlesque of the traditional stage Irishman, who has, for years, outraged every man and woman of Celtic ancestry by gorilla-like buffoonery and grotesque attempts at brogue."[41] Despite being included in the appendix of Gregory's *Our Irish Theatre,* such a positive pronouncement by a prominent Irish American is rarely mentioned in the critical discussions of the Abbey's reception.

Instead, another letter to the *Boston Post,* a letter that was later reprinted in the *Gaelic American,* is typically referred to as the letter that initiated the hostilities.[42] This is the screed written by Dr. J. T. Gallagher containing these fulminations: "I never saw anything so vulgar, vile, beastly and unnatural, so calculated to calumniate, degrade and defame a people and all they hold sacred and dear . . . Nothing but hell-inspired ingenuity and satanic hatred of the Irish people and all they hold dear could suggest, construct, and influence the production of such plays . . . [They] are not only anti-national and anti-Catholic, but anti-Christian . . . Through every play one purpose runs. And that is to show that the Irish people are too savage, crude and unreliable to be trusted with Home Rule."[43] In contrast to such heated rhetoric, one finds in the "A Looker On" column of the *Pilot,* but not in the scholarly literature on the controversy, this measured discussion of the plays and players: "With all admiration for the well known chivalry, bravery and purity of the Irish people as a race, we must admit that there have been conspicuous instances of the lack of these qualities in individuals of Irish blood. On these the dramatist must seize if he is to make an effective play. The typical Irish home, the typical Irish woman in her purity of character and the man in his quick wit and chivalry are materials for a eulogy or a poem rather than a drama." The article concluded with these sensible insights about dramatic art and dramatic advertising: "The playhouse is not the place to seek delineation of national character. For that we have the history, the literature, the poetry of the nation. The playhouse depicts exceptional character of whatever race under exceptional strain and conditions. The trouble with the 'Irish Players' is the title they have taken and the trick of the press agent to work off this and the plays themselves to get them talked about and sell chairs at the Plymouth."[44]

A week after that piece was published, the *Pilot* announced that it would again attempt to provide for its readers evenhanded coverage of the controversy: "Determined to get an impartial and just criticism of these dramas The Pilot sent to witness them, one whose profound knowledge of the Irish character and language is unquestioned, and whose interest in the welfare of Ireland and her institutions is well known, Rev. Michael P. Mahon of St. Mary's Church, Georgetown. Fr. Mahon has not only read the plays, but has attended several performances."[45] Father Mahon began his critique by lauding the actors: "There is a great deal to praise in the program presented by the Irish players at the Plymouth Theatre. Their interpretation is excellent. They are so natural on the stage that it takes some time to realize they are acting, and in the meantime the hearer is fascinated." But he concluded the introductory paragraph with a note of measured disapprobation: "It is regrettable, however, that in so much excellence there should be some serious blemishes." Father Mahon's main criticism was that the Abbey dramatists had failed in their expressed goal of presenting a true portrait of Ireland: "The dramatists of the Irish National Theatre set out to portray Irish life and character. It is clear that they have failed in this. Irish character is as vast in its range as human nature itself, and to depict it in a few plays or within a few years would be a tremendous undertaking. Indeed it would be impossible and we should not take the attempt seriously." In this critique one discovers an obscure parish priest gently, and reasonably, dismissing the grandiose claims of William Butler Yeats about the feasibility of what his National Theatre had done and could do.

But along with his gentle critique, Father Mahon also specifically praised the "splendid allegory" of Yeats's *Cathleen ni Houlihan* and admitted the "good time" an audience could have with William Boyle's *Eloquent Dempsey*; Mahon went so far as to say, "In fact, we can enjoy any one of these beautiful playlets or plays and recognize certain phases or Irish life very faithfully portrayed in them." Father Mahon did, however, spend much of the remainder of the critique discussing the negative aspects of *The Playboy,* which he described as "a trial, an enigma . . . an insult to the Irish race." He repeated the accusation that the play was an attack on the morals of Irish peasant girls, but he also claimed that the play "attacks revealed religion" and "is offensive to any one who takes his religion seriously." But even his denunciations of the play were leavened by some appreciation for Synge's talent: "The play is thoroughly demoralizing and made more so by the scintillations of wit and gleams of humor. It is a comedy at best and there is danger of taking it too seriously." Mahon concluded his critique by once again praising the company as a whole, and by asking his readers to show the Irish Players patience and courtesy: "If we give the Irish National or Literary Theatre time enough, it will treat us to what is grand and noble and refining in Irish character. There is no use in losing our tempers. These people are only beginning and they could not injure Irish character if they would. If time and space allowed, we would dwell with pleasure on the meritorious qualities with which so many of these plays are so replete."[46] And so in Father Mahon's critique one finds generally friendly praise for the repertoire of the Irish Players, specific criticism of the content of Synge's *Playboy,* and an implicit dismissal of Yeats's claims that the plays presented a realistic portrait of Ireland.

Though they were in the minority, opinions like those expressed by Father Mahon can be found in other American Irish publications. For instance, in the *Irish World* one can find, unexpectedly for sure given its editors' vehement opposition to the tour, an extremely interesting discussion of the Abbey productions in the "Currai an tSaogail" column. This article began by noting, "We may say at the outset that we disagree with many of the attacks which have been made upon the 'Abbey' founders, principally those which charge them with sinister motives." It went on to say, "It should be remembered . . . that when the 'Abbey' was founded we had no Irish drama; we have had the most brilliant dramatists and actors in the English-speaking world, but no Irish drama, in Irish or in English." Next the article made the bold claim that "the question brought into discussion through the presentations of the Abbey players, therefore, is more important than their success or failure, or the character of one or more of their plays."[47]

Like Father Mahon, however, the author of this piece did not praise Synge, and in fact *The Playboy* was judged to be devoid of "any poetic flights, the expression of an idea we would like to retain, a sentence which we would like to remember, an interesting figure or character, grotesque or otherwise," in sum "a repulsive and atrocious production, which not for one moment or one passage even faintly reflects the genuine." The author then turned his attention to Yeats, whom he called "a success in comparison to Mr. Synge" but a failure nonetheless in his ability to capture the spirit of the peasants of Catholic Ireland. Yeats was advised to "stick to his lyre and his pagans and his fairies, and the secular side of modern Irish humans if he touches them at all." This condescending advice was leavened by some genuine appreciation:

"When at his best he handles the lyre with a more artistic hand than anyone singing in English today."[48]

The reasonable points made by Father Mahon and the "Currai an tSaogail" columnist are in fact nearly identical to points made by the publication Lady Gregory and her devoted scholar-followers have so often painted as the intractable Irish American enemy; one finds in the September 30, 1911, *Gaelic American* this simple argument: "William Butler Yeats has done much for Irish literature and Synge has made some brilliant contributions to it, but their proper line is not in presenting pictures of present day Irish peasant life."[49]

A Cracked Looking Glass

Despite its headline—"Irish Players Well Received in Boston"—the majority of that September 30 *Gaelic American* front-page article is not really a report of the Irish Players' opening night reception but rather a fascinating refutation of claims Yeats was making in the American press to publicize the tour and defend Synge. A close reading of this article proves how problematic it is for a scholar like Kenneth Cox Lyman to claim: "Completely ignored were the well-publicized facts that the story [of *The Playboy*] was based on an actual incident in the west of Ireland and that much of the language had been transcribed from peasant speech word for word . . . It is probably true that many [Irish Americans] had never heard of Synge, let alone read one of his plays, but no matter: the everlasting enemy abroad had come to camp on Manhattan's shores!"[50] Lyman is of course alluding here to Synge's claims about the authenticity of the play's language and plot. Yeats had repeated these claims in a piece published in *The Forum* magazine, quoting Synge: "Any one who has lived in real intimacy with the Irish peasantry will know that the wildest sayings in this play are tame indeed compared with the fancies one may hear at any little hillside cottage of Geesala, or Carraroe or Dingle Bay." In the same piece, Yeats himself claimed: "An old man on the Aran Islands told me the very tale on which 'The Playboy' is founded, beginning with the words, 'If any gentleman has done a crime, we'll hide him. There was a gentleman that killed his father and I had him in my own house six months till he got away to America."[51] Rather than ignoring these claims, the *Gaelic American* piece tried to deconstruct them.

Regarding the language of the play, the *Gaelic American* frankly admitted that Irish peasants were in the habit of telling wild stories around the hearth, "full of grotesque and impossible incidents"; but, the article protested, "these extravagant productions are avowedly inventions and no one takes them as anything else." Thus the article disqualified the manner in which "these fantastic tales about heroes, giants, old hags and fairies are given as the excuse for presenting 'The Playboy of the Western World' as a true representation of life in the West of Ireland." Regarding the plot of the play, the article chillingly acknowledged the brutal violence that so often had accompanied Ireland's colonial history: "The law was made by the enemy and administered by the enemy, and partisan judges and packed juries did England's work without scruple or mercy. If the Irish people did not resist the law they would have been exterminated . . . That the people sympathized with and aided the man who killed an evicting landlord, an agent or a bailiff is true and there is no need to apologize for the fact. The same is true about killing informers, political or agrarian."[52] But of course the article denied that any such sympathy would have been extended to a parricide or common criminal.

Furthermore, the article explained away both of Synge's claims by suggesting that Irish peasants were only too willing, too ready, and too able to perform the part expected of them by English visitors, and Anglo-Irish ones as well. In this context, Yeats is described as follows: "[He] is not an enemy of the Irish people, but a friend—a born Irishman who has done a great deal for Irish literature, but he misunderstands the character and mind of the Irish peasant as badly as if he were only an English tourist." The implication is of course that such tourists are continually duped by the tall tales and bulls of feigning peasants, or as the *Gaelic American* put it: "Every Irish wag is ready at a moment's notice to fill the credulous Englishman with stories of horrors and monstrosities . . . Every Irishman can tell a story about fooling the cockney tourist. The present writer has a score of them, but two or three will suffice." As one example, the article's author offered this anecdote: "'Where are you coming from, Pat?' asked the English tourist of a man he met on the road. 'From Killinaman, sir,' replied the peasant. 'Killing a man,' exclaimed the Briton in horror. 'Yis, sir,' said the peasant. 'And where are you going now?' asked the Englishman. 'I'm going to Kilmore,' calmly replied the countryman. And the Englishman got out of the terrible country at the earliest possible moment." Reading the *Gaelic American* article, one familiar with modern Irish drama cannot but be reminded of George Bernard Shaw's *John Bull's Other Island,* specifically when Aunt Judy describes the mendacious driver who brings the Englishman Broadbent into the village of Roscullen: "Arra would you mind what the like of him would tell you? Sure he'd say whatever was the least trouble to himself and the pleasantest to you, thinking you might give him a thrupenny bit for himself or the like."[53]

Whether or not the writer of the *Gaelic American* piece had read Shaw's play is not clear, but it is obvious that he was familiar with Synge's preface to *The Playboy,* for the article is at pains to debunk the authenticity Synge and Yeats were so desperate to ascribe to the play: "All Synge's painstaking study of the people and his copious note taking bore some fruit in his mastery of their manner of expressing their thoughts, but he failed utterly to get an insight into their true character." The *Gaelic American* contrasted Synge's anthropological excursions among the peasantry of Catholic Ireland with the typical background of its own readership: "In every city and large town in America there are more men and women from those Western counties than in Dublin— bright, intelligent people who have made their way in the world—and they know the innermost thoughts of the people, not through taking notes or sojourning for a while among them, but because they are themselves a part of them." This was the audience Yeats so offended by insisting on the realism of Synge's work.[54]

Yet in his article "The Gallous Story and the Dirty Deed: The Two *Playboys,*" Edward Hirsch highlights the fact that "dismissing the reactions" of Synge's audiences "has been the fundamental strategy adopted by almost all critics" and thus "it has been axiomatic for several generations of Synge critics to summarize the controversy by stating that the Dublin (and later the Irish-American) playgoers had narrow political and moral values but no literary or aesthetic values."[55] As has been shown, these objections are typically attributed to a combination of Catholic prudery and nationalist oversensitivity, with a dash of working-class ignorance thrown in for good measure. But John Quinn, for one, did indeed recognize that Irish American objections to *The Playboy* were of a literary nature; in the midst of the controversy Quinn wrote to Douglas Hyde, "Everybody whose name happens to be Kennedy or Shaughnessy or Murphy or Moriarty seems to think he is a born critic of the drama."[56] It is ironic, but perhaps not surprising, that Quinn's biographer B. L. Reid misses the point of this remark entirely by using it to illustrate the claim that "what particularly infuriated [Quinn] was that works of art were being denounced often in pure ignorance of their contents and by persons and principles that bore no relevance to art."[57] Actually, what seems to have particularly infuriated Quinn was that works of art he admired were being denounced with principles of literary criticism by persons who Quinn, and later Reid, assumed were ignorant of art, or who disagreed with Quinn's artistic judgments.

Yet Reid's take on the events is the standard-issue critical interpretation that one finds echoed in the scholarship on this incident. For instance, Kenneth Cox Lyman asserts, "Neither the *Gaelic-American* nor the *Irish-American* made any attempt to appraise artistically this or any other play presented by the Abbey Theatre during the New York engagement,"[58] and "the majority of these earnest nationalists had little time or desire to understand the universal nature inherent in all great art,"[59] while Edward Abood contends: "The interest of Irish-Americans in the purely theatrical aspects of the company was slight. Rather, they were concerned almost exclusively with the Abbey's representation of Ireland."[60] Abood is of course right to identify "representation" as the key issue in the whole affair, and it is certainly true that Irish American audiences were convinced that the representation of Ireland onstage had political consequences, but it should also be self-evident that the question of "representation" in a supposedly realistic drama is one inherently concerned with the theatrical aspects of that production.

Therefore, what Hirsch reveals, and Reid, Lyman, and Abood all illustrate, is that scholars have created the inaccurate impression that every Irish American who protested *The Playboy* was a rabid Fenian, a boorish plebeian, and/or a priggish Catholic and thus either illiterate or anti-literate, a-theatrical or anti-theatrical, un-artistic or anti-artistic.

And such a portrait reinforces the misleading and elitist dichotomy that Yeats, Lady Gregory, and eventually George Bernard Shaw constructed to help explain away the confrontation between the Irish Americans and the Irish Players—namely, "the eternal dispute between the man of prose and the man of imagination" that Yeats's father, John B. Yeats, described for *Harper's Weekly*,[61] "the old battle between those who use a toothbrush and those who don't" that Lady Gregory identified after the Dublin *Playboy* riots,[62] the great divide between the artist and the philistine "sham Irish peasants" that Shaw would envisage in the conflict between Irish Americans and the Irish Players.[63] And it seems as though this dichotomy became so internalized by literary critics and literary historians that it went largely unchallenged for nearly three-quarters of a century.

Only in the last few decades have scholars begun to complicate this narrative by giving serious consideration to the concerns and expectations of the audience. And what Hirsh and John Harrington, as well as Shaun Richards and David Cairns, have all persuasively discussed is a process in which Synge, and later Yeats and Gregory, the Abbey actors and actresses, and most of the play's American reviewers misrepresented *The Playboy* to its audiences as a realistic work. Hirsch demonstrates how "Synge's claims to linguistic and ethnographic fidelity created expectations . . . which were then exploded by the violent and unrealistic mode of *The Playboy*."[64] Those famous linguistic and ethnographic claims—"I have used one or two words only that I have not heard among the country people of Ireland" and "anyone who has lived in real intimacy with the Irish peasantry will know that the wildest sayings and ideas in this play are tame indeed, compared with the fancies one may hear in any little hillside cabin"—these claims were of course included in Synge's defensive preface to *The Playboy*, the preface the *Gaelic American* had tried to disprove.[65]

In their essay "Reading a Riot: The 'Reading Formation' of Synge's Abbey Audience," Richards and Cairns provide details showing how the supposed realism of Synge's play was further reinforced by the naturalism of the acting and staging, including a set that was the exact dimensions of a typical Irish cottage of this time: twelve feet wide and twenty feet long, with a ceiling that sloped from a height of twelve feet in the front to eight feet in the back. They also quote program notes from an earlier tour of England which described the Irish Players as "all familiar with the ways of the Irish peasantry" and desirous "to put upon the stage the actual life and aims of the peasants they have so carefully studied in their native land."[66] And John Harrington cites articles from magazines like *The Outlook,* and newspapers like the *New York World,* that in the run-up to the Abbey tour continually contrasted the popular sentimental comedies of Dion Boucicault with the allegedly more accurate plays of Synge. Harrington puts the responsibility for such advance publicity squarely on Yeats and notes the irony of the situation to come: "The claims to realism that would be the source of great dissent were not advanced by the *Gaelic American* but by the Irish Players."[67]

A further irony that may be added is that in the years just before the tour, one finds in Yeats's journals a kind of appropriation of some of Oscar Wilde's insights. In an entry from this period Yeats wrote: "Active virtue as distinguished from passive acceptance of a current code is therefore theatrical, consciously dramatic, the wearing of a mask . . . One notices this in Plutarch's *Lives,* and every now and then in some modern who has tried to live by classical ideas, in Oscar Wilde, for instance."[68] Yet the mask that Yeats wore in America in 1911, the mask of an active stage manner producing realistic drama, is totally at odds with the role Wilde, in "The Decay of Lying," suggested was the appropriate one for artists. In that essay denouncing realism, one of the two speakers engaged in the dialogue admits: "I can quite understand your objection to art being treated as a mirror. You think it would reduce genius to the position of a cracked looking-glass"; the other responds, "A great artist invents a type, and Life tries to copy it, to reproduce it in a popular form."[69] So how strange it is to find Yeats arguing that *The Playboy* held a mirror up to Ireland, and Synge himself having argued that his characters were mere facsimiles of Irish peasants rather than original creations. Wilde's judgment of such writers, as pronounced in his dialogue, was harsh indeed: "If a novelist is base enough to go to life for his personages he should at least pretend that they are creations, and not boast of them as copies."[70]

Other well-known Irish writers expressed more explicit views on the purportedly realistic nature of Synge's drama. Though it was not expressed in the context of the events of 1911–1913, James Joyce would, years later, offer an opinion of Synge that sounds more like the opponents of *The Playboy* than defenders like Yeats, remarking to his friend Arthur Powers: "I do not care for [Synge's work] . . . For I think that he wrote a kind of fabricated language as unreal as his characters were unreal, for in my experience the peasants in Ireland are a very different people from what he made them to be, a hard, crafty and matter-of-fact lot, and I never heard any of them using the language which Synge puts into their mouths."[71] Brendan Behan had his own uniquely profane take on the matter, telling Richard Seaver: "Synge . . . stuck his fucking ear to the fucking wall to overhear how the peasants really talk, then put it into his fucking plays as though he'd made it up himself! Damned thief!"[72]

The prevalence of this discourse about the "realism" of Synge's work, a discourse that Yeats instigated, pervades much of the public debate that took place in the days surrounding the play's debut in both Boston and New York. And this discourse was not limited to the pages of the Irish American weeklies. In Boston, Mayor John "Honey Fitz" Fitzgerald delegated his secretary, the Harvard-educated William A. Leahy, to evaluate whether *The Playboy* was obscene.[73] Leahy reported, "If obscenity is to be found on the stage in Boston, it must be sought elsewhere." But he added, unaware no doubt of the way Synge had prefaced his play or Yeats had been trying to defend it: "The mistake, however, lies in taking the pictures literally. Some of these playwrights, of course, are realists or copyists of life and like others of their kind they happen to prefer strong brine to rosewater and see truth chiefly in the ugliness of things. But as it happens the two remarkable men among the playwrights are not realists at all. Yeats and Synge are symbolists, and their plays are as fantastic and fabulous as the Tales of the Round Table."[74] The mayor also sent his daughter, the future Rose Fitzgerald Kennedy, mother of JFK, to see the play. As a refined, educated young woman, she knew that what she was watching was supposed to be Art, but she nonetheless had mixed emotions seeing the Brahmins being entertained by a play depicting rowdy, bog-trotting Irish. It is telling that the historian Doris Kearns Goodwin describes the play as a satire and frames Rose's response as an inability to accept it as such, when in

1911 the young woman clearly realizes that the play's art is supposedly bound up with its faithful depiction of the peasantry.[75]

In a letter to the editor of the *Advocate,* a J. D. Hackett (who, one assumes, was John Dominick Hackett, a brother of Francis Hackett and E. Byrne Hackett, all three of whom had been founding members of John Quinn's New York branch of the Irish Literary Society)[76] defended the play against charges that it was misrepresenting Irish peasant life. Hackett argued that the play was obviously a farce, and he spun Yeats's comments in the *Forum* to mean that the play represented the "mind of Ireland" in the sense that Synge's characters all spoke with lyric beauty. Hackett concluded the letter by reminding readers, "Those who are not obsessed by the idea that the play is a libel on Irish life have given it nothing but the most extravagant praises."[77] Rather than defending the play as a fantastic allegory like Leahy, or a beautiful farce like Hackett, one James P. Conway wrote a letter to the editor of the *New York Sun* before the New York premiere defending the feasibility of the plot on the basis of his own personal experiences witnessing his fellow Irish peasants engage in violence and lawbreaking.[78]

On the morning of the day the play was to be performed, the *New York Times* published the professional opinion of Seamus MacManus, the Irish playwright and short story writer from Donegal who happened to be in New York on a lecture tour at the time of *The Playboy's* debut. During a lengthy interview in which he lamented that Yeats was now receiving a British pension, MacManus remarked, "Some of the plays are beautiful, some of them vile, and some of them are not Irish at all." He praised Yeats's *Cathleen ni Houlihan* as fine, lovely, and beautiful but dismissed *The Playboy* as ugly and "un-Irish." To buttress his claims, MacManus stated, "I may say without egotism that there are very few who know our people, our people of the remote mountains and islands, better than I." He then contrasted his own knowledge with that of Yeats and Synge, and by implication Lady Gregory, "Mine is the knowledge, not of the outsider who goes among them filled with sympathy if you wish, like Yeats and Synge, but the truer, surer, soul knowledge of him who is one of them, lived their life, saw with their eyes, heard with their ears, felt their joys and their woes, knew them from the soul to the skin." Implicitly portraying himself as a realistic author, MacManus told the interviewer, "I know all of their little shortcomings, and have never, through fear of the outcry of the thin-skinned or the snobbish, feared to set my people down as I found them, their foibles blended with their virtues." Ultimately, MacManus dismissed the possibility of *The Playboy*'s plot on account of "two qualities I have never set down for our people because these two qualities I never discovered among them, and they are vulgarity and immodesty."[79]

MacManus's interview was reprinted in the *Gaelic American*,[80] alongside a review of *The Playboy* that had first been published in the *New York Evening Post*.[81] After the disturbance on opening night, that anonymous drama critic for the *Post* recognized that much of the sound and fury was a direct result of the play's presentation of itself as a seemingly realistic work:

> Now it is all very well to say that there is much more in this play than appears on the surface, or that appears to the dull and unappreciative soul. Whether it is really a bit of melodramatic extravaganza, or a fantastic satire, in which the Irishman, as he is, is contrasted with the Irishman upon the stage, as he is supposed to be; whether it is surcharged with subtle symbolism, or filled with lamentations of a later Jeremiah, is nothing at all to the purpose. None of these abstract, spiritual, and sweetly intellectual intentions are denoted, or suggested in the play itself—least of all in its actual presentation. A play must be judged, can only be judged, by its effect and apparent purpose. There is not a line in the "Playboy" that contains a hint that it is in any respect freakish, or more or less than it professes to be, a study from nature in the nude. Mr. Synge, in a foreword, pledges himself—probably with some measure of artistic disingenuousness—that it contains virtually no phrase or word which he had not heard from living peasant lips. If this does not mean actual and precise realism, what does it mean? . . . Is there any cause for wonder because they have brought offense to decent Irishmen who do not know a parable or an allegory when they see one? . . . And unfortunately, the Irish Players, through their want of practical theatrical training, are incapable of throwing into relief the picturesque fancy, the poetic diction, and the characteristic humor which constitutes the only real value of the piece.[82]

Illustrating the *Post* critic's perceptive analysis about the effect of the play on a typical Irishman was a James Reidy, one of the men ejected from the theater on opening night.[83] In comments made to a reporter for the *New York Evening Mail*, Reidy argued: "It is put on the stage as a real picture of Irish life among the western peasants. It is no more a true picture of Irish life than it is a picture of life in the jungles of Africa."[84] But in a letter to the editor of the *Sun*, published after the play had premiered, Patrick Quinlan of the Bronx took the likes of Reidy to task:

Sir:

Permit a real Irishman, not a mollycoddle, to make a brief statement in reply to the critics, or more correctly, the faultfinders of John M. Synge and the Irish Players. "They don't talk like that in Ireland," said one thin skinned Hibernian, and scores of pious frauds joined in the chorus. I will ask them have they read Grattan's reply to Corry? Have they forgotten O'Connell's unworthy and ungenerous attack on Coppinger? And all of us remember Timothy M. Healy's scurrilous speeches denouncing Parnell. We can never forget the "Katie O'Shea petticoat" speech, the "Don't speak to the man at the wheel" speech, and the Castle Corner incident, when lime was flung in Parnell's eyes. The outrageous abuse of the late Miss Parnell at a suffragist meeting will not soon be forgotten. And last but not least, the historic scenes in Committee Room XV. Who on reading them can belittle John Synge? . . . Why don't they openly and decently admit they are a bunch of inverted snobs and stay away?[85]

More than a week after *The Playboy*'s uproarious debut in New York, the *Advocate* included a commentary provided by Pat Bell in his "Snapshots" column which also identified the crux of the complaint against *The Playboy* in its lack of realism, what he called its "perverted exaggeration." While confessing that he hadn't "seen any of Synge's plays on the stage," Bell claimed he had "read several of his plays some time ago." He admitted to having found the plays "amusing . . . delightful and original." Despite missing out on *The Playboy*, Bell had seen the Irish Players perform Lady Gregory's *Rising of the Moon* and *Spreading the News*, and T. C. Murray's *Birthright*. Bell judged these plays very positively because of what he perceived to be their faithful depiction of Irish life:

> The three sketches I saw . . . carried me back again to familiar scenes and people. I was like a good many others, presumably, no longer a denizen of a "skyscraper" city, and for the few hours my eyes were glued to the stage I was verily living again in the dew-kissed soil of Ireland. The entertainment this night at least was racy of the soil—Irish—and that, too, mind you, without the least bit of the customary devices to emphasize the fact. There were no green banners waving. No national airs were played. Not a note of any kind was heard. "the play's the thing," and the play certainly was the thing. Well, the audience came to see the Irish Players portraying Irish life, and dramatic art solely seems the aim of the Irish National Theatre.

In regard to the actual players, Bell also noted their accuracy: "One thing is certain there is not an actor on Broadway who could do the work of any of the Irish Players. Only one who is Irish and thoroughly knows his characters with all the schooling that that entails can do the Irish pieces justice."[86]

The accuracy of the plays was further deliberated in a scholarly article titled "Irish Drama and Irish Views," written by a Dublin Jesuit named George O'Neill and published in the *American Catholic Quarterly* in April 1912. Not surprisingly, Father O'Neill's judgment was harsh: "It is with regret and without passion that I speak of the Abbey Theatre plays as a systematic propaganda of calumny."[87] He took particular umbrage at Yeats, whose rhetoric in defense of the National Theatre dated back to *Countess Cathleen*: "During twenty years this same ingenious dodging between realist pretension and symbolic excuses has been recurrent."[88] As for Synge, Father O'Neill attempted to debunk the myth of the artist-as-anthropologist who objectively records his peasant subjects: "We have been told that Synge's portraits of the Irish peasantry must be truthful because of his close study of the originals. Admitting the fact, the argument is quite fallacious . . . Art, good or bad, is always selective. The personal equation cannot be eliminated and is sometimes a huge factor. It was emphatically so with Synge. Synge used themes named from Ireland to express—himself!"[89] Reading that, one may be shocked to discover that the priest's indictment of Synge sounds much more like Oscar Wilde's view of the artist than does Yeats's defense of Synge, for Wilde had written, "The justification of a character . . . is not that other persons are what they are, but that the author is what he is."[90]

The Fabian versus the Fenians

In December 1911, the author of *John Bull's Other Island* and *The Shewing-up of Blanco Posnet* inserted himself directly, and no doubt merrily, into the fray surrounding the Irish Players. The issues surrounding the protests against *The Playboy* that have been discussed in this chapter can be brought into even clearer focus by examining this fascinating tangent to the controversy. A close reading of George Bernard Shaw's analysis, expressed via two newspaper dispatches, demonstrates the many ways it can be interpreted as a kind of ur-criticism of the whole incident which many subsequent commentators have parroted.

The impetus that impelled Shaw to consider the controversy was a formal report made by the Drama Committee, Central Council, Irish County Associations of Greater Boston that was printed first in the *Boston Post,* then in the Irish American press. It read in part:

> Out of 160 delegates to the Central Council, 150 are peasants or the sons of Irish peasants. They know their Ireland as children know their mother, and they have no hesitation in affirming that the vulgar, raucous, ewe-houghers and incendiaries, retching drunkards, degenerate women, religious imposters, fratricides and parricides depicted in these alleged Irish plays no more represent the peasantry of Ireland than the Apaches of Paris or the Thugs of British India. If the company be Irish, their offence is exceedingly heinous in so ably misrepresenting the native character; if they are not an Irish company, then they are obtaining audiences under false pretenses.

Speaking specifically of *The Playboy,* the report noted the absence from the play of any admirable or honest character and then claimed this was unprecedented in English literary history: "Call the roll of English and Irish dramatists, names familiar to students of English dramatic literature—Shakespeare, Johnson, Massinger, Fletcher, Wycherly, Congreve, Otway, Garrick, Sheridan, Goldsmith, Keefe, Murphy, Knowles, and single out any of their productions where all the characters without exception are vicious, depraved and vulgar." In contrast, the authors discussed how, in *The Tempest,* Shakespeare used Ariel and Miranda to balance the monstrousness of Caliban and the foulness of Sycorax. The report also attempted to refute the very goal of the Irish National Theatre by suggesting that Boucicault, one of the arch-conjurers of stage Irishry, was a superior dramatist to Synge:

> They come they tell us, to elevate the Irish drama! to eliminate the buffoon comedy, to destroy Boucicault and all his works. Boucicault gives us the "Wake" of Conn, ridiculous and objectionable no doubt, with Father Tom Dolan, a good hearted and kindly priest, although he is pictured as fond of his pipe, which after all is no great crime for even an Irish soggarth. The poor Rope-makers' daughter of Garryowen, the Colleen Bawn and Ana Chute, the noble and impulsive Irish heiress, are fine creations. Conn himself is a generous harum scarum. We find generosity, wit and triumphant true love. What do we get in Synge's 'Playboy'? Unnaturally aroused female emotion and drunkenness, relieved by parricide and parental blasphemy—dramatic orgies.[91]

Shaw's response to all of this, in the form of a faux interview, appeared first in the December 9, 1911, *New York Evening Sun.* It was later reprinted in many of the New York dailies, as well as in the *Gaelic American* and the *Advocate.* The piece began by ridiculing the American Irish in general, and John Devoy in particular:

> I warned Lady Gregory that America was an extremely dangerous country to take a real Irish company to . . . [T]here are not half a dozen real Irishmen in America outside that company of actors . . . You don't suppose that all these Murphys and Doolans and Donovans and Farrels and Caseys and O'Connells who call themselves by romantic names like the Clan-na-Gael and the like are Irishmen! . . . Devoy? That's not an Irish name . . . Depend upon it, his nurse told him he was devoid of something or other—possibly of Irish blood—and he caught it up wrongly and thought she meant that his name was Devoy . . . No; he would never talk about the Clan-na-Gael if he were Irish.

Shaw then continued his assault on the Clan by claiming that their version of Irish nationalism was symbiotically and sycophantically dependent on England:

> We have these Clan-na-Gael Irishmen in Dublin; they come over from Liverpool in the cattle boats. You know what the name means: the collectors of gold . . . Shall I tell you what they did in Dublin to the Irish players? There was a very great dramatic poet, who died young named John Synge—a real Irish name—just the sort of name the Collectors of Gold never think of. Well, John Synge wrote a wonderful play called "The Playboy of the Western World," which is now a classic . . . Well, sir, if you please, this silly Dublin Clan-na—Gael . . . struck out the brilliant idea that to satirize the follies of humanity is to insult the Irish nation, because the Irish nation is, in fact, the human race and has no follies, and stands there pure and beautiful and saintly to be eternally oppressed by England and collected for by the Clan.

One notices here that Shaw's interpretation of *The Playboy* as a satire is, of course, quite different from the realistic interpretation that had been advocated by Yeats. Nevertheless, Shaw skillfully turned the tables by accusing the American Irish of being guilty of the very charge many of them had been making against the Irish Players—namely, that of perpetuating the stereotype of the stage Irishman:

> In the plays of [Yeats] you will find many Irish heroes, but nothing like "the broth of a boy." Now you can imagine the effect of all this on the American pseudo-Irish, who are still exploiting the old-stage Ireland for all its worth and defiantly singing "Who fears to speak of '98" . . . Their notion of patriotism is to listen jealously for the slightest hint that Ireland is not the home of every virtue and the martyr of every oppression, and thereupon to brawl and bully or to whine and protest, according to their popularity with the bystanders. When these people hear a little real Irish sentiment from the Irish Players they will not know where they are.

Eventually, Shaw addressed the statement of the Boston Irish directly, in the process de-romanticizing Irish American immigrants and deconstructing the emigrant/exile trope:

You will observe that they begin by saying that they know their Ireland as children know their mother. Not a very happy bit of rhetoric that, because children never do know their mothers; they may idolize them or fear them, as the case may be; but they don't know them . . . They declare they are either Irish peasants or the sons of Irish peasants. What on earth does the son of an American emigrant know about Ireland? Fancy the emigrant himself, the man who has left Ireland to stew in its own juice, talking about feeling toward Ireland as children feel toward their mother. Of course a good many children do leave their mothers to starve; but I doubt that is what they meant.

Shaw then derided the criticism that Irish Americans dared level against the play on literary grounds:

No doubt they are peasants . . . for they feel toward literature and art exactly as peasants do in all countries; that is, they regard them as departments of vice . . . No real Irish peasants would pretend for a moment to be an authority on literature; but these fellows put down the names of all the famous playwrights they ever heard of, beginning with Shakespeare . . . And now will you please look at the list of refined, high-minded British dramatists whom they cite as the superiors of our modern Irish ones. To begin with, Wycherly! . . . Wycherly is purer than Synge. Congreve—their next selection—Congreve . . . is the writer whose delicacy is to put Lady Gregory to shame . . . But Lady Gregory . . . will simply walk over the Clan–na–Gael unless it has the sense to understand that she is the greatest living Irishwoman, and that cultivated Americans will attach much more importance to anything she says or does than to the splutterings of Bostonian sham Irish peasants.[92]

After Shaw's essay had been published came the incident in Philadelphia when the whole cast was actually arrested. At this point, Shaw issued a more concise statement effectively summarizing the views expressed in the first. Shaw's razor wit and sharp sense of humor are again revealed, but his celebrated progressivism is certainly tempered by the suspicion that much of his sympathy for the brotherhood of man simply could not quite endure the mental trip across the broad Atlantic. The *Times* published the dispatch under the headline "Shaw Scores Philadelphia":

The occurrence is too ordinary to be worth any comment. All decent people are arrested in America. For that reason I refused all invitations to go there. Besides, who am I that I should question Philadelphia's right to make itself ridiculous? I warned the Irish Players that America is being governed largely by a mysterious race, probably one of the lost tribes of Israel, calling themselves American Gaels. It is a dangerous country for genuine Irishmen and Irishwomen. The American Gaels are the real Playboys of the Western World. We are none the less grateful on this side to Col. Roosevelt for his public and, no doubt, representative, expression of contempt for this blackguardly agitation against art and literature which has made the names of Synge, Yeats, and Lady Gregory famous, and has called the attention of Europe to the fact that Ireland is a nation with specific and splendid national genius, and not merely a province of England.[93]

One scholar calls this rather modest second dispatch from Shaw "a masterpiece of satire" and claims that "such eminent criticism was difficult for the *Gaelic American* to rebut, so the paper changed the emphasis in its criticism from the play to the personalities supporting it."[94] This claim conveniently ignores the fact that Shaw had engaged in just such an ad hominem attack on John Devoy in his original piece. And conveniently, the version of Shaw's dispatch that appeared in Gregory's *Our Irish Theatre* leaves out the attack on Devoy.[95]

Actually, the *Gaelic American* did indeed attempt to rebut GBS by reproducing Shaw's interview under this ironic headline:

BERNARD SHAW'S GREATEST MASTERPIECE

In Interview With Himself He "Knocks Spots" Out Of All His Previous Productions—Enlightens The World On Irish Names, Irish Drama, Irish Organizations, American Drunkenness And Blasphemy And His Own Greatness—Only Genuine Irish Are the O'Shaws, O'Synges, MacYeatses, O'Gregorys, MacPersses And O'Greggs— Saint Augusta O'Gregory Will Down The Horrid Anglo-Saxon Clan-Na-Gael

This *Gaelic American* piece also added a spirited and sardonic introduction calling Shaw's article "the best comedy yet produced by the new Ireland" and noting that "the delicate touches of sarcasm and irony, together with the wide knowledge of history, ethnology, genealogy, national character and land tenure, the intimacy with . . . the inside secrets of the Clan-na-Gael, learned by intuition, bear eloquent testimony to the universality of the dramatist's genius and the colossal character of his intellect." The *Gaelic American* then facetiously admitted that "the Kellys, Burkes and Sheas, Doolans, Murphys and Flanagans, who were driven to America by the O'Shaw land agents, leaving their poor mothers to starve in Ireland . . . are not Irish at all but Hibernian Blanco Posnets, who know nothing about the theatre, or about anything else"; and furthermore, "The Cromwellian planters' progeny who have taken their places in Ireland are the real Irish, the 'new Ireland,' and have the 'Irish revival' all to themselves."[96] In a separate editorial, the *Gaelic American* also scored with this one-liner referring to Shaw's business dealings with New York theater producer Arnold Daly: "Of course, nobody takes George Bernard Shaw seriously, except those who have financial dealings with him."[97]

No doubt it was retorts like these that John Harrington had in mind when he noted that "the *Gaelic American*'s campaign also had much more wit than is generally remembered."[98] But it was not just the *Gaelic American* among the Irish American press that printed pieces striving for wit as they sparred with Shaw, Yeats, Lady Gregory, and the Irish Players. The *Advocate* printed a series of poems about the controversy by a Stephen M. Faherty of New York. Most of Faherty's verse is dull and dour, but one poem, written to the tune of "The Wearing of the Green," included this rollicking stanza:

> O here comes Lady Gregory, says she they do offend
> The Irish all are amadauns they fail to comprehend
> They've Synged my darling "Playboy" in spots he's really raw
> Piped loud the dreary oracle, 'I told you so,' Pshaw.
> An Patrick dear, hold you no fear a voice people have bann'd
> This canting knave and atheist forever from our land
> This freak of freaks whom we thought wise is but a thing of straw
> A gaseous bag of self conceit, who punctured it, Pshaw.[99]

A more successful effort, perhaps, is "A Letter from the Playboy Himself" sent to the *Irish-American* from Chicago and printed on its February 17, 1912, front page. The first paragraph read in part:

Editor Aveelish:

I am writing you lest the people of the great world might be thinking that it's dead itself I am. Since the day I left Pegeen Mike in Mayo "to go romancing through a romping lifetime" I never got such treatment as was given me and my gallant heathen Company in Chicago . . . Here, surely, in this distant windy place we can find no one who would be putting words on the people telling them of our Art. Instead they do be slighting our greatness like we were nothing but mountain goats lepping the rocks in the crags of the Burren.

Yours for Art's sake,
Playboy Eile[100]

Obviously, these pieces are not quoted in order to argue for their rhetorical merit as polemic or as poetry or as parody, but rather to highlight once again the simple truth that much of the backlash against the Irish Players was in one way or another of a literary nature.

Theater of the Absurd

In addition to the absurdity of George Bernard Shaw chastising a man who shared his view of the Irish peasant as a cunning teller of tall tales, and the absurdity of an Irish Jesuit echoing Oscar Wilde in order to denounce John Synge, and the absurdity of William Butler Yeats, the visionary poet credited with bridging the gap between romanticism and modernism, miring his theater in a discourse about the realism of its drama, there was a plethora of other ridiculous incidents related to this controversy that it would be remiss of me not to discuss. When Yeats and Lady Gregory threw down the gauntlet by having the Irish Players perform *The Playboy* in Boston, it must be admitted that the controversy did spontaneously combust into the firestorm of overstatement, exaggeration, vitriol, and racial abuse on which many scholars have focused their commentaries.

Not surprisingly, the issue of the directors' Ascendancy background came raging to the fore as articles and letters to the editors of the American Irish papers lambasted Yeats and Gregory. The two swiftly went from being referred to as the respected founders of the Abbey

Theatre to being derided as "the British Government pensioner and his female Loyalist assistant"[101] whose modus operandi was "to confirm and present a striking instance of the old English slander that the Irish sympathize with murder and are by nature uncivilized, barbarians and law breakers."[102] A Gearoid MacCarthaig of Skowhegan, Maine, whose letter to the *Irish World* was published under the headline "A Shameless and Mercenary Crew," was even more chauvinistic in describing the Abbey directors as "not Irish," as "the effete spawn of the intruders," and as a "neurotic, decadent, non-Gaelic class" who "furnishes the world with such hybrid abortions as Shaw, Moore and Synge!"[103]

Of course, prejudice on the part of the participants was not limited to the American Irish protesters. In her chapter on *The Playboy* in America, Lady Gregory makes it abundantly clear that she perceived "the enemy" to be composed almost wholly of working-class riffraff and sheeplike Catholics. After the opening night riot in New York, she wrote, "In the box office this morning they have a collection of spoils left by the enemy (chiefly stink-pots) and rosaries"; she also duly noted the rather plebeian occupations of those detained by the police in New York: "Ten men were arrested. Two of them were bar-tenders; one a liquor dealer; two clerks; one a harness-maker; one an instructor; one a mason; one a compositor; and one an electrician."[104] In Philadelphia, where arrest warrants were issued for the entire cast on the grounds that they were performing indecent plays, Lady Gregory noted with astonishment, "Our accuser is a liquor dealer."[105] This haughty tone is echoed by B. L. Reid in his biography of John Quinn: "In Philadelphia the company was arrested, on the warrant of a liquor dealer, and charged with putting on a sacrilegious and immoral performance. Quinn went twice to the city for periods of several days and secured a writ of habeas corpus. In the hearing he savagely cross-examined the complaining publican."[106] This ridiculous seller of spirits was none other than Joseph McGaritty, a man prominent historians have credited as being the reviver of the Clan na Gael in North America, the rescuer from bankruptcy of Patrick Pearse's St. Enda's School, and the chief Irish American ally of, and fund-raiser for, Eamon de Valera during the Anglo-Irish War—in other words, a publican of some importance![107] McGarrity also scribbled verse in his spare time. His papers, at Villanova University, include an unpublished poem titled "On Verses by Yeats in 'The Smart Set'" that mocks Yeats as an imitator of Robert Burns who spends his time and British pension money in London.[108]

The socio-religious stereotypes and claims about racial essentialism that informed both sides of the controversy were, of course, nothing new in regard to the Irish question, and as was often the case, they tended to veer toward the absurd, such as when a Chicago alderman named Michael McInerney, who supported prohibiting performance of *The Playboy*, responded to a question about whether Lady Gregory was Irish by stating: "There's a difference in being from Ireland and being Irish. There are lots of people in Ireland that aren't Irish. If you're born in a stable, that doesn't make you a horse."[109] McInerny's statement is included in the oft-cited appendix to *Our Irish Theatre*, but whether McInerny knew, in uttering it, that he was borrowing the Duke of Wellington's famous analogy that dismissed any suggestion of the Irish origins the Iron Duke abhorred, or whether Lady Gregory, in publishing it, realized that the ultimate declaration of unsullied Ascendancy Saxonism was being used by an Irish American politician to dismiss the Irish origins she so valued, is not at all clear; but it is ironic indeed.

Another oft-quoted piece of sublime ridiculousness is this claim made by the *Gaelic American* about the Abbey's barefooted actresses: "No such feet ever came out of Ireland before. They were typically Anglo-Saxon feet—big clumsy and flat—that would make as large an impression on soft ground as the hoofs of one of Guinness's float horses. Irish women have the daintiest feet in Europe."[110] A few weeks later, apparently forgetting about the women's big, clumsy, flat Anglo-Saxon feet, the *Gaelic American* tried to instigate a controversy between the actresses and management over a supposed contract dispute by using some familiar nationalist tropes: "They appealed to Lady Gregory, but their appeals fell on a heart of stone—a heart trained in the pitiless school of Galway landlordism, accustomed to trample on Irish feeling and treat the mere Irish with contempt and cruelty. Lady Gregory held them to their contract: it is in her English blood to play the tyrant and she could not throw away the opportunity. She brought them here to insult the Irish people and hold them up to contempt, and, like Shylock, she demanded her pound of flesh."[111] The actresses later refuted these allegations via a letter to the *Gaelic American* which was subsequently printed under the wonderfully contentious headline "Denial from Irish Girls: Say They Did Not Protest against the Vile 'Playboy' and Got Their Money—Do They Also Approve Robinson's Viler 'Harvest' and Expect Decent People to Respect Them?"[112]

As the reference to Shylock's pound of flesh in the previous paragraph might suggest, there was also a thread of anti-Semitism mixed in with the protest against the Anglo-Irish managers of the Abbey. The *Gaelic American* imagined a kind of Jewish-nativist conspiracy against the Irish among the mainstream American press. After *The Playboy* had been allowed a performance in Providence, one article, featuring the subheadings "Nativist Bigots Delighted" and "Nativist Wasps Delighted," chastised "the Knownothing scribes of Providence" and "the anti-Irish editorial wasps who rushed to the assistance of the anti-Irish Irish players in defense of 'freedom of theatre' when that freedom puts the Irish in an odious light."[113] After the New York premiere, an editorial, titled "Jew Papers and Irish Readers," fulminated against "the outburst of malignant abuse and misrepresentation of the Irish people in Jew-controlled daily papers of New York" and "the impudence, ignorance, and cheap flippancy of the scribblers from the banks of the Jordan in lecturing the Irish people on a subject on which the Irish are fully informed and the lecturers wholly ignorant."[114] The *Gaelic American* and other Irish weeklies insinuated that the mainstream press was lying in order to perpetuate Irish stereotypes: "No violence was used; no violence was intended, so it had to be invented in order to justify abuse, and the Semitic papers were equal to the occasion."[115] A subsequent letter printed in the *Gaelic American,* but originally sent to the editor of the *New York World* and never published, concurred, claiming that "the protest against the 'Playboy' was dignified" and that accounts of "vegetables, rotten eggs, potatoes, apples, Walthams [i.e., watches] and 'stink pots' which 'rained on the stage' are only the coloring of reporters who prefer exaggeration to accuracy."[116] The *Gaelic American* admitted only that "one foolish man threw a potato" and "another excited man threw an apple and another pelted his watch at them"; but it claimed that this was the extent of the fusillade.[117] About this watch, Thomas N. Brown would later comment sardonically: "The Irishman in New York who protested the *Playboy* by throwing his watch onto the stage was a higher, if less picturesque, social type than the savage Molly Maguires of the Pennsylvania hills. If nothing else, the old passions had been diluted by prudence—the watch thrower retrieved his possession at the stage door."[118]

However accurately or inaccurately it may have been reported, and whatever the caviling details, it was not lost on observers that the *Playboy* disturbance in New York was a farce that certainly did have an all-Irish cast. The *Advocate* reprinted this observation from the *New York Press:* "It was an Irishman's play, produced by an Irishwoman and presented by Irish players. The disturbers have Irish names, and so have the police officers who looked after throwing them out of the theatre. It was an Irish magistrate who tried the case and fined the obstreperous ones."[119] That magistrate was Joseph E. Corrigan, who, by a strange coincidence of transatlantic literary history, would later find himself involved in the initial court proceedings taken against the *Little Review* magazine for publishing James Joyce's *Ulysses.* To these dramatis personae, we might add the names of the night court lawyers, Dennis Spellisy and John T. Martin; the arrested men were named O'Callaghan, Cassidy, Casey, Byrne, Neary, O'Connor, Kelly, O'Coffey, Harford, and Gambler; the chief complainant against the rioters: Rosina Emmet of Washington Square.[120] Miss Emmet was a niece of the great Irish patriot whom Yeats, after being guaranteed a hefty payday by John Devoy, had memorialized in 1904.

Another result of the decision to perform *The Playboy* was that other pieces in the repertoire abruptly became targets of derision. The old criticisms of Yeats's unorthodox religious views resurfaced. For instance, the *Advocate* ran an article by Corrig O'Sheen titled "W. B. Yeats and His Work," suggesting that *The Countess Cathleen* was "even more pernicious" than *The Playboy.*[121] Shaw's one contribution to the repertoire, *The Shewing-up of Blanco Posnet,* was frequently chastised for having been banned in England for its blasphemy, and after it was performed during a matinee at Yale in front of Chief Cowles of the New Haven police, who was there to consider censoring *The Playboy,* the bungling chief suppressed parts of Shaw's play thinking that it was Synge's.[122] Lennox Robinson's *Harvest* was persistently condemned because one of the main characters cries out, "I hate Ireland." And T. C. Murray's *Birthright* was repeatedly denounced for presenting a fatal conflict between two brothers vying for their father's land. Louis Sherwin of the *New York Globe and Commercial Advertiser* reported the following reaction to the climax of *Birthright* on opening night in New York: "Loud murmurs were heard in the theatre, and sporadic hissing . . . Why the worthy folk should have objected was a perfect mystery to me until I heard a stanch Hibernian declaring: 'They're not Irish: that was a dirty trick to smash out the light before he attacked the other man. NO IRISHMAN EVER TOOK SUCH AN UNFAIR ADVANTAGE!!!' To which his sweet-voiced companion, replied exquisitely: 'I wish it was Lady Gregory they were choking.'"[123]

The views of the sweet-voiced Celt who wanted to see Lady Gregory strangled were echoed in an article written by Mary F. McWhorter, national chairwoman, Ladies Auxiliary, Ancient Order of Hibernians, Irish History Committee, published in a March 1913 issue of the *National Hibernian*. McWhorter appraised the Abbey's second American tour, which took place from December 1912 to April 1913, and spent the bulk of its time in the American Midwest. Writing from Chicago, McWhorter suggested that the repertoire as a whole inspired one to be "possessed of an insane desire to seek out Lady Gregory or some one else connected with the plays and then and there commit murder." McWhorter's article had begun by admitting that "*The Playboy* is bad and very bad," but the main thrust of the criticism was that the other plays, while seemingly harmless, each included "an insidious dig" at things Irish American audiences held sacred.[124]

And so McWhorter went down the list offering her interpretations: in Lady Gregory's *Rising of the Moon* "our patriotism is attacked"; T. C. Murray's *Maurice Harte* illustrates that the accusation "said by our enemies that to have a priest in the family is to be considered very respectable by the average Irish Catholic family, and to bring about this desired result we are willing to sell our immortal souls"; Gregory's *Workhouse Ward* "gives you nothing more edifying than the picture of two hateful old men snarling at each other in a truly disgusting manner," while her *Coats* "gives the picture of two seedy, down-at-the-elbows editors, who . . . are thinking unutterable things about each other"; William Boyle's *Family Failing*—"the worst of the output"—"is a strong witness in favor of that old fallacy, so often repeated by our enemies, that it was not the cruelty of English laws that sent us forth as wanderers, but our lazy, idle, shiftless ways"; and St. John Ervine's *The Magnanimous Lover* "presents the nasty problem play" and "puts into the mouth of the Irish peasant girl" horrible words. Yeats did not escape McWhorter's scrutiny either. While admitting that his *Cathleen ni Houlihan* is "beautiful," she suggested that "everyone knows Yeats wrote this before he became a pagan and went astray"; in contrast, "his *Countess Kathleen,* written since then, is a weird thing" that teaches "a rather dangerous lesson."[125] McWhorter had the chronology of Yeats's two plays absolutely backwards, but this only highlights how an average Irish American could have perceived Yeats's career trajectory: from earnest champion of Ireland's cultural and political nationalism to esoteric promoter of paganism and anti-Catholicism.

In concluding her article, McWhorter stated: "The plays taken as a whole have no literary merit. The backers preach about Art with a capital A, but they have no artistic merit, for art is truth, and the plays are not true."[126] Such an analysis resembles just the kind of criticism Wilde had discussed in "The Decay of Lying": "They will call upon Shakespeare—they always do—and will quote that hackneyed passage about Art holding the mirror up to Nature, forgetting that this unfortunate aphorism is deliberately said by Hamlet in order to convince the bystanders of his absolute insanity in all art-matters."[127] It is worth noting for the final time that the conceptual frame for this kind of inane, if not insane, criticism of the Abbey plays was suggested, first and foremost, by the artists themselves.

CHAPTER 5

Meet The New Gossoon, *Same as the Old Gossoon*

THE ABBEY PLAYWRIGHTS IN
IRISH AMERICA, 1931–1939

As READERS LEARNED in chapter 4, when William Butler Yeats arrived in America in 1911 to publicize the tour of the Abbey Theatre's Irish Players, he gave a variety of interviews in which he presented *The Playboy of the Western World* in particular, and the repertoire of his National Theatre in general, as a much-needed realistic antidote to the sentimental and melodramatic plays that were so synonymous with stage Irishness. In her survey of Irish American theater, Maureen Murphy provides a nice description of the typical features of these kinds of so-called Irish dramas: "blushing colleens, broths of boys, genial parish priests, neatly thatched cottages, carefree songs and dances—all lightly laced with poitin and patriotism."[1] Those kinds of Irish plays, remember, had, in 1897, provoked the famous "Manifesto for Irish Literary Theatre," in which Yeats, along with Lady Gregory and Edward Martyn, imagined a national theater that would "show that Ireland is not the home of buffoonery and easy sentiment, as it has been represented, but the home of ancient idealism."[2]

Yet in her article "Players in the Western World," Adele Dalsimer argues that the Abbey's later, less infamous American tours of the 1930s abandoned "the experimental or expressionistic dramas that were part of [the Abbey's] repertory" in favor of "the social comedies that had been very popular in Dublin." Dalsimer contends that these "carefree pieces of make-believe . . . had none of the satiric or somber overtones characteristic of the earlier comedies of Synge, William Boyle or Lady Gregory." For Dalsimer, representative pieces of carefree make-believe included Lennox Robinson's *The Whiteheaded Boy* and *The Far Off Hills,* Brinsley MacNamara's *Look at the Heffernans,* and George Shiels's *Professor Tim* and *The New Gossoon,* the last of these described by Dalsimer as "the hit of the 1932–1933 season."[3]

To buttress her claims about the inferior content of these comedies, Dalsimer quotes a few perceptive reviewers who noticed this shift in style and substance: in 1933 a critic from the *Boston Herald* noted that "the old indignant denial of the Irishman as a mere figure of low comedy is no longer stressed," while in 1934 a reviewer for the *Toronto Mail* observed: "This [kind of cozy comedy] was not the sort of thing on which the famous Dublin Theatre built its renown . . . [I]t was the very thing against which the Abbey Theatre rebelled, as giving too limited an idea of Irish talents."[4] Though not mentioned by Dalsimer, one could add here the acerbic commentary of the influential drama critic George Jean Nathan, who in a 1937 *Newsweek* article title "Erin Go Blah" wrote: "The infelicitous fact remains that, lovely and musical speech aside, the present Abbey Theatre Company has put the dub in Dublin. Not so long ago one of the finest acting organizations in the world, it is now a caricature of its former self."[5] Dalsimer concludes her essay by lamenting that by the mid-1930s, "the 'real' Irish play had become a conventional comedy dealing with marriage or property differences suffered and settled in an Irish setting," and furthermore, the typical Irishman presented onstage by the Abbey "was now a simple, jovial fellow endowed with a thick brogue and a lilting voice."[6]

If these definitions of Irish play and stage Irishman call to mind John Ford's film *The Quiet Man* and/or Barry Fitzgerald's performance as the matchmaker in that film, that's no coincidence. It was on these later tours that Fitzgerald established the reputation that would later make him a scene-stealing Hollywood character actor. In an essay examining Fitzgerald's career, Adrian Frazier notes that during this period, for Abbey actors like Fitzgerald, it was character that mattered, not plot or atmosphere. As a result, "the productions of *Juno and the Paycock* and *The Plough and the Stars* that toured America in the early 1930s . . . meandered comically towards unhappy endings, with startlingly vivid low-life characters sporting their eccentricities in front of cheap, painted scene flats." The metamorphosis of Sean O'Casey's "serious plays" into "Dublin character comedies" was no minor theatrical revision. According to Frazier, "O'Casey's great Dublin plays . . . held the stage throughout the 1930s wherever English was spoken." And in particular, *Juno* had become "the world's favourite Irish play since its 1924 debut."[7] *Juno*, along with O'Casey's 1923 Abbey debut, *The Shadow of a Gunman*, are often credited with saving the National Theatre from bankruptcy. W. B. Yeats himself admitted to O'Casey, "If you had not brought us your plays just at that moment I doubt if [the Abbey] would now exist."[8] While O'Casey's plays did eventually mutate into comic productions, it is important to note here their origins as realistic depictions of Irish sociopolitical tragedy set amid the most radical changes to the Irish body politic since the Act of Union in 1801. Those changes were instigated by the Easter Rising of 1916, accomplished during the War of Independence of 1919–1921, and finally settled following the Civil War of 1922–23.

Set inside a Dublin tenement during that civil war, *Juno and the Paycock* depicts a few months in the life of the Boyle family: epic layabout Captain Boyle and his crony Joxer Daly; Boyle's beleaguered wife, Juno; his aspirational but vain daughter Mary; and his doomed son Johnny, a crippled veteran of Easter week who has turned informer on his old comrades in arms. *Shadow* is set during the War of Independence, and its tragic plot hinges on a case of mistaken identity among tenants in another Dublin tenement. Donal Davoren is a poet who his neighbors think is a covert IRA volunteer. When a real volunteer hides a bag of grenades in the tenement but then dies in action before he can retrieve them, it results in the death of an innocent young woman named Minnie Powell.

In the third play of his Dublin trilogy, *The Plough and the Stars*, O'Casey once again depicted the suffering and death of innocent women and rebel men by dramatizing the months before and the days after the Easter Rising. The play centers on the plight of Nora and Jack Clitheroe, a young couple expecting their first child, and includes an eclectic cast of colorful neighbors, including the loquacious alcoholic Fluther Good, a doctrinaire communist named the Young Covey, a working-class Protestant woman named Bessie Burgess, a poor old woman named Mrs. Gogan, and her tubercular daughter Mollser. The tragic action of the play is set in motion when Jack, against Nora's wishes, returns to the Citizen Army so that he can fight in the rebellion. In one notable scene set in a pub, excerpts from patriotic speeches written by Padraic Pearse are read offstage, while characters, including a prostitute named Rosie Redmond, drink and squabble. Performed at the Abbey in 1926, after the National Theatre had begun receiving a subsidy from the Free State government, the play provoked the rioting of audience members, including widows like Hanna Sheehy-Skeffington, who felt the play desecrated the memory of the Easter martyrs. Following the riots, Yeats chastised the Abbey audience: "You have disgraced yourselves again. Is this to be an ever-recurring celebration of the arrival of Irish genius? Once more you have rocked the cradle of genius."[9]

Yeats's comments made obvious allusion to the 1907 *Playboy* riots, but in stark contrast to the genius of Synge, who had to defend his acquaintance with the Catholic peasants he depicted onstage by recourse to his years of anthropological fieldwork, the genius of O'Casey resulted from personal intimacy with his setting and character types. Born John Casey, he was a self-educated working-class Dublin Protestant who had learned Irish and Gaelicized his name. Inspired by the labor leader Jim Larkin, he joined James Connolly's Citizen Army, but quit when he saw that nationalist goals were usurping the socialist ones. He did not take part in the Easter Rising, and his three Dublin tenement plays dramatized the terrible human cost of revolutionary violence and civil war on Dublin's laboring poor.

Not surprisingly, these tragic plays that so powerfully and provocatively challenge the ideologies of physical force nationalism—even if they were performed as character comedies and starred the irrepressible Barry Fitzgerald—were greeted with circumspection by republican elements within Irish America. In January 1933, at the end of the Abbey's tour, Fianna Fáil, Inc., of New York and the United Irish-American Societies objected to the Free State subsidy of a national theater that produced something like *The Shadow of a Gunman* or *Juno and the Paycock*—or *The Playboy of the Western World*. But unlike the 1911 *Playboy* protests, these objections resulted neither in a widespread campaign against the plays in the press nor in public protests or riots in American cities where O'Casey's dramas were performed. Rather, as Dalsimer notes, the mode of attack was backroom political pressure, namely, presenting to the consul general of Ireland a formal protest complaining of the plays' "filthy language, drunkenness and prostitution."[10]

One Irish American who on this occasion vehemently defended O'Casey in particular, and the Abbey repertoire more generally, was a man named Patric Farrell. According to a brief profile in *Time* magazine published in 1927, Farrell, described as "a young man with social connections in Manhattan," had co-founded the Irish Theatre at Sheridan Square with eleven other members, "including a clerk from Bog of Allan named Sean Dillon, a Dublin sign painter, a Drogheda school teacher, a traveler named Rex Moore McVitty who came originally from Tandiragee, and two professional actresses, one from Athlone, one from Wicklow"; Farrell's co-director was "Miceal Breathnach, a Galway engineer."[11] In 1929 the group staged a performance of O'Casey's *The Silver Tassie* that Brooks Atkinson gave a middling review.[12] Later Farrell opened the Irish Theatre and Art Rooms at the Hotel Barbizon, which he eventually rebranded as the Museum of Irish Art at the Ritz Tower.[13] In response to the charges made by Fianna Fáil of New York and the United Irish-American Societies in January 1933, the *New York Times* reported that Farrell sent an additional resolution to the Irish consulate, arguing that the Abbey plays "do not malign the Irish people . . . but even if they did, there is no reason why they should be barred so long as they represent worthwhile Irish art." Farrell closed his letter by suggesting the Abbey should receive an even bigger subsidy.[14]

The following year, in a speech to the Dáil, President Eamon de Valera acknowledged that some of the Abbey's plays provoked "shame and resentment among Irish exiles."[15] De Valera threatened to withdraw the subsidy, but the Abbey directors resisted the interference, and ultimately the two parties compromised, agreeing on a declaration that would be printed in all programs distributed in America stating that while the Free State government subsidized the Abbey Theatre, it could not accept responsibility for the repertoire. Later in 1934, O'Casey's work would once again be attacked in America, this time for moral rather than political reasons, but in this instance, the weight of the Abbey was not behind him.

O'Casey had famously broken with the National Theatre, and Yeats in particular, when in 1928 the old man said no to *The Silver Tassie,* an experimental expressionist play O'Casey had written about the horrors of the Great War as experienced by a Dublin lad named Harry Heegan. It debuted in London rather than at the Abbey, and O'Casey followed it with an even more experimental play, *Within the Gates.* Set entirely inside a public park, the play is populated by allegorical characters: a prostitute, a capitalist, an evangelist, an atheist, a poet-dreamer, and a bishop—who turns out to be the prostitute's natural father. The play opened in London in February 1934 and arrived in October in New York, where it was praised by consistently pro-O'Casey reviewers like Brooks Atkinson and George Jean Nathan. In his chapter on the New York reception of *Within the Gates* in his book *The Irish Play on the New York Stage,* John Harrington notes the historical irony of the play's opening on Broadway simultaneously with the traveling Abbey productions of O'Casey's older Dublin plays (that is, the productions addressed earlier that presented *Juno* and *Plough* as character comedies starring Barry Fitzgerald). But more ironic than this mere coincidence is the silence with which O'Casey's new play was greeted by the Irish American press. Harrington notes that the *Gaelic American* "never even mentioned *Within the Gates.*"[16]

But the play certainly was mentioned in the Catholic periodical press. In *The Commonweal,* a lay Catholic journal founded in 1924, Grenville Vernon concluded, "Mr. O'Casey's poetry has gone to his head and obscured many things, among them dramatic unity, good taste, sound philosophy and common sense."[17] In *America,* Elizabeth Jordan admitted that that she was appalled by the play, "both in its substance and by the manner of its reception." Jordan described the play as "a black and slimy pocket full of crawling things" and warned readers that "there is not a single decent human being" in it.[18] This particular criticism about the total absence of any ethical characters resembled the protest of the Irish County Associations of Boston that had so aroused George Bernard Shaw during the *Playboy* controversy. During that uproar the Irish citizens of Boston never succeeded in banning Synge's play, but unfortunately for O'Casey, *Within the Gates* provoked enough Catholic outrage to sway the censors to prohibit the play from opening there.

Time magazine reported the events leading to the ban in a brief story titled "Boston v. O'Casey."[19] First, Father Russell M. Sullivan of the Boston College Council of Catholic Organizations approached Mayor Frederick William Mansfield, a Catholic. Next, Mansfield sent the city censor, Herbert L. McNary, to see the play in New York. Then, after reading McNary's report, Mansfield concluded that O'Casey's play was "nothing but a dirty book full of commonplace smut." In a letter to the editor published in *America,* another Jesuit, Terence L. Connolly, tried to defend the censorship of the play by the city authorities as a kind of protest against another less obvious kind of censorship: "The action of the censor here in Boston was merely a dignified rejection, under the statutes, of the false art and bad morality which theatrical censors had decreed we must accept under the perils of being stigmatized as prudes, ignoramuses and mid-Victorians."[20] A few weeks before the censorship decision, Father Connolly had published another denunciation of O'Casey's work in *America.* In that piece, Connolly claimed that in the Dublin trilogy, O'Casey had "violently attacked patriotism and every other manifestation of idealism in his native country . . . with all the devastating cynicism of an embittered propagandist." As for *Within the Gates,* Connolly dismissed it as exhibiting the "technical fault" of the "inappropriate injection" of lyric attempts into drama, and a "moral fault" of impudently treating prostitution, "a theme that until [O'Casey's] time was never portrayed upon the stage in his native country."[21]

John Harrington notes that the controversy around O'Casey's play in Boston "did not follow the precedent" of the 1911 *Playboy* controversy in that O'Casey's producers did not intellectually challenge the protesters or financially capitalize on the protests.[22] Yet it is worth noting here that while the 1911 tour managed by Lady Gregory is typically credited with creating favorable publicity that helped improve the bottom line, it is a fact that the less controversial, less critically acclaimed, and supposedly less artistic 1932–33 tour was the Abbey's most financially successful one. In his 1934 memoir *Whatever Goes Up*, George Tyler, who had been one of the managers employed by Liebler & Co. during the Abbey's early tours, noted how much more popular and profitable the 1932–33 tour was than the earlier ones: "Every blessed time [we brought the Abbey over] New York was at best apathetic. And now here's the funny thing. Last year another company came over from the Abbey Theatre, a much less able and less experienced lot, and cleaned up during one of the worst seasons Broadway ever saw. There's no sense whatever in that."[23]

Adele Dalsimer's insights, discussed earlier in this chapter, might provide the logic needed to explain why the better-acted and more artistically accomplished plays of the early Abbey tours were less popular and lucrative than the later ones: the new kitchen comedies and the stage Irishness they employed were much more palatable and enjoyable for American audiences, including, one supposes, Irish American audiences. Dalsimer concludes that this selling out and dumbing down of the Abbey repertoire was a disturbing development, albeit one with a financial silver lining for the Abbey: "American dollars kept the theatre alive when Irish pounds would not support her."[24] Harrington views these changes to the fundamental nature of the Abbey repertoire less as a decline and more like a paradoxical cycle of artist-audience relations: "Having dismissed the popular Irish and Irish-American audience . . . for a higher-class one, and having lost that replacement audience by its own repetitive repertory . . . the Abbey Theatre in New York set about recapturing the original audience rather than addressing the element of repetition."[25] Or in other words, the arrogance of the Irish artists had yielded to the tastes of the Irish American audiences.

But in his autobiography *Curtain Up*, Lennox Robinson, who served as a kind of second in command behind Lady Gregory on the first tour, assured readers that it was not the art but the audience that had changed: "Irish-America had to choose between their rosy dreams and the theatre of Synge and the younger realists. They chose wrong in 1911 and protests continued through 1912 and 1914 but by 1932 when the Players went back a new, more intelligent, a more broad-minded generation had arisen and now our best and most enthusiastic friends across the Atlantic are the Irish."[26] Implicit in Robinson's logic is the idea that a less intelligent, more narrow-minded generation of Irish Americans had passed away. Perhaps he was thinking of Patrick Ford, who had died in 1913 at the age of seventy-six; for his last forty-three years Ford had published and edited the *Irish World,* a soapbox he used to vehemently denounce the Abbey repertoire as he had vehemently denounced economic inequity, "[his] efforts on behalf of the Land League and American labor unions plac[ing] him at the fore-front of those who have worked for social justice."[27] Or maybe Robinson was alluding to John Devoy, who died in 1928 at the age of eighty-five; Devoy spent the last twenty-five years of his life publishing and editing the *Gaelic American,* a mouthpiece he used to become the great enemy of the Irish Players as well as, in the words of *The Times* of London, "the most bitter and persistent, as well as the most dangerous enemy of [England] which Ireland has produced since Wolfe Tone."[28] With the passing of this generation of Irish Americans who had helped Irish peasants win the Land War and Irish rebels win the War of Independence, Robinson suggested, Irish America was finally ready for good theater.

And among the enthusiastic Irish friends across the Atlantic whom Robinson counted among this more intelligent, more broad-minded generation would no doubt have been well-connected young men like Patric Farrell and his colleagues at the Irish Theatre at Sheridan Square. Another group of enthusiastic but less well-connected friends included Daniel Danaher, John Duffy, Joseph O'Reilly, Mary Kelly, Thomas McDermott, Martin Walsh, and John Hughes, a collection of immigrant Irish students enrolled in evening high schools in New York City who were members of the Irish Students League, and who in 1933 founded the Thomas Davis Irish Players, a community theater society whose motto was "educate that you may be free."[29] The group named itself after, and borrowed its motto from, the nationalist poet and jour-nalist whom the young Yeats had championed but the mature Yeats later dismissed as a bourgeois hack.

But evidence suggests that contrary to Lennox Robinson's interpre-tation, the likes of the Thomas Davis Irish Players did not embrace the theater of Synge, or for that matter the theater of O'Casey. It would be forty-nine years after the founding of that group before they put a Synge play onstage (*In the Shadow of the Glen* in 1982), and thirty-nine years before they performed an O'Casey play (*Juno and the Paycock* in 1972). Rather than Synge or O'Casey, the TDIP embraced the theater that the Abbey presented in its later tours, that is, the theater of social comedy. Between 1933 and 1941, when the group temporarily suspended its activities with the outbreak of World War II, they produced, in order, Edward McNulty's *The Courting of Mary Doyle* (1933–1936); George Shiels's *Professor Tim* (1937) and *Paul Twyning* (1938); Brinsley McNamara's *Look at the Heffernans* (1939); Shiels's *The New Gossoon* (1940); and Robinson's *The Whiteheaded Boy* (1941). Following the war, they produced Robinson's *Far Off Hills* (1947) and, again, *The Whiteheaded Boy* (1948); then Shiels's *Professor Tim* (1949) and *The New Gossoon* (1950). These plays were all comedies.[30]

In a 1952 essay on the Abbey for *Poetry* magazine, the famously caustic Eric Bentley wrote: "It was ironic, calamitous, and yet inevitable that the Abbey should sink into the slough of lower middle class respectability and Catholic *Gemutlichkeit,* for in modern Ireland these constitute 'normalcy.' (Something like them constitutes normalcy everywhere.)"[31] Even if it was inevitable that the Abbey's repertoire would veer from Synge to Shiels, from poetic tragicomedy to conventional kitchen comedy, from the highbrow to the middlebrow, that evolution still invites a few questions related to a specifically Irish American context: Were the Thomas Davis Irish Players simply following the lead of the Abbey's management in giving the New York Irish audiences the light social comedy they wanted, or does the TDIP's neglect of Yeats, Synge, Gregory, and O'Casey suggest something more fundamental about the literary and cultural taste of the American Irish?

No doubt these questions can be connected to Daniel Patrick Moynihan's accusation that "those who would most value their Irishness seem[ed] least able to respond" to the literary achievements of "Shaw, Wilde, Yeats, O'Casey, Joyce and the like." Moynihan suggested that middle-class Irish Catholics rejected these influential, iconoclastic modern writers because of a sensibility mired in an attachment to "the Irish cause and the Irish culture of the nineteenth century."[32] A group named after the progenitor of much of that nineteenth-century cultural nationalism might seem like the perfect specimen of those charges. But rather than condemning the lack of interest in the work of Shaw or Wilde, Yeats or Gregory, Synge or O'Casey, rather than frowning upon Irish American audiences' embrace of light social comedy, perhaps we should instead commend this amateur group's engagement during the forties, fifties, and sixties with the work of Shiels and Robinson and McNamara, as well as the work of Brigid G. MacCarthy and Bernard Duffy and St. John Ervine and Daniel Corkery and W. D. Hepenstall and Sigerson Clifford and Louis d'Alton and Bryan MacMahon, all of whom were contemporary Irish writers who had plays produced by Ireland's National Theatre and whose work was later performed by the Thomas Davis Irish Players.[33]

Coincidentally, the TDIP was formed around the same time that Yeats's early dispatches to Irish America were being compiled by Horace Reynolds into the volume that would be published as *Letters to the New Island*. In the preface he wrote for that work, Yeats admitted, "My friends and I have created a theatre famous for its 'folk art,' for its realistic studies of life, but done little for an other art that was to come, as I hoped, out of modern culture where it is most sensitive, profound and learned."[34] Implicit in this statement is an admission that the kind of theater the Abbey had become was not the kind of theater that Yeats had envisioned when he began conceptualizing a new kind of drama in 1890 or when he founded the Irish Literary Theatre in 1899. Yet the admission does not go quite far enough, because in 1934 Yeats was still pretending that the Abbey was essentially the theater of Synge and Gregory, when in actuality it had become the theater of George Shiels. No doubt this was an outcome too horrible for the poet to contemplate, so Yeats clung to the rhetoric he had employed in 1911.

Yeats had been more honest and more candid in a letter he wrote to schoolboys in San Jose, California, circa 1924, a letter reprinted in the collection of essays *Theatre and Nationalism in Twentieth-Century Ireland*. In his letter Yeats admitted that the Abbey's "new dramatists" wrote plays that dealt with "the life of the shop and workshop, and of the well-off farmer" and set them "as a general rule, in or near some considerable town" and populated them with conventional characters speaking stilted dialogue. Yeats lamented that these new Abbey drama-tists "introduce such characters so often that I wonder at times if the dialect drama has not exhausted itself—if most of those things have not been said that our generation wants to have said in that particular form." And he actually questioned if "perhaps, having created certain classics, the dramatic genius of Ireland will pass on to something else."[35] Reading this letter, one cannot help feeling Yeats's own exhaustion with and disappointment in the theater he had helped create.

That the grand dream of a young Celt in London—the dream of a poetic drama inspired by ancient Irish legends, a poetic drama that would replace the commercial melodrama and farce of the Victorian stage, in the process inspiring the imagination of a new Ireland—that this dream did not quite come true does not, of course, diminish the boldness of the original vision, nor does the fact that Yeats so often entangled his dream in an ugly and disingenuous discourse about realistic drama. Such a positive judgment on his legacy was articu-lated when he died in 1939 by the *Gaelic American,* which published an extended encomium that praised "Ireland's Greatest Poet" for his efforts in founding the National Theatre, the admitted "center" from which "the whole new Irish literary fever spread." The tribute made no mention of the fractious events of 1911–12; instead it focused at length on the apex of his popularity in Irish America, namely, the speech Yeats had delivered in 1904: "the stirring address to a distinguished audience of 4,000 who had jammed the Clan-na-Gael meeting at the Academy of Music that was a memorial for that great apostle of Irish liberty, Robert Emmet."[36]

While the *Playboy* controversy may have been omitted from Yeats's obituary, attentive readers of the *Gaelic American* would have been reminded of it two weeks later when the front page blared this headline:

"STAGE IRISHMAN" STRUTS AT THE
LYCEUM THEATRE. "MRS. O'BRIEN
ENTERTAINS" INSULTS IRISH

Don't Rotten-Egg This Degrading and Vile Caricature
But Boycott It. Easily Most Vulgar Presentation In
Half a Century. Writer is Renegade with Irish Name[37]

The advice to boycott rather than egg the play shows once again that the events of 1911–12 had taught some of the American Irish a lesson about handling renegades with Irish names who produced work that was vile, degrading, and insulting.

It also helps explain the way they treated another Irish writer, an expatriate Dubliner whose attempts to use his fiction to forge the uncreated conscience of his race would enact the advice Oscar Wilde had given but Yeats had forgotten, or at least obscured: "Literature always anticipates life. It does not copy it, but moulds it to its purpose."[38] James Joyce's purpose in writing his books would be regarded by many Irish Americans with as much suspicion as that of Yeats and Synge and O'Casey had been; but the articulation of that suspicion would bear little resemblance to the wariness expressed so vociferously about the famous Abbey playwrights. Despite the success the Jesuits had in getting O'Casey's drama banned in Boston, perhaps the fiasco of the *Playboy* riots taught other patriotic Irishmen exiled in America that it was more cunning to silently ignore, begrudge or sneer at opponents instead of confronting them in the public sphere.

CHAPTER 6
Through a Bowl of Bitter Tears, Darkly

JAMES JOYCE AND THE AMERIRISH, 1917–1962

"IF MANY IRISH took offence at the naif boastings of *The Playboy* it is a little terrifying to know what will be thought of this book." So wrote a reviewer for the *New York Globe* about James Joyce's *Portrait of the Artist as a Young Man.*[1] And yet just a few years later, in 1926, American man of letters Thomas Beer claimed, "To-day I know Amerirish who would have a colic if they read 'A Portrait of the Artist' or 'Ulysses' but who brag about James Joyce."[2] One implication derived from the juxtaposition of these provocative statements is that Irish Americans had learned the lessons of the *Playboy* debacle well: they would not read what they considered to be the unpatriotic, irreligious, and obscene literature produced by Joyce, but instead of making fools of themselves by publicly denouncing his work as anti-Irish, anti-Catholic, and immoral, they would instead take pride in his notoriety as an influential, world-famous author. Or to put it another way: Irish Americans would boycott the Joycean logos but embrace the Joycean logo.[3] Yet, as we shall see, it was not the Irish American press who embraced Joyce.

By the time Beer made his claim, an American edition of *A Portrait of the Artist as a Young Man* had been published in December 1916 under the imprint of W. B. Huebsch. Huebsch also published American editions of *Dubliners* in December 1916, *Chamber Music* in September 1918, and *Exiles* in May 1918.[4] *Exiles* had also been staged in 1925 by the Neighborhood Playhouse, an off-Broadway little theater group based on the Lower East Side of Manhattan.[5] *Ulysses,* because it had been banned from the mails in the United States as a result of legal action taken against the work while it was being serialized in the *Little Review* during 1919 and 1920, could not, of course, be legally read by the American Irish until 1934. But the famous Shakespeare and Company edition of *Ulysses* published in Paris in 1922 was a notoriously popular piece of contraband, one customs officer allegedly exclaiming: "Oh, for God's sake, everybody brings that in. We don't pay any attention to it."[6]

The publication and performance of Joyce's works were thus met with widespread critical attention in American intellectual circles. The Jesuit journal *America* was actually among the first to comment on Joyce, reviewing *Portrait* in a brief, unsigned, and derisive note published in the February 3, 1917, issue. The reviewer dismissed the novel as "the work of one of those decadent Irishmen, so noisy just now, who scorn quotation marks, write foul words, give detailed descriptions of unseemly thoughts, deeds and conversations, and who no longer have any faith in the church of their baptism."[7]

In contrast to the editors of *America,* many other reviewers who were prominent bookmen of Irish Catholic birth or extraction offered positive views of Joyce's work. Francis Hackett, for example, who, like Joyce, had attended Clongowes Wood before emigrating stateside, reviewed *Portrait* in the March 3, 1917, *New Republic.* In an article titled "Green Sickness," Hackett admitted that the work was "not entirely pleasant"; but he also described it as having "such beauty, such love of beauty, such intensity of feeling, such pathos, such candor, it goes beyond anything in English that reveals the serious malaise of serious youth." Hackett insightfully concluded by prophesizing about a trinity of forces that Joyce had treated in a way that was shocking to a great number of America's Irish Catholics: "Many people will furiously resent [Joyce's] candor, whether about religion or nationalism or sex," though, he admitted, "candor is a nobility in this instance."[8]

Two months later, John Quinn, corporate lawyer, art and manuscript collector, and patron of W. B. Yeats, wrote an article for the May 1917 *Vanity Fair* effusive in its praise for Joyce. Quinn provided a biographical sketch and a summary of all Joyce's work up to that point, and he added Joyce to the pantheon of "modern Irish writers" which included, in Quinn's estimate, Yeats, Lady Gregory, A.E., Synge, James Stephens, and Padraic Colum. Perhaps responding to Hackett's review, Quinn wrote of Joyce: "He has the sincerity of genius. Let a man be ever so frank and plain-spoken, as Joyce is, if he is sincere, he is not vulgar or 'unpleasant.'" In closing, Quinn noted "what a fine, hard, great piece of work it is."[9]

Padraic Colum, Abbey playwright, poet, unimpeachable nationalist, and, since 1914, resident of New York, also did his best to provide American readers with some accurate impression of Joyce and his work. In an article for the May 1918 *Pearson's Magazine,* Colum ascribed the "strange" foreignness of *Portrait* to its Catholicism. He explained: "James Joyce's book is profoundly Catholic. I do not mean that it carries any doctrine or thesis: I mean that, more than any other modern book written in English, it comes out of Catholic culture and tradition— even that culture and tradition that may turn against itself." Colum also confessed that the book describes "many squalid and vicious things" but concluded, "The pure ecstasy of poetic creation has been rendered in it as in no other book that I know of."[10]

Following their notices of *Portrait,* both Hackett and Colum reviewed *Exiles* in articles published in October 1918. While both praised Joyce's obvious talent, neither critic was enamored with the work, proving that they were not mere propagandists for Joyce in America. In *The New Republic,* Hackett wrote disapprovingly: "Exiles neither creates a perfect conviction of being like human experience nor quite recalls experience in terms anything like its own . . . There is an unreality around certain passages in Exiles that suggests the literary alchemist vaguely striving to transmute pretty theories into honest flesh and blood."[11] In *The Nation,* Colum contrasted the innovative nature of *Portrait* with the derivative features of *Exiles:* "The play is in Ibsen's form, without

the symbolism that haunted Ibsen's plays and without his conclusive-
ness and his climaxes."[12]

And so in Hackett and Colum, and in John Quinn, one finds Irish
Catholic representatives of those "discriminating seekers of brains in
books" to whom Huebsch had initially advertised Joyce on the back
cover of the *Little Review*'s March 1917 issue. But what of those Irish
Catholic readers who sought things other than "brains" in their books,
those who perhaps purchased books about the old country in the hopes
of finding a patriotic expression of cultural nationalism or a flattering representation of the national character, or those who maybe just
enjoyed reading a good yarn set amid the familiar scenery of their Irish
childhoods? Such readers, one imagines, would have turned not to *The
New Republic* or *Pearson's* or *The Nation*, and certainly not to *Vanity
Fair*, but to a reference guide such as Stephen J. Brown's *Ireland in Fiction: A Guide to Irish Novels, Tales, Romances, and Folk-Lore*, a second,
expanded edition of which was published in 1919.[13] Brown was a Jesuit,
another alumnus of Clongowes Wood, and a prolific bibliographer.
His earlier published works include *A Reader's Guide to Irish Fiction* in
1910 and *A Guide to Books on Ireland* in 1912.[14] Though his guides were
printed in Dublin and London, evidence suggests they were widely
disseminated among the Irish in America. Today, a century after its
publication, a WorldCat search shows that the 1919 edition of *Ireland
in Fiction* remains on the shelf at more than seventy libraries in North
America. Besides being owned by many Catholic colleges and universities, as well as by the public libraries of "Irish" cities like Chicago
and Philadelphia, Brown's book is also held by institutions as diverse
as Yale, the University of Hawaii at Manoa, and the Louisville Free
Public Library.

And what did this widely disseminated and, one must assume, influential shaper of Irish American taste have to say about Joyce and his
work? About the man, Father Brown noted his education at Clongowes
Wood, Belvedere, and University College, but curiously and incorrectly
claimed that "he held for a long time a position in the consular service
at Trieste." In the same biographical note, Brown also mentioned Joyce
as the author of *A Portrait of the Artist as a Young Man*, but the novel
was dismissed as a work resembling "the reminiscences of Geo. Moore

(q.v.) in its entire absence of reticence and of the ordinary amenities of publicity."[15] Brown did devote a full entry, number 823 on his list of over seventeen hundred titles, to *Dubliners*. It reads: "Seventeen genre studies in the form of stories picturing life among the Dublin lower-middle and lower classes, but from one aspect only, viz., the dark and squalid aspect. This is depicted with almost brutal realism, and though there is an occasional gleam of humor, on the whole we move, as we read, in the midst of painful scenes of vice and poverty. His characters seem to interest the Author in so far as they are wrecks or failures in one way or another. He writes as one who knows his subject well."[16]

Father Brown, it should be noted, was not alone among bibliographers and librarians in his treatment of Joyce. William S. Brockman examined American and British library journals published in the 1920s and early 1930s; his examination of that evidence highlights "the involvement of librarians with the suppression of what even then was a prominent work."[17] But Brown's dismissive judgments about the merit of Joyce's work were not limited to the pages of his magisterial guides. The June 26, 1920, edition of the *Irish World*—which in those days still "boasted nearly 120,000 readers"[18]—included an article by Brown titled "The National Idea in Novels." This essay basically provided another list, this one of novels that had rendered in fiction some stage of the Irish struggle for nationhood. Brown first noted novels depicting the Elizabethan Wars, the Wars of Confederation, and the Williamite Wars; this was followed by a discussion of works about the rebellions of the United Irishmen, the Young Irelanders, and the Fenians; the final part of the article examined narratives dealing with the Home Rule, Gaelic League, and Sinn Fein movements. Though Brown admitted that his list made "no attempt at completeness," one would naturally expect to have been mentioned in this final category the novel that has so well dramatized for millions of readers the polarizing effect of Parnell, as well as the nationalist enthusiasm that the Gaelic League and Sinn Fein inspired among Catholic college students during this period. But while contemporaries of Joyce such as St. John Ervine, Lennox Robinson, Brinsley MacNamara, and James Stephens were mentioned, there was not a word about Joyce, nor a hint of the existence of his monumental *Portrait*.[19]

Just below Father Brown's article, though, was printed a large advertisement for "Two Booklets That Irish Americans Must Read" by an author named Joyce. Yet the ad was not for James's *Dubliners* and *Portrait* but for a certain J. St. George Joyce's two "Gems of Irish Propaganda"— "Manual of Sinn Fein: In Question and Answer" and "Erin Then and Now: A Pocket History of Ireland."[20] Even more ironically, in the same issue of that paper an autobiographical book written by a J. A. Joyce was hailed as "a work of genius"—but the praise was not for James Augustine Joyce's *Portrait* but rather for the late Irish-born Kentuckian, Civil War veteran, and all-around raconteur Colonel John Alexander Joyce's memoir *A Checkered Life.*[21] Scouring through the microfilmed archives of the *Irish World* or the *Gaelic American,* the other prominent Irish American newspaper of this period, searching for any trace of Joyce's presence, one actually turns up a wealth of such synchronicity: championed are the works of a famous Irish novelist who had indeed been a member of the consular service in Trieste, but that writer is Charles Lever, not James Joyce; commended are the careers of men who shared a youthful residence at the Martello Tower in Sandycove with Oliver St. John Gogarty, but those men are Arthur Griffin and Seumas O'Sullivan, not James Joyce; celebrated along with O'Sullivan are the works of a plethora of penmen named Shem—Seumas MacManus, Shaemas O'Sheel, Seamus O'Duilearga, but never Seamus Seoighe.

Another Seamus whom the newspapers, Irish American or otherwise, could not possibly ignore was the debonair Tammany politician James "Jimmy" Walker. The child of an Irish immigrant, Walker was famous for his tailored suits, for his carousing with chorus girls, and for his memorable quip that he had "never yet heard of a girl being ruined by a book." That comment is often credited with ensuring the defeat of the Clean Books Bill that John Sumner's New York Society for the Prevention of Vice helped bring before Walker's state legislature in 1923.[22] But unfortunately for James Joyce, in 1921 Sumner had already played a successful role in getting *Ulysses,* because of its obscene power to supposedly ruin young women, banned from the United States.

And yet, in his article "Joyce, *Ulysses,* and the *Little Review,*" Jackson R. Breyer pointed out that Sumner, so easily vilified as a puritanical bogeyman, was "not ultimately responsible for the legal action."[23]

Breyer elucidates how the little magazine edited by Margaret Anderson and Jane Heap that first published the early sections of *Ulysses* had been suppressed by the post office in January 1919, June 1919, and January 1920, all prior to Sumner's involvement in June 1920.[24] In his discerning book *James Joyce and Censorship*, Paul Vanderham builds on Breyer's analysis by examining postal records in which the *Little Review* is labeled "a publication of Anarchistic tendency" and in which documents related to its suppression are filed under "Subversive Literature, WWI." Vanderham concludes that "the motives behind the postal suppressions were not only moral but political."[25] And in fact Sumner, the moral crusader, became involved only after a series of remarkable events described eloquently by Vanderham:

> Desirous of increasing subscriptions, [Anderson] sent an unsolicited copy of the July–August number to the daughter of a prominent New York lawyer. Thus, just as Homer's storm-tossed hero was welcomed on the shores of Phaecia by the daughter of King Alcinous, Princess Nausicaa, so Joyce's *Ulysses* was received into the domestic realm by a privileged young woman. Unlike Homer's heroine, however, the lawyer's daughter was offended by the stranger's nakedness. She complained to her father who drew the case to the attention of the District Attorney of New York County, Joseph Forrester, who in turn sought the advice of the expert in such matters: *Ulysses* was thus brought to the exacting moral attention of John Sumner.[26]

The identity of the young woman who blushed reading of Leopold Bloom's self-pleasuring has never been discovered, but the whimsical suspicion that she was a lace curtain Irish Catholic, a convent student home on summer break, and that her father was a member of the Clan na Gael certainly would add even more irony to an already intriguing story.

Enraged by the chain of events orchestrated by Anderson was John Quinn, who, in typical fashion, had been aiding Joyce in a variety of ways—offering patronage, securing publicity, providing pro bono work as unofficial literary agent and legal adviser. Quinn, despite his years of fraternizing with bohemian artists, remained at heart a shrewd, pragmatic New York lawyer who well knew the difference between abstract aesthetics and practical legal matters. Quinn had made his position clear, to no avail: "There are things in 'Ulysses' published in number after number of 'The Little Review' that never should have appeared in a magazine asking privileges of the mails. In a book, yes. In a magazine, emphatically no."[27] When Anderson welcomed the potential prosecution because of the publicity it would provide for her magazine and the opportunity it would afford to put the principle of obscenity on trial, Quinn dismissed such notions with a very conservative legal argument: "Law is changed by public opinion, discreetly organized and not by flagrant violations leading to convictions."[28]

Quinn arranged a friendly lunch meeting with Sumner during which he was able to persuade the crusader to withdraw the complaint on the promise that Joyce would stop publishing *Ulysses* in the *Little Review*. Whether Joyce would not agree unequivocally to that demand or whether Sumner could not get the district attorney to drop the charges is not clear; but in any case, the deal fell through and the case went to trial. In a letter to Ezra Pound, Quinn noted that this was "not a case where Sumner or Comstockery, or the Society can be honestly knocked," and he fulminated, "Don't for God's sake write to me any more about the illiberality of the United States, or its laws." Quinn, maintaining that the statute was "identical with the British Act" and "not so strong as the French Act" or "the Belgian Act," concluded by advising Pound, "So don't blow off at your typewriter with the idea that this is a sign of provinciality, or anything peculiar to America."[29]

When the preliminary proceedings began on October 21, 1920, Quinn was arguing in the Jefferson Street Police Court before Magistrate Joseph E. Corrigan, a second-generation Irish American and a nephew of Archbishop Michael Corrigan, New York's conservative prelate from 1885 to 1900; unlike his uncle, the judge was a progressive man and a friend of Quinn's.[30] Coincidence would have it that Corrigan had been involved previously with proceedings related to Irish literature: he had passed sentence on the *Playboy* rioters nine years earlier. Quinn hoped he would dismiss the case, but Corrigan refused to do so, instead retiring to his chambers to read the offending passage. When Corrigan eventually returned, he gave Quinn the opportunity to speak in defense of a dismissal. Quinn began by making an argument resembling the famous defense of *Madame Bovary,* but with a twist: like the advocate for Flaubert, Quinn claimed that filth deterred, but he also argued that beauty corrupted. To support this point, Quinn compared Joyce to one dear, dirty Dubliner, Jonathan Swift, while contrasting him to another, Oscar Wilde: the "strong hard filth" of Swift and Joyce were presented in stark opposition to "the devotion to art of a soft flabby man like Wilde." Next, Quinn tried to argue that to be legally obscene a work must be "filthy in result, pragmatically filthy," which he claimed the "Nausicaa" chapter was not; Quinn reasoned: "If [the average person] understood what it meant, then it couldn't corrupt him, for it would either amuse or bore him. If he didn't understand what it meant, then it could not corrupt him."[31] Corrigan listened attentively but responded that anyone could understand "the episode where the man went off in his pants," which was "smutty, filthy within the meaning of the statute."[32] The magistrate set bail at twenty-five dollars and held the defendants over for trial in the Court of Special Sessions.

Quinn attempted to have the case moved to the Court of General Sessions, where there would be a jury trial, but he was unsuccessful. And so the trial began on February 14, 1921, "covered by reporters from several New York daily newspapers."[33] None of the Irish American weeklies based in New York publicized the proceedings, despite the fact that there were numerous Irish parties involved in addition to Joyce and Quinn. Quinn's adversary was Assistant District Attorney Joseph Forrester—whom Quinn described as "an Irish Republican, formerly a Sinn Feiner but now a revolutionary militant."[34] And doing the adjudicating was Judge McInerney, joined on the three-person panel by Judge Moss and Chief Justice Kernochan. Unlike the proceedings against the *Playboy* rioters, this was not an all-Irish affair. In her autobiography, Margaret Anderson described the panel thus: "There were three presiding judges—two with white hair who slept during the major part of the proceedings and a younger man, a Norwegian. Two years later Jane [Heap] met him at a party. Why on earth didn't someone tell me you were Norwegian? he asked. I could have changed that verdict for you."[35] During the trial, when Forrester tried reading from the offending passage, one of the white-haired, nodding judges refused to allow the potentially obscene material to be read in the presence of a beautiful young woman seated in the gallery. Quinn sardonically informed the judge that he was speaking of Miss Anderson, the indicted editor, but the judge was incredulous and stated that she must not have known what she was publishing.[36] When Forrester did start reading, he was soon stopped by the judges, who declared they would read the episode on their own during a week's adjournment.

When they reconvened for final arguments, Quinn admitted that certain passages were disgusting, but he repeated his earlier claim that an average reader would become bored or amused, not aroused, by the material. Forrester's response was angry, loud, and excited, leading to one of Quinn's best-remembered legal arguments:

> Just look at him, still gasping for breath at the conclusion of his denunciation, his face distorted with rage, his whole aspect apoplectic. Is he filled with lewd desires? Not at all. He wants to murder somebody. He wants to send Joyce to jail. He wants to send these two women to prison. He would like to disbar me. He is full of hatred, venom, anger, and uncharitableness. He is my chief exhibit as to the effect of "Ulysses." It may make people angry and make them feel as though they wanted to go out and tomahawk someone or put someone in jail, but it does not fill them with sexual desires.[37]

Quinn believed his "frank appeal to the three Judges' ignorance" had persuaded the two who were "consciously ignorant"; but in Quinn's view those two had succumbed to the will of the third judge, whom Quinn deemed "unconsciously ignorant."[38] Anderson and Heap, who were furious about Quinn's cynical, unsuccessful defense of the novel, were fined, and the novel was effectively banned from American publication on the basis of the ruling. Quinn was not particularly upset about the fine levied on the *Little Review,* and in fact he hoped it would put the little magazine out of business. But Quinn was genuinely dejected that the trial had resulted in the lost opportunity for an American edition of *Ulysses.* The prosecution for obscenity did lead to one unintended consequence, however. It was during the trials that Quinn had planted in Joyce's mind the germ for the idea that would become the deluxe private edition published by Shakespeare and Company in Paris on Joyce's fortieth birthday, February 2, 1922.[39]

One review of *Ulysses* that followed the Paris publication of that deluxe private edition appeared in the *Freeman* magazine, July 19, 1922. The author was Padraic Colum's wife, Mary, née Mary Gunning Maguire in County Sligo. Like her fellow New Yorker Quinn, Mrs. Colum did not deny that the book had disgusting aspects: "The revelation of the mind of Marion Bloom in the last section would doubtless interest the laboratory, but to normal people it would seem an exhibition of the mind of a female gorilla who has been corrupted by contact with humans." In concluding the review, Mary Colum even admitted that "some attempt is being made by admirers to absolve Joyce from accusations of obscenity in this book." In response to her own rhetorical question—"Why attempt to absolve him?"—she answered: "It is obscene, bawdy, corrupt. But it is doubtful that obscenity in literature ever really corrupted anybody."[40] Reading this, one wonders if Jimmy Walker had been perusing the *Freeman* on the train to Albany and/or taking his opinion about literature and society from Mrs. Colum.

Nevertheless, Mary Colum's review is less important for its frank discussion of obscenity than for its remarkably insightful commentary on the novel, commentary that in many ways echoed and expanded upon her husband's earlier insights about Joyce—insights that highlighted both Joyce's Irishness and his Catholicism: "'Ulysses' is one of the most racial books ever written, and one of the most Catholic books ever written; this in spite of the fact that one would not be surprised to hear that some official of the Irish government or the Church had ordered it to be publicly burned. It hardly seems possible that it can be really understood by anybody not brought up in the half-secret tradition of the heroism, tragedy, folly and anger of Irish nationalism, or unfamiliar with the philosophy, history and rubrics of the Roman Catholic Church." Later in the review, speaking of the intellectual portrait of Stephen Dedalus drawn within the pages of *Ulysses,* Colum asked: "Where has the peculiar spiritual humiliation that the English occupation of Ireland inflicted on sensitive and brilliant Irishmen ever been expressed as in this book? Where has the aesthetic and intellectual fascination of the Roman Catholic Church ever found subtler fascination? . . . Has the Catholic Church ever been described with such eloquence?"[41]

The assertions of Joyce's Irish Catholicness made by both Colums is certainly interesting when viewed through the lens of contemporary scholarship on Joyce's reception. In his study *Our Joyce*, Joseph Kelly suggests that prior to 1914, Joyce wrote to "improve his country" and to "rescu[e] his own class—the newly enfranchised but economically stagnant, educated, urban Catholics—from what he considered a disabling cultural nationalism." But after 1914, "Ezra Pound and T. S. Eliot changed Joyce from an Irish writer into an avant-garde, cosmopolitan writer, shucking off his parochial husk to make him serve their literary movement."[42] Kelly's view is shared by Joseph Brooker in the first chapter of his study *Joyce's Critics*.[43] What one finds in the Colums, then, is perhaps an early and astute attempt to combat such an internationalist avant-garde understanding of Joyce's work by stressing that Joyce was writing out of a particular national-religious tradition and writing to a particular national-religious audience; furthermore, the Colums argued that an awareness of the concerns of that specific national-religious tradition was essential to any sophisticated understanding of Joyce's work.

Another early advocate in America for Joyce as a particularly Irish author was Ernest Boyd, a Dublin-born intellectual who had resigned from the British consular service and settled in New York. Boyd had omitted Joyce from the first edition of his work *Ireland's Literary Renaissance*. But in the second edition of 1922, Boyd not only included Joyce in the pantheon of Irish writers but also attempted to combat "the effort now being made to cut [Joyce] off from the stream of which he is a tributary," an effort Boyd feared would "leave this profoundly Irish genius in the possession of a prematurely cosmopolitan reputation, the unkind fate which has always overtaken writers isolated from the conditions of which they are a part."[44] Rather than Ezra Pound or T. S. Eliot, Boyd faulted Valery Larbaud, one of Joyce's French champions, for the distortion of Joyce's literary identity.[45] But whoever was to blame, Boyd left readers with no doubt about the importance of Joyce's national origins: "The fact is, no Irish writer is more Irish than James Joyce; none shows more unmistakably the imprint of his race and traditions."[46] Boyd reiterated and refined these ideas about Joyce's essential Irishness in articles for the *New York Times Book Review* and the *New*

York World, and in the explanatory notes for the Neighborhood Playhouse production of *Exiles* staged in February 1925.[47]

According to his biographer, John Quinn resented the efforts of those like Boyd and the Colums who tried to stress Joyce's "merely parochial provenance" and thought that "booming *Ulysses* as 'a European event,' not an Irish event," would deny "the Irish patriots a chance to assail it as they had assailed *The Playboy of the Western World* as a 'libel' upon Ireland."[48] While Quinn sometimes granted Pound the credit for coming up with this European strategy, he also liked to take that credit for himself. The fascinating thing about the strategy, however, is not so much who devised it but that for Quinn at least, it had less to do with international modernism than with the internecine warfare among the Irish. In a private letter, Quinn had predicted, "The patriots will claim that 'Ulysses' is not a picture of Irish life and is incorrect and immoral."[49] It is certainly understandable why Quinn would have expected such a reception, but the fact of the matter is that Irish American patriots raised nary a whisper against *Ulysses* in their newspapers.

The conspicuous exclusion of any discussion of Joyce in the pages of the Irish American press offers a striking instance, albeit in a totally different context, of what Lawrence Weschler has described as the presence of "felt absence."[50] And this "felt absence" of Joyce raises a number of questions: Did the Irish American weeklies boycott Joyce because, even though they considered his work a libel on Ireland, they sought to avoid drawing attention to the supposed libel as they had done to *The Playboy?* Or did they ignore him because of the efforts of Pound, Eliot, and Larbaud to de-nationalize Joyce had succeeded in obscuring that Joyce was an Irish author writing fiction not only set in Ireland but also deeply engaged with Irish issues? Or did they shun him because of the ecclesiastic judgments provided by the likes of *America* and Father Brown? Or were they too preoccupied with the political upheaval that occurred in Ireland between 1916 and 1922 to care about the rise of a talented but controversial native novelist? Or, like James Stephens, the Dublin-born author, did Irish Americans simply feel that "[*Ulysses*] is too expensive to buy, and too difficult to borrow, and too long to read, and from what I have heard about it, altogether too difficult to talk about"?[51] The answer to all these questions is probably some elaborate synthesis: the reluctance of Irish Americans to look foolish and provide free publicity to their foes, the ambiguity of Joyce's nationality, the reputation for obscenity and blasphemy in his work, the difficulty of his style, the basic unavailability of his most famous work, and the focus on political developments rather than literature and culture probably all contributed to Joyce's absence from the pages of the Irish American journals during this period.

And yet, in the ensuing years, when the Irish Free State became a more stable reality and when Joyce had firmly established himself as a world-renowned Irish writer, only the *Advocate* paid him any mind. The March 5, 1927, issue reprinted from the editorial page of the *Roscommon Herald* a piece lambasting "the new school of writers in Dublin whose abominable writings have made Ireland a foul smell in the nostril of other countries" and in particular "a degenerate named James Joyce" who "issued a book entitled 'Ulysses,' which in its vileness could only be compared to a reeking cesspool." The piece then went on to mention a petition in support of *Ulysses* "signed by all the European works of literature, whose chief aim is to undermine the people's faith in Christianity."[52] The petition in question was published on February 2, 1927, and supported Joyce in his fight against a New York "booklegger" named Samuel Roth, who, from July 1926 to October 1927, published, without Joyce's authorization, fourteen abridged episodes from *Ulysses* in a magazine called *Two Worlds Monthly*. The protest against this piracy was supervised by Joyce, authored by Ludwig Lewisohn, revised by the lawyer-poet Archibald MacLeish, and signed by 167 prominent members of the American and European intelligentsia. About the petition, Leo Hamalian has observed, "Probably never before (or since) have so many famous names of illustrious men of letters been assembled together on one page," although Hamalian also sardonically claimed that "two of the alleged 'signatories' were dead at the time; eighteen of them could not read English and about thirty 'signatories' denied ever having signed the petition."[53] The *Advocate*'s editors followed the reprint about the petition with news that they thought would pique Jasper Tully, the publisher of the Roscommon paper: "at a recent meeting of an Irish literary group in New York City," a speaker who had once written a preface to *The Collegians* nevertheless "lauded Joyce and belittled [Gerald] Griffin."[54] A quick Google search reveals that none other than Padraic Colum wrote an introduction to Griffin's novel, which was published in Dublin by the Talbot Press in 1918 and in New York by the Frederick A. Stokes Company in 1920.

Despite having led readers to believe in his degeneracy, the June 3, 1939, *Advocate* at least paid Joyce the courtesy of noticing *Finnegans Wake*. In the "Review of Irish and Catholic Books and Authors" column, John Francis Kelly displayed an awareness of Joyce's entire oeuvre as well as his significant influence on other writers. Kelly also revealed an understanding of the fundamental nature of the book: "Former residents and people who know Dublin of the years 1895–6–7 and 8 will find much amusement dissecting the lines and getting at the meaning of the words and names." But for Kelly, such amusement had its limits: "Word puzzles in their way are entertaining and at times funny. But one does not want an entire book with every page a puzzle, a conundrum, a headache." Ultimately Kelly concluded, "But with all due respect to Joyce and his genius, and to the influence he wields among the young writers today, this reviewer must class Joyce as a failure."[55]

In contrast to the *Advocate,* the *Gaelic American* and the *Irish World* continued to ignore his prominent presence on the international stage while highlighting the accomplishments of other, much more obscure Joyces. During 1933 and 1934, for instance, amid the widespread coverage of the *Ulysses* trial and its appeal, one finds neither a condemnation nor a defense of the writer, nor even a discussion of his embattled novel. But in the *Irish World,* one does find Robert Dwyer Joyce's "Boys of Wexford"—verse authored by a long-dead poet celebrating the doomed insurrection of 1798.[56] And in the *Gaelic American* one discovers a posthumous article by the antiquarian Patrick Weston Joyce on Celtic domiciles.[57] In May 1939, as the literary world saluted the long-anticipated publication of *Finnegans Wake* and Joyce was featured on the cover of *Time* magazine, one finds in the Irish American press no celebration of this labor of love, language, and learning, nor even a passing mention of this work so long in progress, but on the front page of *The Irish World* there was an account of a hurling match between Kerry and Galway, the latter squad no doubt composed of at least a few descendants of the tribe Joyce.[58] And most egregiously and most sadly, when Joyce died in 1941, one searches the *Gaelic American* and *Irish World* in vain for an encomium, an obituary, or even a simple death notice, but one finds nothing, though one does read about the passing of a Michael Joyce of Limerick, who "represented his native city in the English Parliament" and who was "twice mayor of Limerick and for many years Alderman of the Corporation."[59]

The question why Joyce was afforded this silent treatment must once again be addressed. Perhaps the most reductive explanation is that editors of the *Irish World* and the *Gaelic American* were indeed following clerical counsel. For instance, in an article for *America* titled "Ulysses the Dirty," Father Francis Xavier Talbot responded to the lifting of the federal ban on *Ulysses* by advising the burial of the subject:

> As far as Catholics are concerned, the case of *Ulysses* is quite clear. Judge Woolsey states that the effect of the book is "emetic"; he does not find it to be "aphrodisiac." It is truly emetic. Our most emetic reactions would be caused not so much by its vulgarity, nor by its indecency, but by its rampant blasphemy. Only a person who had been a Catholic, only one with an incurably diseased mind, could be so diabolically venomous toward God, toward the Blessed Sacrament, toward the Virgin Mary. But the case of *Ulysses* is closed. All the curiosity caused by the extraneous circumstances of its being banned is over. It has now subsided into just a book. It will be discussed, undoubtedly, in the little literary pools of amateurs and young Catholic radicals. But for the most part it is in the grave, odorously.[60]

During the course of the complicated series of legal proceedings that ultimately led to the removal of the ban on *Ulysses* in the United States that so disgusted Father Talbot, it is perhaps not shocking to note that the process of liberalization was orchestrated by two Jewish men, Random House publisher Bennett Cerf and attorney Morris Ernst, and then validated by three Protestants, first by Judge James Woolsey, and later by Judges Learned and Augustus Hand. In his excellent study *James Joyce and Censorship,* Paul Vanderham presents a team of Republican-appointed federal prosecutors who had no stomach for keeping *Ulysses* banned and who were relieved they had lost their case. Vanderham writes: "The U.S. Attorney's Office was also content with [Woolsey's] decision . . . [Assistant U.S. Attorney] Nicholas Atlas 'seemed delighted.' [Chief Assistant U.S. Attorney] Sam Coleman . . . welcomed Woolsey's decision. [U.S. Attorney] George Medalie . . . must have agreed with his assistants, for he did not initiate an appeal of Woolsey's decision."[61] Morris Ernst described Coleman not as one who tanked the case but as "a highly skilled and honorable lawyer" who "carried with vigor his duty of searching for truth by adversary relationships and, unlike other or most prosecutors, was not interested in producing convictions."[62]

Conversely, the forces who sought to maintain the conservative status quo were all Irish Catholic Democrats who had been appointed following the election of FDR in 1932: U.S. attorneys Martin Conboy and Francis Horan, who appealed Judge Woolsey's ruling, and Assistant U.S. Attorney General Joseph B. Keenan, who approved the appeal. Vanderham at least gives these earnest Irish Catholic lawmen credit for carrying out an appeal that, "however misguided its intention, had the virtue of bringing about the vindication of *Ulysses* on saner grounds than those of the Woolsey decision."[63] For Vanderham, those "saner grounds" include the acknowledgment that certain parts of *Ulysses* were indeed legally obscene, but that "the benefits of artistic freedom generally outweigh the harm that such freedom may cause."[64] Vanderham has less praise for the narrow thinking of Judge Martin Manton, who of course dissented from the Hands' majority decision to uphold Woolsey.

Interestingly, at the start of the appellate trial, Conboy stated his case against *Ulysses* with this succinct description of the novel: "This is an obscene book. It begins with blasphemy, runs the whole gamut of sexual perversion, and ends in inexpressible filth and obscenity."[65] In a reminiscence about the *Ulysses* trials published years later in the *James Joyce Quarterly*, Morris Ernst noted how Conboy's appeal attempted to buttress the government's claims about the text's titillating and dangerous obscenity by also ascribing "the outworn penal sanction of blasphemy" to the novel. Ernst described Conboy's representation of the novel as "one day in the life of a Hungarian anti-Christ Jew," a representation Ernst saw not as anti-Semitic but, rather, in line with the view that Joyce was "a Catholic renegade." With the certainty of hindsight, Ernst claimed, "This line of attack was not disturbing to me even though Judge Manton . . . was the lone dissent and, without carrying the inference to an extreme, it must be noted that Manton was a Roman Catholic." Interestingly, "the absurdity of the Conboy position was made clear" to Ernst when he later related Conboy's argument to Joyce in Paris. Ernst asked Joyce, "When did you leave the Church?" According to Ernst, Joyce replied, "That's for the Church to say," which Ernst interpreted as meaning that Joyce had never really left.[66]

Evidence suggests that Joyce did not share Ernst's interpretation of the trials, and had his own fascinating analysis of the "campaign which was organised by the Irish and Catholic elements in America against the proposed repeal of the ban" on *Ulysses*. In comments made to his first biographer, Herbert Gorman, Joyce suggested that Irish American opposition was based not on the supposed blasphemy or even on the obscenity of the text but on a perceived lack of patriotism in the author: "There can be little doubt that the defamatory article . . . written by Mr. Michael Lennon of Dublin . . . alleging that the author of *Ulysses* had amassed 'ample means' by . . . entering the British government propaganda service in Italy at a time when the British government was carrying on a war of its own against the nationalist forces in Ireland . . . had no small effect in forming the virulence of this campaign."[67] In another communication with Gorman dictated by Joyce to Paul Leon, the same article by Lennon was described this way: "It was highly libelous and defamatory both to [Joyce's] father and himself and in fact there is little doubt that the fact of its publication having gone without legal challenge had an extremely harmful effect on the artistic career of [Joyce] in the U.S.A."[68]

The article to which Joyce referred was published in the March 1931 issue of the *Catholic World*, a magazine published in New York City by the Paulist Press. Lennon was an old Dublin acquaintance whom Joyce had hosted in Paris, which made the betrayal even worse: "So much for Ireland's hearts and hands," he wrote to another old Dublin friend.[69] In addition to the false allegation that Joyce had been in the pay of the British, Lennon also revealed the details of Joyce's elopement with Nora and debunked the idea that Joyce was in any way the son of a gentleman or the descendant of Irish Catholic nobility. While Joyce considered these revelations libelous and defamatory, the contemporary reader is likely to be more shocked by Lennon's literary evaluations.

Portrait is called "a wretchedly constructed affair" which "suggests that with more care the author might have done better"; *Dubliners* shows an author who "lacks even the typically Irish capacity for clever phrase-making"; *Ulysses* is "not so much pornographic as physically unclean"; *Work in Progress* is "a confession of literary failure" that resorts "to the word building devices of *Alice in Wonderland*." Lennon concluded this remarkably poor attempt at criticism by conceding that "Joyce certainly can write good literary articles" and as a result "might be able, some day or other, to give us fine, strong prose in which Catholics could take pride. That is to say, he may have a future as an essayist." But in Lennon's view, "as a poet, or novel-writer, he will always fail."[70]

The sour tone and dismissive judgments of Lennon's article can also be discovered in the reminiscence Oliver St. John Gogarty, by then living in New York, provided for the *Saturday Review of Literature* upon Joyce's passing. Published under the title "The Joyce I Knew," it alerted readers that Joyce "came from the lower middle class" and had a father who spent his "little income" on "drink and good fellowship while his wife who was delicately nurtured was left to feed her starving sons and daughters as best she could." While admitting that "no man had more erudition at so early an age," Gogarty suggested "Joyce's social status or the lack of it precluded him from the company of [George Russell]," while "his effrontery to Yeats shut him out of the band of geniuses for which Lady Gregory was advertising for the Abbey." Contrasting Joyce to Yeats, Gogarty described a nihilistic Swiftian anarchist: "With savage indignation against all that was bad form and was holy, Joyce, a disheveled harbinger of the Bolshevic [*sic*] revolution, flung himself away from beauty and harmony to howl outcast for the rest of his life through the dark recesses of the soul." Gogarty implied that Joyce's first publication, a slim book of poetry, was his best work, though in praising it, he also managed to turn the title into a scatological joke: "The lovely simple notes of pure lyricism which are to be found in Chamber Music (named in mockery after the sound he made by kicking accidentally a night jar) died away and maniacal rage against all things established took their place in a brothel in his lacerated heart." Later in the piece, Gogarty summed up his portrait of Joyce by labeling him "a great repudiator: he repudiated Ireland, he repudiated the Church, he repudiated the Classics and his more intelligible self." Recognizing that it was Joyce's later, supposedly unintelligible work that gained him acclaim, Gogarty went on to say, "I hope that the adulation, even though it may have been undiscriminating, of the literary dilettantes of Paris soothed his heart insatiable for fame." The article concluded with Gogarty once again diminishing Joyce's work in light of Yeats's: "But those whose gaze is clear and undimmed and steadfastly fixed on the Vision Beautiful as Yeats' was, must see what nonsense this vast concordex represents."[71]

Padraic Colum responded to Gogarty's article in a letter to the editor published in the *Saturday Review of Literature*. Colum suggested that "Gogarty fails completely in his approach to James Joyce the writer" by not understanding "the tragedy and compassion that James Joyce got into 'Ulysses' and . . . 'Finnegans Wake.'" Colum also claimed that "Yeats had a high admiration for 'Ulysses'" and had "read thoughtfully 'Finnegans Wake.'" The letter concluded with Colum's contention that Joyce "had the highest admiration for Yeats."[72]

Echoes of the jaundiced opinions of Lennon and Gogarty as well as the positive view of Colum can all be found in the *Advocate* in the weeks after Joyce passed away. The *Advocate* had been the only Irish American weekly to offer Joyce the courtesy of a death notice, though it made him share it: "Two great Irishmen have passed away within a few days of each other—James Joyce, author of 'Ulysses' and other famous literary productions, who died in Zurich, Switzerland, Saturday last, and Sir John Lavery, the famous Irish portrait painter, who died Friday last at Kilkenny, Ireland. Both were unsurpassed in their separate fields of endeavor. Like the late William Butler Yeats, they excelled in their own specialty and wrote and worked from an incomparable angle. All three were endowed with wonderful imaginative faculties and were inimitable, each in their own particular phase of endeavor."[73]

Despite the respectful obituary, the *Advocate* was unable to resist subsequently dishonoring the memory of the dead man. The mean-spirited retrospective was written by John J. Doyle and is worth quoting at length for its strikingly inane critical judgments:

The passing of James Joyce in far-off Switzerland brought forth many long news articles and several editorials on the author of Dubliners and the Portrait of the Artist as a Young Man. There was the same confusion of thought in the articles as there was when Joyce's magnum opus "Ulysses" was under discussion. After the latter book had been accepted Joyce had the chance to write a really great one, such as Eugene Sue or Victor Hugo or William Carleton produced. He tried to run from Ireland by going to Paris, but he was unable to shake it off. He had the further difficulty of not having been able to adopt a new country and write about it. In a sense Joyce spiritually was a man without a land. His gift for stream-of-thought and the arrangement of his ideas . . . and characters were ruined by his failure to give them soul and spirit. Except when dealing with himself, and then only at rare moments, his figures of men are all bodies devoid of intellectual gifts charm, spirit or soul. He told us what they did from sunrise to sunset and after, in the slums and resorts of the dregs of mankind and the hapless fallen. But never what they thought or felt. Therein was Joyce's great weakness. His characters won't live. Carleton's "Art Maguire" or the Broken Pledge will live as long as men imbibe too freely and too much. Had Joyce gone to the villages and mountains and islands as Synge did, he might, while there close to the earth, sea and sky seeing men in their natural state instead of in the Diggs of Dublin, have written himself into immortality. His ego was too great . . . His success as a painter of ugliness was transient and trifling. His learning was lost and he passes on soon to be forgotten.[74]

Doyle's suggestion that Joyce told readers what his characters did but never told readers what those characters thought or felt makes it pretty clear that the columnist was writing out of his hat. Nevertheless, the piece is notable for reasons besides its condemnation of Joyce. An Irish American journalist judging Carleton a superior Irish novelist simply shows that Doyle had remarkably old-fashioned tastes in literature, as does his championing of Hugo and Sue. But an Irish American journalist holding up Synge's career as the literary paradigm to which Joyce should have aspired is quite flabbergasting, given Synge's history in Irish America. While the praise for Synge demonstrates the extreme malleability of literary reputation, it also, in fairness to Doyle, sounds vaguely like the criticism the young Yeats had leveled against so many of his cosmopolitan compatriots fifty years earlier. Beneath this disparaging piece on Joyce appeared—perhaps further highlighting the pettiness of the *Advocate*'s editors, but more likely just displaying again the synchronicity of the Irish Catholic universe—a notice that "Martin Conboy, former United States Attorney for the Southern District, will be the principal speaker at an open meeting of the American fraternity Sons of Erin in the Hotel Commodore, Tuesday evening, January 28."[75]

The following week, the *Advocate* mentioned Joyce's death a third time, and once again belittled his legacy with misleading and unintentionally ironic claims. To wit: "Had he preached beauty or brotherhood or even sought a new era for the world or a new spiritual thought for his own people he would have left landmarks or bright chapters in Ireland's story." Despite these ridiculous contentions, the column also managed to make a rather astute point about writers being by far Ireland's most notable and valuable commodity: "Were it not for Irish writers we sometimes would scarcely know there was such a place as Eire." While admitting that Joyce "was better known among Americans, French and English than in his own country," the author pointed out that "in the end Ireland got the publicity." Cataloguing how "so many of Ireland's great writers"—Goldsmith, Moore, Speranza, McGee, Wilde, Yeats, and now Joyce—went "to Tir-Nan-Og from foreign lands," the article concluded presciently, "Indeed it is no figure of speech to say that the Wild Geese tradition is sustained by Irish poets, writers and artists" whose dust "like the race from which they spring" is "scattered to the four winds."[76]

When he died and his body began the slow process of turning to dust, the treatment Joyce endured in death at the hands of certain New York clergymen was sadder and even more astonishingly shoddy than the treatment he had endured in life at the hands of Irish American jurists and journalists. Some of the jurists and journalists may have acted, after all, in literal good faith, and been genuinely concerned about the effect of Joyce's fiction on the morals of American citizens or on the souls of Catholic readers; but for Joyce's soul the priests seem to have troubled not at all. According to Mary Colum, "When Joyce died and some of his friends in New York wanted to have the customary Mass said for him, every priest approached, even the Jesuits whose pupil he was and for whom he preserved a great respect, refused on the grounds of Joyce's alienation from the Church." According to Colum, the chaplain of Columbia University, Father George Ford, finally did have "the customary prayers said," but she indignantly contrasts this treatment with that for "people far less Catholic than James Joyce like Paderewski and George Cohan [who] were given all the rites, and in the Cathedral." Colum's explanation for Joyce's status as persona non grata was that "he had done the unforgivable thing in English-speaking Catholicism: written freely of sex."[77]

While perhaps a bit too reductive, Colum's explanation does provide one possible reason why Joyce, in death, suffered one final exclusion by Stephen J. Brown, who, still writing about literature and guiding readers, co-authored *A Survey of Catholic Literature,* which was first printed in 1945. Inside the second edition of 1949, one reads with amazement the following passage, with emphasis added: "Irish Catholic Writers in modern times have produced a considerable mass of fiction. It includes *no great names,* but on the whole compares favorably with any similar body of fiction elsewhere."[78] Brown compiled a list of thirty-two writers: Michael and John Banim, Gerald Griffin, William Carleton, Charles Kickham, Canon Sheehan, Katherine Tynan, M. E. Francis, Padraic Colum, Seumas MacManus, Rosa Mulholland, Alice Dease, James Murphy, Seumas O'Kelly, Brian O'Higgins, Canon Joseph Guinan, Maurice Walsh, Daniel Corkery, Aodh de Blacam, Joseph O'Neill, Dr. J. H. Pollock, Francis MacManus, Annie M. P. Smithson, Patricia Lynch, Francis MacManus, Patrick Purcell, Philip Rooney, John D. Sheridan, Michael MacLaverty, Kate O'Brien, Maura Laverty, and Mary Lavin—yet never mentions James Joyce.[79] To add injury to this insult, prior to enumerating his list, Father Brown had acknowledged "Dr. Oliver Gogarty" as "a writer who loves to indulge in the pastime known as *épater le bourgeois.*"[80] But apparently the shocks provided by Joyce's fiction were judged too pernicious to mention.

Yet the attempts by bibliographers and newspapermen and priests to ostracize Joyce from the Irish Catholic tradition were futile; for in the same year that second edition of Brown's Joyce-less survey of Catholic literature was published, L. A. G. Strong was writing: "Priests and ministers of religion are infrequently good judges of art: and art is one way of revealing the truth. The Catholic artist should be of all the best qualified to reveal truth fearlessly, but those who are set over him are too

often timid or blind to any truth but their own . . . [Joyce] led a dedicated life: and those who would condemn him need to be very sure that
their own faith is as clear and their integrity as strong."[81] Strong's study
The Sacred River: An Approach to James Joyce was published in London in
1949 and in New York in 1951. During the next decade a remarkable—
pardon the pun—bloom of criticism on the Catholic dimensions of
Joyce's art appeared. In the seven years from 1952 to 1959 alone, the
following essays and monographs appeared: "The Catholicism of James
Joyce: A Portrait of the Artist as Apostate" by Sam Hynes in *Commonweal;*[82] "James Joyce: Doubting Thomist and Joking Jesuit" by Arland
Ussher in his book *Three Great Irishmen: Shaw, Yeats, Joyce;*[83] *Joyce and
Aquinas* by William Noon, S.J.;[84] *Joyce among the Jesuits* by Kevin Sul-
livan;[85] *The Sympathetic Alien: James Joyce and Catholicism* by J. Mitchell
Morse;[86] and, appropriately, *Our Friend James Joyce* by Mary and Padraic
Colum, the first book-length work on Joyce by his longtime advocates
in Irish Catholic America.[87]

Surely the work of these scholars helped make Joyce more palatable
for many Catholic readers. But at what cost? The contemporary critic
Jeffrey Segall has suggested that many of these authors "frequently muted
[Joyce's] anti-Catholicism."[88] In Segall's analysis, "the darker side of
Catholicism that Joyce was so familiar with is often effaced from" the
"revisionist readings" of such "Catholic intellectuals."[89] Segall claims that
for these Catholic scholars, "the question was not whether Joyce's fiction could be admitted into the canon of great literature, but whether his
work proved that he was among the saved or the damned." And to prove
he was among the saved, they "labored mightily to establish the view that
[Joyce] was not a blasphemer or an atheist or a pornographer."[90] Segall
is correct is surmising that the state of Joyce's soul was no minor matter
for Catholic readers. When I attended Cathedral Preparatory Seminary
in Elmhurst, New York, in the early to mid-1990s, I vividly recall a collection of critical essays on Joyce held by the school library that included
a handwritten inscription on the title page, an inscription along the lines
of "his art will save him from the fires of hell."[91]

The era of revisionist Catholic scholarship on Joyce also included
seminal works such as Hugh Kenner's *Dublin's Joyce,*[92] and of course
Richard Ellmann's *James Joyce,* the still authoritative biography.[93] Cer-

tainly these two works also highlight Joyce's inescapable Irish Catholic background, though these two preeminent scholars suggest very different visions of Joyce's religiosity: *Dublin's Joyce* depicts a disdainful, highly ironic mocker of the modern world's spiritual barrenness, whereas *James Joyce* presents a joyful, sincere secular humanist. Another, much less influential piece of Joycean criticism from this period is Herbert Howarth's volume *The Irish Writers, 1880–1940*. At the start of the chapter that concludes this 1958 study, Howarth writes:

> An Irish priest in Pittsburgh, where I finish this book, tells me that though the Irish now recognize Joyce as a great writer, they refuse to take him "too seriously." If so, it is a way of dodging what he tried to say to them. He intended, certainly at the beginning of his life . . . to make a moralist's impact on his people. But there is a respect in which their reception is right. He did not want the Irish to receive the moral with a long face. He assumed the contrary, that they would only understand his viewpoint if they read him farcically.[94]

In the opinion of one such long-faced Irish American reader, however—a Mr. John C. Delaney of 35 Garetson Road, White Plains, New York, whose annotated copy of Howarth now resides in the Ryan Library Irish Collection at Iona College—Joyce certainly was not a great writer. Mr. Delaney began reading Howarth, according to his own notation, on "4/26/62: Feast Our L'Good Counsel!" and finished, just a week after Bloomsday, on "6/21/62: Mary Ellen's graduation dance from St Bernard's." Mr. Delaney also scribbled on the back page of his copy this final judgment: "Joyce is particularly ludicrous. The obscenity of his meanings are [*sic*] based oftentimes on blasphemy and uncontrolled deceit and obscurity. If its meaning is of any consequence then why the necessity of countless critics and investigators enmeshed in the thought of messianism?"[95]

Fifty-three weeks after Mr. Delaney finished reading Howarth's book on the Irish writers, Joyce's reputation was such that another Irish American was comfortable alluding to him in a speech before the Irish parliament. Describing Irish immigrants such as his great-grandfather, John Fitzgerald Kennedy proclaimed: "They came to our shores in a mixture of hope and agony, and I would not underrate the difficulties of their course once they arrived in the United States. They left behind hearts, fields, and a nation yearning to be free. It is no wonder that James Joyce described the Atlantic as a bowl of bitter tears."[96] Lovely image that, but of course the quote from *Ulysses* is actually "bowl of bitter waters" and refers to Dublin Bay, not the Atlantic Ocean.[97] But this only proves that Joyce's writings had indeed become safe and sound enough to be misunderstood and misrepresented by proud and supposedly pious Catholic Ameririshmen, or at the very least, proud and supposedly pious Catholic Ameririshmen who had graduated from Harvard.

CHAPTER 7

Receptions of an Irish Rebel

BRENDAN BEHAN IN IRISH AMERICA, 1960–1964

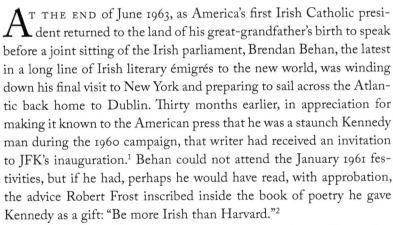

AT THE END of June 1963, as America's first Irish Catholic president returned to the land of his great-grandfather's birth to speak before a joint sitting of the Irish parliament, Brendan Behan, the latest in a long line of Irish literary émigrés to the new world, was winding down his final visit to New York and preparing to sail across the Atlantic back home to Dublin. Thirty months earlier, in appreciation for making it known to the American press that he was a staunch Kennedy man during the 1960 campaign, that writer had received an invitation to JFK's inauguration.[1] Behan could not attend the January 1961 festivities, but if he had, perhaps he would have read, with approbation, the advice Robert Frost inscribed inside the book of poetry he gave Kennedy as a gift: "Be more Irish than Harvard."[2]

Behan had spent his formative years not as a student at Harvard or Oxbridge or Trinity or even University College, but as an Irish prisoner of the British crown, an experience described vividly in his autobiography, *The Borstal Boy*, which had been published to great acclaim, first in London by Hutchinson in 1958 and then in New York by Knopf in 1959. The thoroughly Irish voice who narrates that book suggests that while James Joyce may rightly be described by Thomas Kinsella as the first modern Irish author to speak for "the shamrock lumpen proletariat,"[3] Behan was the first to achieve acclaim for work that communicated almost entirely via the idiom of that raggedy class. Frost's advice to President Kennedy only adds to the irony of the observation made less than three years after JFK's inauguration by Daniel Patrick Moynihan—a Harvard professor by way of New York's Hell's Kitchen neighborhood—the observation that Behan was "Irish indeed" and hence shunned by America's middle-class Irish Catholics.[4]

To prove his point, Moynihan noted that Behan had been banned from marching in the 1961 Saint Patrick's Day parade.[5] Behan had been invited to participate by the Fordham University Gaelic Society, but in announcing the decision, the chairman of the parade's formation committee, the Honorable James J. Comerford of the Court of Special Sessions, explained to the *Daily News:* "We have a semi-religious, almost sacred feeling about this parade and it's not the place for a man seeking publicity . . . We don't want a personality in the parade that has been advertised extensively as a common drunk." In the same article Behan responded to the ban with two of his classic bons mots. The first offered a new theory on what happened to the snakes of Ireland following their expulsion by Saint Patrick: "They all came to New York and became judges"; the second chastised what Behan called "the professional Irishmen" of New York, who were, in the playwright's view, "terribly anxious to pass as middle-class Englishmen."[6]

The latter of Behan's retorts, and indeed Moynihan's analysis of the ban, both imply that at the root of the problem was a class issue: that Behan was simply too rough, too rowdy, and too ribald to be allowed anywhere near the respectable proceedings on Fifth Avenue. This narrative is complicated a bit by Michael O'Sullivan's revelation of a "bourgeois taint" in the Behan family tree that Brendan concealed all his life. (Moynihan's own working-class genealogy has also been challenged: New York City mayor Ed Koch memorably quipped that "Hell's Condominium" was the more appropriate designation for the senator's place of birth.)[7] Nevertheless, it's also a truism that perception is reality, and Behan's ban certainly was perceived by some as rooted in his public identity a working-class hero. Take, for instance, Edward J. Casey, chairman of the Jersey City Saint Patrick's Day Committee, who, after the New York snub, invited Behan to festivities across the Hudson River. Casey told the *Daily News:* "We are sure he will be very much at home and welcomed in the spirit of true, down-to-earth Irishmen . . . This is no lace curtain Irish celebration. His appearance will enhance our St. Patrick's Day affair rather than degrade it."[8] Behan gladly accepted Casey's invitation and, after arriving in Jersey City on the seventeenth, proclaimed: "At one end of the Holland Tunnel lies freedom. I chose it."[9]

The hypothesis that Behan was banished to Jersey City because he was "Irish indeed" and therefore unpalatable to the lace curtain snobs is a popular one. It is employed by Ulick O'Connor in his biography of Behan. Describing "the respectable New York Irish" who made up the County Associations—a group he dubs the "Communion Breakfast crew"—O'Connor writes: "Often their parents and grandparents had been immigrants from the old country. They had a sense of insecurity. Brendan reminded them of an image they were trying to live down. The Ireland they had learned of through their parents was largely rural. They missed a lot of Brendan's Dublin wit while reacting against his fairground hurly-burly."[10] In March 1961, it is not hard to imagine how certain upwardly mobile but insecure members of the Irish American community could have viewed Behan this way, especially in contrast to the other Irishman who was so prominent in the public consciousness: JFK. In such a scenario, the newly inaugurated president obviously represented the success, suaveness, and sophistication of the American Irish, shining as a beacon of a bright future; whereas the playwright reminded them of the drunken antics of the stage Irishman, lurking like a specter from the past, haunting Irish America at its moment of greatest triumph. The physical essence of each man could only have reinforced such impressions. In Brendan Gill's description of Behan, one can see the antithesis of the thin, fit, and tanned president: "a roly-poly, aggressively unathletic-looking young man, with . . . a skin of uncanny pale whiteness." This ghostly pallor was attributable "to the fact that it was his habit to collide as little as possible with broad day-light—he bloomed at night, in bars where the stink of sweat, smoke, and spilled beer was perfume to him."[11] And so, the story goes, bour-geois Irish Americans trembled behind their crucifixes, shunning this vampiric spawn of the night.

But there is a problem with this narrative: it is both reductive and inaccurate. Consider, for example, Judge Comerford, that seeming embodiment of middle-class Catholic philistinism and lace curtain snobbery, that English-imitating snake of Behan's imagination. The truth is that the judge had much more in common with the writer than Behan, his biographer, or the judge himself could have imagined or would have cared to admit. Like Behan, Comerford was born and bred in Ireland; like Behan, Comerford had spent his youth in the IRA; like Behan, he had spent his manhood struggling to become a working-class intellectual: Comerford had put himself through Columbia University and Fordham Law School toiling as a ticket agent for the IRT subway at night while attending classes during the day.[12] At Columbia, his master's thesis had even focused on the Transport Workers Union.[13] O'Connor's implication that a man like Comerford, a man who, incidentally, had arrived in New York in 1925 at the height of the Jazz Age, could not grasp Behan's wit is simply not persuasive. What Comerford objected to was not so much Behan's Dublin tenement substance but rather his self-promoting style. In a similar way, the reaction Behan inspired among Irish Americans was related to a variety of factors in addition to class, factors that can all be recognized in the reception of Behan's first Broadway play, *The Hostage,* a reception that took place six months before the Saint Patrick's Day imbroglio.

When Behan set foot in America for the first time, arriving at Idlewild Airport on September 2, 1960, he was already a successful and critically acclaimed literary phenomenon. *Borstal Boy,* his autobiography chronicling his youth in British penal institutions, *The Quare Fellow,* a play about the last hours of a man condemned to death by hanging, and *The Hostage,* the English-language version of a play originally written in Irish about an IRA captive being held in a Dublin brothel, had all been hailed in London as the brilliant work of a new and genuinely Irish talent. Kenneth Tynan, the influential drama critic for the *Observer,* offered this famous estimation of Behan's genius and the tradition from which that genius sprang: "It is Ireland's sacred duty to send over every few years a playwright who will save the English theatre from inarticulate dumbness."[14]

But by 1960, in addition to his literary fame, Behan had also earned a reputation as a brawler and boozer of legendary proportions. After spending most of his teen years and early twenties incarcerated for IRA activities, he had burst into the transatlantic consciousness through a combination of pen, pint, and pugnacity. A dissertation on the reception of Irish drama in New York that was approved the same year Behan arrived on Broadway stated, "One of the most promising of the new Irish dramatists is Brendan Behan, a gargantuan-featured, high living, uncompromising young man who resides in Dublin when he is not in prison."[15] Events that had contributed to this reputation include the following: in 1954 he had physically attacked the poet Anthony Cronin following a dispute related to a libel case brought by another poet, Patrick Kavanagh; in May 1956 he had appeared sauced out of his mind on Malcolm Muggeridge's BBC program *Panorama;* in the summer of 1959 he had been roughed up by the doorman at the Wyndham Theatre in London when he tried to disrupt a performance of his own play; and in November 1959 he had been linked in from Dublin on Edward R. Murrow's CBS show *Small World,* after which Jackie Gleason, the other guest that evening, described Behan's incoherent performance as "not an act of God, but of Guinness."[16]

In terms of his critical reception among the intellectual world of which Irish Catholics were a part, the off-Broadway premiere of *The Quare Fellow* elicited comment from both the *Catholic World* and *Commonweal* in the early months of 1959. The *Catholic World* offered a generally positive review written by Euphemia Van Rensselaer Wyatt, who concluded, "If strong food is digestible, *The Quare Fellow* offers real values not only against the death sentence but as the work of a new talent."[17] In *Commonweal,* critic Richard Hayes was much tougher: "The international clamor over 'The Quare Fellow' seems to me one of the esthetic mysteries of the decade. Apart from a certain scurrilous drollery, it is fatally uninteresting, and as a document of compassion . . . it dwindles into a kind of garrulous morbidity." It is interesting to note how Hayes's review nevertheless ordained Behan as the heir to Sean O'Casey: "Mr. Brendan Behan stands, by virtue of his antecedents, his intention, his moral commitments and his method, in the line of O'Casey's succession." The review saw both O'Casey and Behan as lacking, however, when compared to Yeats and Synge, in whom "a vastly finer sensibility is at work: speech and tone are elevated to a magnificent enterprise in language."[18] Despite this harsh criticism, then, the *Commonweal* article clearly rated Behan as part of an established canonic line of succession in Irish drama: Yeats to Synge to O'Casey to Behan.

A year later, in March 1960, *Commonweal* ran another article about Behan under the headline "An Irish Success." The author, Sam Hynes, once again cast Behan as the latest genius in a celebrated literary line that included "Yeats and Shaw and Joyce and O'Casey." But Hynes was aware that this tradition was already in danger of becoming a mere caricature of itself.

> There is another, and more strictly literary, sense in which Behan is at the mercy of his Irishness—I mean the Irish idiom in which thus far he has written. Not only the speeches of Irish characters, but the whole of *Borstal Boy* is written in a colloquial style which is often close to being a parody of itself . . . The speech is firm and effective in its use of Irish rhythms and phrases, but even so it is near the edge of that Erin Go Bragh style which one associates with Irish tenors and music hall comedians and Saint Patrick's Day on Amsterdam Avenue. Over the years since Synge and the early Yeats, Irish habits of speech have accumulated such a weight of whimsy and sentiment as to make them virtually unusable for the serious writer.

Furthermore, Hynes noted a destructive psychological impulse toward "self-contempt" and "disgust and aimless rage" underlying this tradition. Hynes noted that Irish writers "have found it easy, even natural, to destroy, with comedy or with withering irony, the follies of their countrymen."[19]

The professional literary opinions of Richard Hayes and Sam Hynes do not, of course, necessarily represent the views of a typical Irish Catholic American in 1960. But evidence from the Irish American weeklies suggests something connected to their insights. Specifically, it seems as though some Irish Americans did recognize a canon of Irish writers whom they resented for relentlessly attacking the perceived follies of Irishmen, particularly those Irishmen of Catholic and/or nationalist persuasion. This canon, it should be noted, was no longer being generated out of the Abbey Theatre. The Abbey's role in Irish and Irish American culture at the dawn of the 1960s can be guessed at from an advertisement for the film *Broth of a Boy* that ran in the January 2, 1960, *Advocate:*

> "BY ALL MEANS, GO!
> A DARLING OF AN
> IRISH MOVIE—HEARTILY RECOMMENDED!"
> —*Phidona, Herald Tribune*
> "The Abbey Players and
> Barry Fitzgerald are as charming
> as a soft summer's day. It all turns out as happily as a Gaelic
> fairy tale."—*Weiler, N.Y. Times*
> "FUN TIME AT THE MOVIES!"
> A froth of a film—Gaelic charm and
> Laughter prevailing all around!"—*Thirer, Post*[20]

This darling, charming, fun, frothy film was a based on Hugh Leonard's play *The Big Birthday,* about the world's oldest man, which had debuted at the Abbey in January 1956. The film is notable as Barry Fitzgerald's last performance on the silver screen, and it was no doubt heavily promoted because it had been filmed on location in Ireland and "Made Entirely in Eire."

Obviously, then, it was not the likes of *Broth of a Boy* that piqued some Irish Americans. Rather, it was Sean O'Casey, whose work the Abbey had discovered, but then rather famously rejected, leading the playwright to bid Inishfallen a permanent fare thee well. The week after Hynes's article about Behan appeared in *Commonweal,* the *Advocate* published a letter to the editor from an Edmund O'Rourke denouncing *Juno and the Paycock,* which had recently been aired on local television in New York:

> From platform, Press and Play, we have recently been plagued by a series of presentations which unjustly degrade, humiliate and ridicule the Irish people, their faith and their national aspirations. The latest and perhaps the most offensive in this series is O'Casey's "Juno and the Paycock" lately seen on Channel 13 T.V.
> Housing a choice collection of bums, drunks, hypocrites, parasites

and a disgusting caricature of a sniveling "patriot," it is the unholy creation of a man divorced from God and Country. But this is O'Casey, brilliant craftsman and supercynic, whose well constructed plots connote a false integrity and are intended to promote an atheistic philosophy that seeks to plant the seeds of contempt and ridicule for belief in God and the moral values which sustain our concept of human dignity . . . Defenders of O'Casey and others of his kind, charge that we are oversensitive and cannot take criticism. This is the bunk. On the contrary, our lack of vigorous protest is responsible for the fact that we are slandered with comparative impunity.[21]

There are many layers to this letter: resentment of O'Casey's satire, an attack on O'Casey's communist sympathies, and the acute awareness that the Irish were viewed as "the crybabies of the Western World" for complaining about how they were represented.[22]

Besides the *Advocate*, Irish Americans who wanted to complain about O'Casey had another popular forum in the *Irish Echo*. The paper had been founded in 1928 by an immigrant from Monaghan known as Charlie "Smash the Border" Connerly. Despite the provocative name of its proprietor, the early *Echo* was more interested in covering sports at Celtic Park than politics in the North of Ireland.[23] But after the paper was taken over by the Grimes family in 1955, it "steadily evolved into a paper covering both the immigrant Irish and Irish American community, not just in New York, but also in the surrounding states of the north east and beyond." In terms of its politics, the *Echo* espoused a "constitutional nationalist ethos" though "many readers openly supported the IRA."[24]

With this context, let us look at the August 20, 1960, *Echo*, in which one finds a review of David Krause's *Sean O'Casey: The Man and His Work*. The gist of the notice is that Krause overlooks O'Casey's communist leanings because he is "a sympathetic American liberal" who agrees with "O'Casey's opposition to Irish nationalism and formal religious worship."[25] In the same issue of the *Echo*, columnist Frank O'Connor tied O'Casey to Behan in a somewhat cryptic piece titled "Behan the Terrible." O'Connor chastised O'Casey for his attacks on Catholic Ireland while simultaneously claiming that the drama of both O'Casey and Behan bore no relation to the realities of contemporary Ireland:

The Irish, of course, have not cornered the market in irrelevancy; they just spend more time at it than anyone else . . . Behan does it in "The Borstal Boy," "The Quare Fellow" and, I'd say, in "The Hostage," too, though Coras Tráchtála [the Irish Export Board] might dispute that with me. [Behan's] stuff does fit the minister's speech in Enniscorthy like a glove, 'tis all for export: life, justice, faith, betrayal, hatred, ciga-rettes, drugs, stout, guards, ropes, scaffolds . . . I have had a unilateral argument (that means he hasn't answered my letter) with Seán O'Casey on the subject. One reason he might not have answered is that I sent along a review I did of Seáno, in which I said his psyche, outlook, was determined by the fact that he grew up a poor Protestant among poor Catholics, when the custom was for Protestants to be rich . . . In effect, in this one-sided argument with O'Casey, my contention was that he should give up throwing rocks through the stained-glassed windows and get after the termites stuck in the bogdale supporting the big house on Kildare Street. But, I suppose Seáno is too removed from Ireland now to know what's going on. Yeats and Synge are dead, so there's noth-ing they can do about it: the young ones like Behan . . . are close enough to it to know, but they're back in the famine, with the leprechauns in the forge, the matchmakers, and the wearing of the Ivy Leaf of the Parnel-lites. Forgotten are the people who are going, going, go . . .[26]

What Behan's contemporary urban dramas had to do with the famine, leprechauns, matchmakers, or Parnell is certainly not clear, and perhaps not surprisingly, O'Connor's column inspired this perplexed response from a John J. Regan of Brooklyn that was published in the letters column of an ensuing *Echo:* "Dear Mr. O'Connor . . . Your remarks re-garding the state of Irish literature, particularly the works of Behan and O'Casey, strike me as strange in the light of the praise being heaped upon them lately."[27]

A fair bit of that heaping, it must be noted, was actually being done within the Irish American press. Brief puffs about the impending opening of *The Hostage* appeared from week to week in the *Echo* as well as in other Irish papers. A representative piece of positive publicity was headlined "'The Hostage' First Was Written, Played in Irish" and informed readers: "On translation it was produced by Joan Littlewood at her theatre at Stratford East, London, with such success that it was chosen to represent 'Britain' at the Paris international theatre festival last year. It was also staged in Sweden."[28] Another informed readers, "Miss Celia Salkeld [is] the only member of the original cast of Brendan Behan's 'An Giall,' which received its first performance in Gael-Linn's Damer Theatre in 1958, who is going to New York to play in the Broadway production of its translation, 'The Hostage'"[29] Clearly, these notices invoked Behan's reputation as an international literary celebrity while also trying to establish his Gaelic bona fides.

But in regard to the notorious man himself, the papers did not gloss over his reputation, though many columnists did try to soften it a bit. A good example can be found in the *Irish Echo* published just a week before Behan's arrival in New York; in that issue, columnist Sean Maxwell wrote: "The hilarious Behan, rollicking, fun-loving Brendan . . . who . . . when challenged can scowl and wear the expression of a world's champ getting in for a K.O. Then there is another Behan, who smiles and laughs and sets the world aglow with his wit, good humor, his razor edged sarcasm . . . But whether he is a world away from or at home it must be accredited to Behan that he is one of the world's great playwrights and might well become the greatest as his pen flows rapidly on."[30]

In the pages of the *Irish World,* which in 1951 had merged with its longtime rival the *Gaelic American,* Michael Sheehan presented an even more subdued portrait in two brief notices that appeared in consecutive weeks: "I met Brendan Behan and his wife some days ago on Third Ave. The well known Dublin born playwright . . . enquired for Clarke's on Third Ave. I told him who I was and I regret that I hadn't the chance of speaking longer with him and his gracious wife who are visiting New York."[31] And then: "I met Brendan Behan at The Jager House and rarely have I heard a better Irish Speaker. Brendan has no apologies for speaking the language of Ireland . . . I am glad the versatile Brendan Behan speaks our ancient language."[32]

In the *Advocate,* columnist Pete Lee likewise depicted a Behan who appeared to be in almost direct opposition to the man readers would have expected:

The Behans, complete with entourage, had a captive audience at Costelloe's, world famous Bar on Third Ave., N.Y. last Thursday evening. There was a time when the playwright would have held his audience spellbound with a different type of show, but those wild, rip-roaring days are gone. For the Behan of today, is an astute, though somewhat subdued man who seems to have an ear for everybody, even writers and newspapermen . . . Mr. Behan intends to spend considerable time in the dollar zone, especially if his play "The Hostage" . . . is successful . . . When next I see this gentleman from Ireland, it will be from the Mezz seat on opening night. Until then I will keep in mind the remark which Mr. Behan threw in my direction in parting: "Bieth me at cainnt duth aris." (Translation: I'll be talking to you again.)

Lee's column is unintentionally humorous in its portrait of Brendan's wife, Beatrice Behan, whose maiden name was ffrench-Salkeld. Ms. ffrench-Salkeld was from a family of prominent Dublin artists and intellectuals and she was fluent in Irish, but Lee apparently thought the woman was of Gallic descent; hence his description: "His wife, who is one of the few Gaelic-speaking Parisians, is not what one would call a typical petite French lady."[33]

Two weeks after meeting the Behans, Lee did indeed write about opening night of the play. Lee's judgment was that "'The Hostage' tho [*sic*] at times inclined to be indecent, is nevertheless a very entertaining play." Lee advised his readers that if they were "the proper Bostonian type" who "still live in the 19th Century," the play would provide "the shock of [their] life." But for those who would "like to see something unusually funny, unusually crazy, and unusually indecent," Behan's play was the thing.[34]

But not all the New York Irish were as welcoming of Behan as Sheehan and as accepting of *The Hostage* as Lee. In *My Life with Brendan,* Beatrice Behan recalled the following scene:

> One Irishman stopped us in the street and said to Brendan, "I saw your play. It's a disgrace and slander on the Irish people."
>
> Brendan never liked to hear his work criticised.
>
> "I hope you paid for your seat," he said.
>
> "I certainly did."
>
> "Well, that cheers me up a bit."
>
> "You had no right to put prostitutes in your play. Everybody knows there's not a prostitute in Ireland."
>
> "And what part of Ireland do you come from?"

"I come from Drumsna."

"Drumsna?" echoed Brendan. "You're so fucking poor in Drumsna you couldn't keep a snipe, never mind a prostitute."[35]

Though their critiques were not quite as naïve as the complaint made by the man from Drumsna, some of the very same journals that were puffing and praising Behan also reproved both his play and his persona. This negative material can be grouped into four broad and sometimes overlapping categories of corruption of which Behan stood accused: obscenity, blasphemy, traitorousness, and public drunkenness. The first three charges he shared not only with O'Casey but also with Joyce, Synge, and Yeats; but the last was his own unique contribution to the perceived vices of Irish writers. Knowledgeable readers might be wondering as well about how Behan's sexual appetites factored into his reception. But Brendan Gill testifies that Behan's bisexuality was not known to one of his closest friends in New York during the period when he resided there, and I found no evidence that journalists or readers suspected Behan of such proclivities.[36] Of course if this had been known publicly, it would have linked Behan to the perceived vices of Oscar Wilde in the mind of his detractors.

As it was, Brendan's alcoholism was the thing that attracted negative attention as soon as he landed. The day after Behan arrived, the *Advocate* published a striking front-page headline alluding to a speech by the then-Taoiseach: "IRISH NOT HEAVY DRINKERS SAYS LE MASS."[37] Inside the paper, in the article attached to the headline, the prime minister was quoted lamenting that "there are Irish journalists, playwrights and novelists who seem to think that the surest way to extract royalties from British publishers is to depict the Irish not as they really are but as the British public have been led to imagine them."[38] Behan's reply to these comments was included in a separate note: "It is not the business of Irish playwrights to give publicity to Irish politicians . . . You can say this however. They . . . should not collect income tax off books that they have banned in Ireland."[39] A week later, when Brendan was firmly situated in New York, the *Advocate* published a terse editorial scolding him for encouraging the worst anti-Irish prejudices through his drunken clownish behavior.[40]

A related view of Behan was expressed by Bill Slocum, a columnist for the *New York Journal American.* The unique observation Slocum made about Behan, however, was that in New York, at least, he was not truly getting drunk and disorderly but—even worse—was just performing the sloshed Celt, a role Slocum described as "a caricature of the drunken Irishman . . . 'Paddy the Mick' who hates the English and roars 'up the I.R.A.'" While lumping Slocum in with the insecure and humorless "respectable New York Irish," Ulick O'Connor nonetheless credits the columnist with realizing something many others missed: "Brendan was playing a part. Sober, he remembered the impression that his drinking escapades made on the public, and he was not averse to giving the impression from time to time that he had a few drinks just to live up to his reputation."[41]

After *The Hostage* had debuted, a review in the *Echo* focused not on the playwright's public persona but on the text's offenses against religion. After describing the plot and setting of the play, Mary Jane Grimes wrote:

> Granted, one would not expect the language spewing forth from the inhabitants of such a place to be that of a convent; nevertheless, one is not prepared for the rawness of many of the lines, and certainly not braced for the blatant blasphemy. And here is where the iconoclastic Behan loses all sense of what can be tolerated and what is completely offensive. Several times throughout the play he brings in lines and situations which are so out of order in their mockery of the beliefs and traditions of the Catholic Church as to make the playgoer shake his head in disbelief. Artistically, there is no justification for the inclusion of these incidents. They are deliberately inserted to shock, and in this they succeed.

After this harangue, Grimes actually complimented the acting, the staging, and the set. But she closed her review by again lamenting the performance of the playwright: "There is no doubt Behan could have given us a wonderful evening had he even *tried* to distinguish between good humor and outbursts of bawdiness and blasphemy in the poorest possible taste. As it is, 'The Hostage' is not fit fare for the stage, and certainly not fit fare for the Irish."[42]

Three weeks later, Frank O'Connor provided readers of the *Echo* with an even more derisive review of *The Hostage*. O'Connor once again expressed his ideas (ideas that include some notable praise for Synge) with a unique kind of colloquial invective:

> I stood it for two acts, but couldn't take it anymore . . . There were times when the super-patriots of Ireland showered the stage of the Abbey with rotten apples, potatoes and cabbage. I didn't agree with them then, because, at least, the language of Synge was a thing of beauty and came close to the ancient spirit of Western Ireland. They haven't done that to Brendan Behan's Hostage; there is no need for it; the stage is loaded with garbage, put there by the incompetent Dublin brickie. How this thing ever passed the U.S. Department of Agriculture Customs inspection should be a key point in the election platforms. Only once before have I walked out of a play.[43]

A month later the *Echo* printed an item demonstrating that O'Connor's actions were not unique. Under the headline "Walk-out Protest at Behan Play," it described how fifty people had walked out of the Olympia Theatre in Dublin. According to the report, one of the departing audience members shouted: "I am a Catholic, and I object strongly to this being put on in a Catholic country. It is a disgrace to all our consciences." Another man roared, "If there is any Catholic present who has a conscience, he should walk out."[44]

The negative judgments of these *Irish Echo* pieces are reiterated in the *Catholic World*'s November 1960 issue. In a review written by Professor Stephen P. Ryan of the University of Scranton, the play was described as "a wildly riotous affair which ranges from a few moments of lyrical tenderness through some well-aimed shafts of satire, down to an inexcusable amount of absolute obscenity and blasphemy." In its discussion of obscenity, the review contrasted Behan to James Joyce: "It must be said, however, that Behan lacks the artistic integrity of his more famous predecessor; the bawdy, obscene elements in *The Hostage*, for example, unlike the more notorious passages in *Ulysses*, are only too obviously dirt for dirt's sake."[45] No doubt Ryan's judgment is another fascinating example that could be added to the evidence from the previous chapter in order to demonstrate the extent to which Joyce had become a representative Catholic author. But Ryan's suggestion that Behan had included "dirt for dirt's sake" supports Paul Vanderham's assertion that Judge Woolsey's ruling "became the most widely circulated criticism of the novel."[46] Said another way, Ryan's articulation of the concept of gratuitous obscenity demonstrates how influential the logic and language of Woolsey's decision had become in understanding *Ulysses* in particular and modern literature more generally. And yet it was not gratuitous obscenity but blasphemy that Ryan described as "the most objectionable feature" of the play. While Ryan did grant that Behan possessed "a mastery of the rich, racy argot of the Dublin slum-dweller," that he was "a satirist of no mean proportions," that "the play is always alive, always vibrant, always demanding a response from the audience and getting it," and that "serious students of the theatre will find an interest in [the play] for its dialogue, its use of certain technical devices and dramatic tricks," Ryan concluded by insisting that "the play simply cannot be recommended for the general public."[47]

Behan was offended enough by the accusations of anti-Catholic sentiment in his drama that he fired off letters to the editors of the Irish American press in New York. Behan's letters appeared in the October 29 *Advocate* and the November 5 *Irish World;* the gist of the two letters is the same, but they have slightly different introductions. It is not entirely clear if the letter printed in the *Advocate* was actually intended to castigate that paper, which had, after all, published a rather positive notice on *The Hostage* written by Pete Lee. Mary Jane Grimes or Frank O'Connor from the *Echo* would have been the more obvious target for Behan, but nevertheless, he opened by attacking an unnamed critic's dramatic credentials and accusing him of Puritan bias:

References in your paper to my play, "The Hostage," have not been confined to criticism of my plays on artistic grounds. Your critic has attacked the play on religious grounds as well. Your critic did very well for himself here. He had not seen many plays of any kind, I would think, and such "Irish" plays as he has seen, would be for foreign consumption. The sort of Pat and Molly epics that would move a Dublin audience to hysterical laughter. He is, however, pretty well learned in the language of Billy Graham, and accuses me of insulting the Catholic Church, in which I was bred, born, reared and hope to die, (but not before the run of the Hostage is over). Therefore, for the benefit of this theological theatergoer, I append an extract.[48]

In the letter to the *Irish World,* Behan managed to pay brief homage to the long, illustrious history of that paper while simultaneously slighting the other weeklies by reiterating: "The Irish-American press (of whose existence I was not aware except for the Irish World and the Gaelic American), has been uniformly condemnatory of my play The Hostage. It is not my custom to reply or make public comment on criticisms of my work. As they have seen fit however, to accuse me of insulting the Catholic Church, in which I was born, bred, married, and hope to die, I append the following extract."[49]

Both letters included an excerpt from an article that appeared in the Jesuit mouthpiece *America* in October 1960. That article observed: "While Behan is angry with modern causes and ideas, he loves people. Without love he could not have created a gallery of such vital characters. They are not the sort of people one would choose for associates or want for neighbors. Their morals, manners and profanity are deplorable. But we have to live in the same world with them, and their degradation is an indictment of civilization and a challenge to religion."[50] Compared to the indictments of Yeats, Synge, O'Casey, and Joyce that appeared in *America* across the years, this was a remarkably charitable take on Behan's work. Perhaps this can be explained by the fact that the reviewer, Theophilus Lewis, was not a Jesuit priest but an African American intellectual who moonlighted as a postal worker and who had converted to Catholicism relatively late in his life.

Behan's employment of Lewis's criticism to defend his own religiosity inspired the *Advocate*'s Pete Lee to pen a column denouncing his fellow Irish American journalists and defending Behan's play.[51] But Behan's missive also provoked two pointed responses in the letters to the editor section of the *Advocate*. In one, an Edward F. X. Hughes patronized Behan—"the toothless scribe"—for "rally[ing] to the Church for intellectual aid." Hughes sent in an excerpt of his own that he claimed displayed "a more typical American Catholic viewpoint" than the one expressed in *America.* The excerpt was from the November 1960 issue of *The Sign,* a journal published by the Passionist Fathers; it concluded, "Undisciplined and completely lacking in good taste, this waste of an obvious talent communicates nothing beyond blasphemy, confusion, and the image of a small boy writing dirty words on a back fence."[52] The other letter to the *Advocate* was signed P. O Murcada, who identified himself as someone "who did a small bit of fighting in the cause of Irish freedom." In the letter writer's opinion, Behan was doing an injustice to those who fought for the cause of liberty in Ireland:

> I felt very sorry for all those great Irishmen who died fighting that Ireland may take her place among the nations of the world. They left behind a man who by his antics is bringing our little country and all that love it down to a very low level in the eyes of the world. This man last week just to boost his play and his book that was banned in Ireland went into a restaurant and supposedly drank seven bottles and then started to try and sing some ballad of the Irish Republic. He then went on stage in a supposed state of intoxication to boost up a play that we Irish people would not tolerate, a play that should not be supported. The men that went out in 1916 to free their country were true Irishmen and all that mattered to them was the love of country and not to go into some beer joint and get drunk and start singing some Republican songs to let the public know what great heroes they were. In the words of Padraig Pearse, Ireland unfree shall never be at peace. But to my mind, as long as Ireland has men who have the cheek to write cheap books and produce bad plays about her, she shall never take her place amongst the nations of the world.[53]

The letter writer's outrage at the way Behan boozily utilized Republican songs and slogans to burnish his own public image resonates in a column written by Sean Maxwell for the *Irish Echo* shortly after Behan arrived in New York. At that time, Maxwell complained about the way Brendan and his brother Dominic "created a halo of I.R.A.-ism around their names" only to condemn "the folly of their affiliations and the affiliations of others with such a movement." Maxwell went on to speculate that in New York Behan would "come under a barrage of criticism" for "the simple reason . . . that thousands of Irishmen and Irish mothers have lost their sons in the cause of justice and freedom, and while they have regretted their loss they never regarded it as futile, the way Behan has."[54]

P. O Murcada and Sean Maxwell were obviously not the first to criticize Behan in this way; the playwright had actually written such criticism into the text of *The Hostage*. In act 2, the manager of the brothel,
Meg, sings a republican ballad, "Who Fears to Speak of Easter Week."
This exchange follows:

MEG: The author should have sung that one.

PAT: That's if the thing has an author.

SOLDIER: Brendan Behan, he's too anti-British.

OFFICER: Too anti-Irish, you mean. Bejasus, wait till we get him
back home. We'll give him what-for for making fun of the
Movement.

SOLDIER [to audience]: He doesn't mind coming over here and taking
your money.

PAT: He'd sell his country for a pint.[55]

Behan was clearly demonstrating here an awareness of his reputation
among some of his former comrades in arms. Before he came over to
New York for the debut of *The Hostage,* he even told his publicity manager, Rae Jeffs, that "he had heard that there was some doubt in the
minds of the American branch of the I.R.A. as to whether they would
accept a charity performance of *The Hostage,* or bomb the theatre instead."[56] The criticism Behan received from Irish Americans because of
his reformed republican views never quite became the literal barrage
that Behan joked about or the figurative one that Maxwell predicted.
But it was certainly a major cause of consternation directed toward the
playwright.

Another potential reason for Behan's rejection by Irish Americans in
1960 was articulated by the *Echo*'s Frank O'Connor in a brief response
to that defensive letter Behan had sent to the Irish American press.
O'Connor succinctly rephrased his earlier criticism about Behan's irrel-
evance in terms of the *America* article's claims that he was akin to other
angry young playwrights who raged against contemporary society: "I
wish Ireland did produce a John Osborne; the Irish playwrights are
either up in the clouds looking for Ossian in Tire na n-Og, or down in
nighttown."[57] While the nighttown reference clearly alluded to Behan's

carousing persona as well as the setting of *The Hostage*, O'Connor avoided the charges of blasphemy and political heresy leveled against Behan by others; but O'Connor's reference to Osborne implied that, unlike those of the angry young man of English theater, Behan's dramas were unrelated to the social realities of Irish life. Literary critics have, of course, interpreted both *The Hostage* and *The Quare Fellow* as Behan's bleak assessment of the first four decades of Irish independence. Declan Kiberd, for example, has written, "His shabby boarding-house-turned-brothel setting is a fitting metaphor for the decayed ideals of a free Ireland."[58] But the commentary Behan inspired in the Irish American weeklies does not indicate that his drama was understood in this kind of allegorical way.

O'Connor's assertion about the irrelevancy of Behan's drama thus provides a starting point for understanding a great irony one discovers in reading New York's Irish American newspapers during the months surrounding the premiere of *The Hostage*. And that irony concerns the fact that while Behan did elicit both occasional comment and condemnation in the pages of the Irish American newspapers, the coverage of Behan paled in comparison to the weekly publicity granted the amateur actors of the Thomas Davis Irish Players, who announced that for their twenty-seventh season they would stage John Murphy's drama *The Country Boy* at the Master Institute Theatre on 103rd Street and Riverside Drive during two weekends in November 1960 and one weekend in March 1961.

Murphy's play concerns a young Irish farmer still living at home with his parents who dreams of following his older brother to America in pursuit of success. But when the older brother, along with his obnoxious American wife, return home on holiday for the first time, the pain, privation, and remorse that result from leaving Ireland are revealed. Instead of buying a ticket to America, the younger lad stays behind on the farm and buys his Irish sweetheart a ring.

Certainly this was material to which Irish American immigrants and their progeny could much more easily relate than an IRA kidnapping farce set in a Dublin whorehouse. Not surprisingly, the press notices stressed the topical subject matter of *The Country Boy* as well as the critical acclaim it had received in Ireland. From the *Irish World:*

"Prize winner at the 1960 All-Ireland Drama Festival, this play has been described by Ernest Blythe, director of the Abbey Theatre, as the most notable play to come to the Abbey Theatre for a considerable time. Conceived out of the problems created by emigration, the author, who himself lived in America for some time, has fashioned his material into a straightforward play which is quite out of the ordinary, one which will have particular appeal to an American audience."[59] And similarly, from the *Advocate:* "Rated by critics and audiences alike as the most notable play in the field of Irish drama, it has been a sensational success in Ireland the past two years and is currently playing in many towns and cities throughout the country. Conceived out of the problems created by emigration, its story is close to the heart of every Irish immigrant. You will laugh, and you will shed a tear, because you too have experienced the same thoughts and feelings."[60]

After the play had been performed, the *Advocate* ran a review, signed with the initials C.B.Q. The review opened by noting that the play's "success was due to the humor, sparkling dialogue and vivid characterization as well as to the skill with which the dramatist exploited a theme very pertinent to Irish people—emigration." The reviewer admitted, "It may seem that the play proposed an over-simplified melodramatic solution to a very complex problem," but C.B.Q. nevertheless praised Murphy for his ability to dramatize this issue: "The dramatist's understanding of the emigration problem is deep, and those who know the Irish rural scene will admit the keenness of Murphy's insights into the minds of the old, stubborn, possessive Irish farmer and of the impatient, frustrated son who wishes to marry and settle down at home." C.B.Q. also praised the Davis Players for delivering "a spirited and sympathetic performance" and claimed, "It was remarkable how the director and players covered up certain deficiencies in the weak, dramatic structure of the play." In concluding the review, C.B.Q. delineated those dramatic flaws, particularly "the confusion of moods—comic, tragic and melodramatic" as well as the characters' "vulgarity of language and frequent recourse to the whisky bottle."[61]

Reading this review, one begins to realize that while the resonance of the play's major theme was certainly something that would have made it more accessible and attractive to Irish American audiences than *The Hostage,* there exists another, much more important reason why this amateur production was promoted and puffed week after week in the *Advocate,* the *Irish World,* and the *Irish Echo* while Behan and his Broadway hit were discussed only sporadically. That more important explanation is that the Thomas Davis Irish Players were a long-established institution within the Irish American community in New York. The TDIP had been founded in 1933 and therefore were performing Irish plays in locations around New York City for more than a quarter century by the time Behan arrived in town. Furthermore, the group's actors and directors and stagehands were members of other social, patriotic, cultural, and athletic associations within the community. Take, for example, Patrick Walsh, who was, one notice informed readers, a "Davis Players regular . . . president of the Kilkenny Men's Asso[ciation] and . . . a player member of the Kilkenny Hurling Club."[62] From reading these newspapers, it becomes obvious that these amateur players were part of a wide web of organizations that made up the fabric of Irish American life, and that is why they were so strenuously supported. Of course, this may reflect poorly on the literary and aesthetic standards of the community, but it certainly reflects well on their ability to help and support one another in disparate endeavors.

Almost three years to the day after the Thomas Davis Irish Players performed *The Country Boy* for the final time in upper Manhattan, over in Dublin, Brendan Behan finally succeeded in drinking himself to death. Behan was just forty-one when he died, meaning he had outlived Synge but not Wilde. Behan's passing on March 20, 1964, followed, of course, a mere four months behind John F. Kennedy's assassination, an event that prompted Daniel Patrick Moynihan's memorable phrase: "I don't think there's any point in being Irish if you don't know that the world is going to break your heart eventually."[63] Subsequent to their heartbreaking deaths, both Kennedy and Behan would be embraced as part of the inclusive tradition of "Irishness" that the American president's address to the Irish parliament had suggested—the tradition of Henry Grattan, John Boyle O'Reilly, William Butler Yeats, George Bernard Shaw, and James Joyce—the tradition of patriots, poets, and playwrights capable of expressing "that quality of the Irish, the remarkable combination of hope, confidence and imagination."[64] JFK's induction into this pantheon of remarkable Irishmen was immediate on both sides of the Atlantic, and amazingly, Behan's was almost as rapid on the American side of the Western Ocean. The consternation with which he was viewed by many Irish Americans during his visits in 1960 and 1961—though not nearly as many as Daniel Patrick Moynihan or Ulick O'Connor would lead readers to believe—did not prevent Behan's almost immediate absolution and canonization. Whereas it took decades for Synge and Joyce to earn the widespread accolades their work deserved, Behan was celebrated within days of his passing.

In the *Irish Echo,* the publication that was generally most hostile to Behan during the run of *The Hostage,* the weeks following his death included a number of respectful notices. In the March 28 issue, the columnist Hugh Hardy contributed the most lukewarm note: "Though Behan's boisterous, alcoholic sprees were harmful to the Irish image and something we cannot condone, yet many of his plays such as 'The Hostage' and 'The Quare Fellow' are regarded by drama critics as masterful dramatic works."[65] In the next week's edition, the "Carbery Calling" column contained two paragraphs under the sub-heading "Funeral of Brendan Behan"; the column noted that the funeral was "one of the biggest" in years and that "poor of Dublin" loved Behan for his kindness and charity.[66]

The most touching and surprising tribute featured in the *Echo* came from Sean Maxwell, who had acclaimed and criticized Behan with equal measure in the fall of 1960. Maxwell began the eulogy by discussing his personal relationship with Behan: "We spent some time together behind 'Barbed Wire' twenty years ago. It is often we laughed and chatted together, and so often did we disagree on matters pertinent to Republican ideas." Maxwell went on to describe Behan as "very liberal with his ideas and also with his words" and suggested that "if his life and writings lacked tidiness, it was because of its exuberance." Maxwell castigated those who bemoaned this untidy life—"it is pathetic that so many of his critics have indulged in criticizing the author rather than his works"—and found further justification in the artistic personality: "You cannot walk a straight line and have genius, there's a curve somewhere, or perhaps a failing if you wish to call it so. Brendan had his." The piece closed with these words: "It is sad to think that Brendan

Behan at such an early age has passed on. The Literary world has lost a genius and we are more poor because of it. Ar Dheis De go raibh a anam [May his soul be on God's right side]."[67]

The other Irish weeklies offered similar memorials. In the March 28 *Advocate*, Pete Lee, Behan's great defender among the New York Irish journalists, wrote a heartfelt obituary titled "A Man Called Behan." Lee speculated that future generations of Irishmen "at home and overseas" would bemoan and be haunted by "the fact that in life, they sought at times to ridicule him." The column concluded with these reflections on the personal relationship Lee had with Behan:

It was my good fortune to know the late Brendan Behan. I knew him in peaceful sobriety and I also met him when the bottle had taken its toll. In both cases I met a man of character. I met a man who had come up the hard way, and who owed it to no one. Yet, I met a man who was a real, true Irishman. He was a man with a deep sense of duty towards his fellowman. He felt the pangs of the needy as if he were one of them, and his love for the idle rich could not be described as intense. Yet he tolerated the latter, and in fact, had the years been a little kinder to him, he would one day become one of them. But that was not the dream of Behan. His dream was to become another O Casey, Shaw, Joyce, Yeats or Synge. Had he lived long enough, I feel sure he would have made it. Now that death has claimed him—future generations must judge his works and even his way of life. I sincerely hope that while they may praise his works, they will look with compassion on Behan the man, who made his own breaks and perhaps failed to capitalize fully on them. Let us not forget that Behan was a true Irishman, whether on or off the stage.[68]

The April 4 *Advocate* ran this notice, which certainly demonstrates what his former IRA colleagues thought of him:

BRENDAN BEHAN MEMORIAL MASS MAY 2 IN ST. JOHN'S

Brendan Behan has gone from this earthly scene leaving to his friends the image of a brave intelligent and genuine human being. His sensitive nature revolted at the national servitude of his country and the social oppression of his class. To the end he remained a true rebel, loyal to his principles. During his stay in New York he supported the then existing I.R.A. Prisoners Aid Committee of New York, Inc. spending many pleasant hours with old friends. His many friends and admirers will have the opportunity to pay homage to this great Irishman by attending a memorial mass in St John's Church, 210 West 31st St. N.Y.C. at 9 a.m. Saturday, May 2. At the regular meeting of the Irish Freedom Committee, a motion of sympathy was passed unanimously to Mrs. Brendan Behan, his parents and other relatives; the said motion to be sent to the Irish American press and the leading newspapers in Ireland. The meeting then adjourned as a token of respect to the dead patriot.

On behalf of the committee: Liam Cotter, M.P. Higgins, John Joe Hoey.[69]

That same week, the *Irish World* included a remembrance written by Maureen Patricia Ford titled "Brendan Behan—The Rebel." Ford described him as "a sort of Clarence Mangan, Dylan Thomas and Francis Thompson all rolled into one" and then explained to readers the analogies to these writers. Noting that Behan had visited her newspaper's offices, she described him as "just a big, generous, happy-go-lucky, overgrown boy" whose "love for Ireland" and "contempt for snobbery" were "the motivating forces of his life." And she concluded the piece by speculating, "No matter what barrier may have been put upon Brendan in this life we feel sure that at the end, as he lay dying after receiving the last rites of the Church, Saint Peter flung wide the golden gates for him."[70]

In a subsequent issue, the *Irish World* tried to buttress its argument about the state of Behan's soul by reprinting a story from the *Sunday Telegraph* of London under the headline "Borstal Governor Calls Brendan Behan Intensely Religious." The article quoted Mr. C. A. Joyce, the governor of the borstal institution in England where Brendan spent a number of years as a youth, who described the inmate as "an intensely religious boy." Mr. Joyce went on: "He never lost touch with me over the years—often by telephone at 1 a.m. but never mind. You may think of him as the genius and the drunkard, but I remember him as a boy of 19 who wanted to serve God and who loved his mother and his country."[71]

These memorials to Behan are especially striking when contrasted with the treatment of Joyce, whose death, remember, had barely been noticed in the Irish American papers, whose literary legacy had been judged to be negligible, and whose soul had been treated as beyond the sanctifying grace of the Church. But in a coincidence that recalls how the *Advocate* placed a remembrance of Joyce next to a note about Martin Conboy, the nemesis of *Ulysses*, the *Irish World* placed in the column adjacent to its warm tribute to Behan the following announcement: "On Sunday, April 26th, the 11th annual Communion Mass and breakfast of the Co. Sligo Ladies S & B Association and the Co. Sligo Men's S & B Association will be held with Mass at the Church of Our Savior, 59 Park Ave. at 38th St. Manhattan at 10 a.m. and breakfast afterwards at the Hotel Shelburne, Lexington Ave and 37th St. New York City . . . Judge James J. Comerford will be the guest speaker."[72]

Clearly, after there was Brendan Behan, there was still Judge Comerford.

That last sentence of mine tries self-consciously to echo and invert the superb opening line that begins an article Calvin Trillin originally wrote in 1988 for *The New Yorker:* "Before there was democracy, there was Judge James J. Comerford."[73] Trillin's piece was basically an exposé of the inner workings of the Saint Patrick's Day Parade Committee, in which the journalist presented the selection of the grand marshal as the last example of an efficient, old-school style of boss-rule politics whose main principle, to invoke Senator Moynihan once again, "was not tyranny, but order."[74] Nevertheless, Trillin's article is often cited instead for its observation that while the Italians of New York had in recent years selected Frank Sinatra, Luciano Pavarotti, and Sophia Loren to lead the Columbus Day parade, the Irish, during the same period, had chosen apparent nonentities like John Sweeney, William Burke, and Al O'Hagen.[75] Such evidence is typically used to buttress claims about Irish American parochialism and philistinism. In her work *Irish America: Coming into Clover,* for example, Maureen Dezell quotes the Trillin passage before commenting, "Relentlessly anachronistic, the New York pageant remains pious, proper, dour, defensive while Irish culture on both sides of the Atlantic goes through remarkable flux."[76]

But Dezell's is not the only possible interpretation. The conduct of Comerford's parade committee in the 1980s and, by analogy, the Irish American press in the 1960s can also be viewed as evidence of the strength and self-confidence of the community the Irish established in the new world. To honor a Transit Authority employee who volunteered his time to the parade committee for many years as William

Burke had done, rather than rewarding a rich and famous international music or film star, is not after all very different from championing an amateur play put on by a local theater group rather than drawing attention to an outrageous and notorious Broadway playwright. Both decisions illustrate a community that took care of its own regardless of outside opinion, a community that rewarded involvement and service, a community that did not need to trade on the cultural capital of its celebrities in order to bolster an ethnic identity. Such an interpretation can even be reconciled with Behan's posthumous rehabilitation. For when he died, those who lionized and memorialized Behan did so because the playwright had shared his talent for conversation and song with them over drinks and/or had supported their local Irish causes with his time and treasure. In other words, Behan became one of the American Irish in a way that Joyce and Synge, who had not visited, never could, and in a way that O'Casey, Shaw, Yeats, and Wilde, who had visited, never did.

Conclusions

IN THE SAME March 28, 1964, issue of the *Advocate* that announced Brendan Behan's death, a Thomas J. Fogarty of Woodycrest Avenue in the Bronx wrote a letter to the editor. Fogarty's missive admonished a previous letter-to-the-editor writer, a Michael Fitzgerald of Saint Anselm's parish, also in the Bronx, who had communicated: "Would you be good enough to remind your readers about a wonderful play now at The Blackfriars Theatre, 316 West 57 St. It is about an Irishman, in fact, one of the most brilliant Irishmen of them all, I mean Oscar Wilde. This play deals with his conversion to the Catholic Church. I was spellbound from start to finish. What a beautiful performance!"[1] Fogarty responded caustically to Fitzgerald's praise of the play about Wilde, though it is notable that, unlike some of the outraged American Irish who penned letters during the *Playboy* controversy claiming that Yeats and Lady Gregory were not Irish,[2] he made no attempt to deny Wilde his birthright:

> Oscar Wilde was a clever writer, but unfortunately his conduct was notorious and he served a long prison term in Reading Prison when he was convicted for his acts. After he was released from prison he went to France and died in Paris a few years later. He may have converted to the Catholic Church on his death bed but there is some doubt about this. Mr. Fitzgerald should get familiar with the facts before he writes

to your paper. It is true Wilde was an Irishman but he was no credit to the Irish people. Although the Irish produced plenty of scholars, saints and patriots, it also produced a number or perverts and informers as well as other undesirable characters, and Wilde was in the latter group.[3]

Scholars, saints, and patriots *as well as* perverts, informers, and undesirable characters: perhaps, at long last, at least a few readers of the Irish American press had arrived at a sophisticated view of their history.

Irish Writers in Irish America: 1964 and Beyond

While Fogarty's scornful comments about Wilde counterintuitively suggest the evolution of a broader, less narrow, less idealized conception of Irish character, Fitzgerald's praise for the play about Wilde highlights yet again that Irish writers and Irish literature were a matter of importance to many Irish Americans. The initial welcome afforded to Wilde in 1882, the esteem granted to William Butler Yeats in 1904, the embrace of a whole genre of social comedy popularized by the Abbey Theatre, the many heartfelt eulogies for Brendan Behan in 1964—all this evidence undermines Daniel Patrick Moynihan's assertion that "instead of embracing and glorying" in modern Irish literature, Irish Americans "either ignored it, or if they were respectable enough, turned on the Irish authors, accusing them of bad language."[4] Clearly these writers were not ignored, and if they were "turned on" by Irish American audiences, it was for reasons much more complex than bad language: Wilde was rejected first for his lack of nationalist conviction and later for his homosexuality; Yeats was criticized for lecturing emigrant Irish peasants and their progeny about the supposedly impeccable realism of Synge's wonderfully fanciful plays; O'Casey and Behan were both accused of denigrating the nationalist cause and defaming the memory of republican martyrs. Joyce is the only one of the writers discussed in this book whose initial reception history in Irish America resembles Moynihan's view of things, but by the time Moynihan was writing in 1963, even that was changing, as Irish American scholars like John Kelleher and Kevin Sullivan, among many others, had already begun producing articles and books that critically embraced Joyce's work.[5]

The scholarship of critics like Kelleher and Sullivan belies Moynihan's claim that "when it emerged that the American Irish did not see [the value of a play like Synge's *Riders to the Sea*], their opportunity to attain a degree of cultural ascendancy quite vanished," and "after that began a steady emigration from the Irish 'community' of many of the strongest and best of the young." In other words, Moynihan believed that because they were so embarrassed by the philistine behavior of their Irish Catholic friends and family, the best and the brightest young Irish Americans, finding "little to commend itself in the culture to which they were born," had turned away from their ethnic identity, creating a massive brain drain from Irish America.[6] But in 1963, the same year Moynihan's essay was published, the American Committee for Irish Studies held its first annual conference at Purdue University. This organization had been founded in large part through the efforts of Lawrence McCaffrey and Emmett Larkin, young professors who were both first-generation Irish Americans.[7] And the following year, 1964, Eoin McKiernan, an Irish American originally from Brooklyn, would incorporate the Irish American Cultural Institute in St. Paul, Minnesota. Shortly thereafter, in 1966, the IACI began publishing *Eire-Ireland,* an interdisciplinary journal of Irish studies.[8] Clearly, by the mid-1960s, Irish literature and Irish culture was becoming an area of study and passionate concern in American institutions far more diverse than an ethnic press.

What We Write About When We Write About Irish Studies

And yet that once-upon-a-time narrow American audience for Irish culture, the audience who published, edited, wrote for, and read Irish American newspapers, deserves more attention from contemporary scholars who approach Irish studies from an interdisciplinary, transnational point of view.

For instance, the play the men from the Bronx were arguing about in the pages of the *Advocate* was, more than likely, Micheál Mac Liammóir's one-man show *The Importance of Being Oscar,* which originally debuted on Broadway in March 1961, about nine weeks after *The Hostage* completed its run. Joan FitzPatrick Dean has argued that these two plays, along with Brian Friel's *Philadelphia, Here I Come!*, helped redefine "what American audiences understood as Irish drama."[9] Dean's assertion about the positive influence of Mac Liammóir's drama, as applied to specifically Irish American audiences, is supported and illustrated in productive ways by Michael Fitzgerald's laudatory letter to the editor. But Dean's claims about the groundbreaking influence of Friel's play, among Irish American audiences at least, might be contradicted or at least complicated by looking into the archives of a newspaper like the *Irish Echo*.

Of course, Friel's literary career did not begin with *Philadelphia*, and many scholars have noted that prior to his success as a playwright, Friel's short fiction appeared regularly in *The New Yorker*.[10] A fact less noted by scholars is that eight columns Friel wrote for the Dublin newspaper the *Irish Press*, under the headline "American Diary," appeared in the *Irish Echo* during October, November, and December 1963.[11] These short, slight pieces sketched the humorous experiences of an Irish greenhorn who had just arrived in America's biggest metropolis. Adventures narrated by Friel included checking into, then checking out of, a too extravagant Manhattan hotel; visiting Rockefeller Plaza; trying to condense seven hundred years of Irish history into a brief conversation with a confused elevator operator who thought the Orangemen had taken part in the Easter Rising; using a broken English patois to replace the Tyrone accent nobody he met in New York could understand; visiting the United Nations; opening an American bank account; dealing with a bout of homesickness inspired by seeing an *Echo* headline about the politics of Northern Ireland; and, most bizarrely, narrating the thoughts of a golden Labrador named Fritz who lived on the Upper East Side.[12] Clearly, Friel's writing in these columns, as well as in the subject matter of *Philadelphia*—a play dramatizing both the internal, private life and external, public life of young man about to leave Ireland for America— needed no contextualizing; it was plainly rooted in the sensibilities of a rural, Catholic, nationalist Ireland many readers of the *Echo*, or the *Advocate*, would have known so well. Oscar Wilde's kind of Irishness was a different, less familiar thing altogether.

In her essay, Dean highlights the way Mac Liammóir's play helped in "the reclamation of an Irish identity" for Wilde. Yet, as Dean herself notes, the bulk of this work repositioning Wilde as an Irish writer would be done dozens of years later, in the 1990s.[13] That decade saw a rash of titles such as Davis Coakley's *Oscar Wilde: The Importance of Being Irish;* Richard Pine's *Thief of Reason: Oscar Wilde and Modern Ireland;* Declan Kiberd's chapter in *Inventing Ireland,* "Oscar Wilde: The Artist as Irishman"; and a collection of essays edited by Jerusha McCormack titled *Wilde the Irishman.*[14] In most of these studies, Wilde's alleged sense of Irishness becomes equated with either an openly hostile or, at least, a stealthily subversive relationship to English society.[15] Wilde would no doubt relish the paradox of his current reputation. Not only is he much more famous today in terms of literary reputation, but also he is much more famously identifiable as a quintessentially Irish writer than any of the poets of 1848, the men his mother taught him to revere as a child, or the Fenian exiles, those wild geese who typed and toiled in the shadows of great American cities, their fanatic hearts ceaselessly pumping blood, sweat, money, dynamite, rifles, and propaganda into the land of their birth so that it might be free of English rule. Like the Young Irelanders, these bold Fenian men were very often guilty of the literary sins Yeats would later claim separate the true poets from the partisan hacks: "oratorical vehemence" unleashed via "the rhetoric of the platform and the newspaper."[16] And so John Boyle O'Reilly, John Devoy, and Patrick Ford, never mind the families who published the *Advocate* and the *Echo,* are subjects of no importance to literary and cultural critics who deconstruct the supposedly subversive Irish nationalism of Wilde.

Lest readers imagine I'm creating a straw man argument here, doing an advanced search for the names of the three giants of Irish American journalism in the *Irish University Review* between 1987 and 2017 produces a grand total of one hit. In a biographical essay about Patrick Kavanagh, Augustine Martin renders a scene in McDaid's pub, during JFK's 1963 visit to Ireland. The Dubliners are listening to the American president on the radio when JFK alludes to John Boyle O'Reilly, whose name none of the assembled writers recognize, none except for Kavanagh, who recalls his poetry from a schoolboy anthology.[17] Clearly, readers of the self-described "leading global journal of Irish literary studies," a journal that specializes "in defining and expanding the scope of Irish literary studies," would be just as baffled today as the Dublin literati had been in 1963 about the importance of the work done by O'Reilly.[18] And that work, don't forget, included being the first editor in America to publish the poetry of Yeats and Wilde.

As for Oscar, no doubt the idea is persuasive that his lectures on aesthetics delivered to audiences in the UK and the United States, his clever epigrams uttered around the tables of London clubs, his witty dialogue spoken on the stages of the West End, his brilliant essays written for the British press all helped to lay the groundwork for both modern Irish literature and contemporary Irish culture. And we have the scholarship of the 1990s to thank for insights into that idea. Yet readers of a journal like the *Irish University Review* would also benefit from encountering articles that invite them to consider how the foundations on which modern Ireland was invented were also constructed in significant part by the tireless organizing and fundraising and, yes, writing of genuine Irish rebels in America. Lady Wilde had prophesized about the potential of such men: "There are twice as many Irish now in America as there are in Ireland. They form a third of the population of all the great cities, and are banded together in one powerful organization by race, religion, memory, and hopes. They have also one aim, which is to create a new era in the history of Ireland. This is the fanaticism of their lives—but they bide their time; the individual dies, the nation lives and waits."[19] And in a review of a novel by J. A. Froude, Wilde himself acknowledged their impact: "An entirely new factor has appeared in the social development of [Ireland], and this factor is the Irish-American and his influence. To mature its powers, to concentrate its action, to learn the secret of its own strength and of England's weakness, the Celtic intellect has had to cross the Atlantic. At home it had but learned the pathetic weakness of nationality; in a strange land it realized what indomitable forces nationality possesses. What captivity was to the Jews, exile has been to the Irish. America and American influence has educated them."[20]

It's surely a pity that Wilde did not live long enough to see the terrible beauty Ireland's exiled children in America helped create. One can only imagine what sharp, insightful commentary he might have uttered. More certain than even Wilde's reliable wit is the conviction that there should be room within the field of Irish studies, if broadly conceived, both for the valuable scholarship that uncovers or rediscovers heretofore ignored or obscured Irish contexts surrounding the work of a writer like Wilde, and for scholarship that reveals the neglected but important role Irish American journalism and print culture played not only in Irish political history but also in the history of transatlantic Irish culture. The surprising discoveries buried in the back issues of newspapers and periodicals that await Irish studies scholars are plentiful, and finds such as early poems by Wilde and Yeats or a little-known series of articles by Friel might just be the tip of the proverbial iceberg.

Tales Told of James and John

Whereas scholars who work in the academic field of Irish studies would enrich that field by paying more attention to the role Irish American journalism played in the development of modern Irish culture, journalists who currently work in the Irish American culture industry face a different challenge. In trying to inform their readers about the history of the American Irish, they must guard against falsifying or simplifying the stories they tell. Let us look at two problematic examples, one published in 2008 and the other in 2017, and both appearing in media entities owned by Irish Voice, Inc.[21]

On June 10, 2017, just in time for Bloomsday, the IrishCentral website posted an article titled "Remembering James Joyces' [*sic*] 'Ulysses' on Trial." Rather than chronicling any of the *Ulysses* trials in detail, the article was actually an attempt to summarize and reflect upon the recently published book *The Ulysses Trials: Beauty and Truth Meets the Law,* written by Joseph M. Hassett. In the third paragraph the author of the article, Cahir O'Doherty, wrote: "John Quinn, the Irish-American lawyer entrusted to defend the book, thought it unworthy and at times seemed to even work against his own successful defense. A socially prominent Irish-American lawyer, he neither believed in the book nor troubled himself to understand it." Those claims, to put it mildly, are not supported by the facts. But then comes an even more counterfactual claim: "Support for a compatriot Irishman was a nonstarter for Quinn."[22] Surely this journalist must be unaware of all that

Quinn did for W. B. Yeats, and for Lady Gregory, and indeed for Joyce. And clearly the journalist is unacquainted with the fact that it was Quinn who successfully defended the Abbey's Irish Players when they were arrested in Philadelphia. The article's problematic claims seem to be attempts to paraphrase Hassett's criticisms of Quinn's unsuccessful defense of the *Little Review*'s editors. In an interview with Hassett quoted in the article, the scholar plainly states his view that Quinn's defense was cynical and never forced the court to adjudicate the serious legal issues raised by the text of *Ulysses,* a reasonable critique echoed by, among others, Quinn's biographer B. L. Reid.[23] Hassett's more unusual claim, as reported in the article, is that John Butler Yeats, the poet's father, was the real hero of the whole affair for immediately articulating a more robust, more idealistic defense of the book.[24] Yet the article never mentions to readers that J. B. Yeats's life in New York was subsidized in large part by the patronage of Quinn. The problem here is that all these omissions allow Quinn to be cast as a stock villain (that is, the Rich Puritanical Prejudiced Irish Catholic Guy) rather than as the generous, bigoted, complicated human being he actually was. If, in 1964, it was a paradoxical sign of sophistication for someone like Mr. Fogarty to admit that Ireland produced saints and scholars and perverts and informers and undesirable characters, it is now a sign of simplification to preclude the possibility that a prominent Irish American's personality might be a mix of both positive and negative characteristics.

In contrast to the IrishCentral piece, the October–November 2008 issue of *Irish America* magazine ran an article, "The Battle over *Ulysses,*" commemorating the seventy-fifth anniversary of the Woolsey decision, with an adjoining part of the feature the story of John Quinn, titled "Joyce's Irish-American Ally." That story, written by Tom Deignan, concludes, "Without Quinn's legal and financial support, it is possible that American readers might never have gotten a chance to be dazzled, and baffled, by Joyce's magical prose."[25] Clearly this conclusion shines a more accurate spotlight on the largely benign influence Quinn had on Joyce's career, while at the same time, other parts of the article acknowledge Quinn's failure to adequately defend the *Little Review,* and by proxy *Ulysses,* in the courtroom. This brief portrait of Quinn's role thus manages to be more rounded and accurate, though its retelling of the battles over *Ulysses* is not without its own problematic omissions. The author's decision to forgo any mention of, or even allusion to, Judge Joseph Corrigan or Joseph Forrester or Martin Conboy or Judge Martin Manton—the Irishmen who were, in effect, Joyce's Irish American adversaries—suggests an unwillingness to acknowledge the intra-ethnic conflicts and tensions that are so inherent within the experience of the Irish in America, and indeed the Irish in Ireland. Of course, avant-garde writers and art lovers like Joyce and Quinn are an important part of Irish heritage worth reading about, but so are conservative lawyers and judges like Conboy and Manton. To pretend otherwise is to encourage a view of Irish ethnicity that is less complex, less interesting, and less true, one that celebrates secular saints and the scholars who deify them while banishing the undesirable characters— not perverts or informers in this case, but those perceived to be prigs or ignoramuses.

In the conclusion to his insightful collection of essays *Looking for Jimmy: A Search for Irish America,* Peter Quinn (no relation to John) writes of the men like Conboy and Manton who populated his youth in the Bronx of the 1950s:

> The fundamental narrow-mindedness we suffered from wasn't so much in our attitude to the world as to ourselves. We wanted—we demanded—to be seen in one light and one light only . . . America's best-behaved ethnic group, a big-screen refutation of the lies once spread by nativists. The stage Irishman was okay as long as he looked and acted like Bing Crosby and, hell, if the stage Irishwoman wasn't only a nun but a nun played by Ingrid Bergman with a Swedish accent, well, *Hooray for Hollywood* . . . The Irish in America—at least the Irish I grew up with—were still in the defensive crouch they'd arrived in during the Famine, still sensitive to the distrust and dislike of *real* America, to the suspicions about our loyalty and supposed proclivity to raucous misbehavior. We were forever reminding ourselves—and the rest of America—of how many Irish fought with Washington, how many died at Antietam, and how many won the Congressional Medal of Honor, a litany of self-justification that implicitly accepted that it wasn't enough we'd been here for over a century.[26]

It will be a sad paradox if Irish Americans who, like me, came of age in the 1990s suffer from a different kind of narrow-mindedness and remain crouched in a different, though equally defensive, posture. I fear that those who grew up reading *Irish America* or its sister publication, the weekly *Irish Voice,* and who now receive daily e-mail blasts from IrishCentral, have been encouraged to think of authentic Irishness in one light only, as America's most subversively brilliant ethnic group—not as Bing Crosby's Father O'Malley, but as Oscar Wilde or James Joyce or Brendan Behan or Shane MacGowan; not as Ingrid Bergman's Sister Mary Benedict, but as Speranza or Maud Gonne or Edna O'Brien or Sinead O'Connor. This subset of Irish America seems to be forever reminding itself—and the rest of America—of how many Irish writers fought against the philistines, how many died martyrs for their art, and how many won the Nobel Prize for their banned books and plays, a litany of self-glorification which implicitly suggests it isn't enough that for 150 years most of the Irish in America have been digging canals and ditches, pouring pints and shots, rigging elections and contracts, selling stocks and insurance certificates, building churches and Ancient Order of Hibernians lodges, organizing picnics and Saint Patrick's Day parades, raising families as well as funds for Irish causes, sending as many dollars and cents as they could afford back to the relatives and republicans they left behind, and, yes, publishing and reading Irish American newspapers.

My point in riffing on Quinn's insights here at the end of this book is simply to suggest that today, too much Irish American journalism, and even some historiography, along with Irish cultural products for sale like the Irish Writers line of merchandise, imply that real Irishness is fundamentally connected to a kind of rebellious countercultural impulse.[27] And that implication is just as problematic as the old Irish American journalism and historiography which pretended that "true" Irish identity (that is, Irish Catholic identity) was inherently and unassailably virtuous. And both of those essentializing narratives are just as reductive in their way as the mid-century sociology found in *Beyond the Melting Pot* which depicted American Irish Catholic culture as an ash heap of anti-artistic ignorance.

It was of course F. Scott Fitzgerald, an Irish American from Minnesota who lived for a while in the Bronx, or at least uptown Manhattan, who pronounced that "the test of a first-rate intelligence is the ability to hold two opposed ideas in the mind at the same time, and still retain the ability to function."[28] Phillip Lopate, a Jewish American from Brooklyn, in his meditation "How Do You End an Essay?" invokes Fitzgerald's idea in his praise for James Baldwin, an African American from uptown Manhattan who went to high school in the Bronx. Here is Lopate's analysis of the final lines of Baldwin's profound essay "Notes of a Native Son," lines in which Baldwin tries to reconcile his acceptance of injustice as part of the human condition with his desire to fight injustice wherever he finds it: "The idea of two clashing ideas held suspended in the mind acknowledges the reader's hunger for resolution, without giving in to false simplicities."[29]

In trying to represent, analyze, and resolve the stories of dramatic intersection between Irish writers and Irish American audiences, I have attempted to avoid the false simplicities of reductive, essentialist thinking about Irish American identity. Neither turning away from the notorious and sometimes petty conflicts with famous writers that resulted from Irish American engagement with Irish culture, nor obscuring the disingenuousness and hypocrisy of certain Irish writers as they dealt with an Irish American public who by turns supported and confronted them, the chapters in this book reveal an activist Irish American community with its own print culture and its own notions of the Irish literary tradition, notions and a culture that were not entirely separate from or ignorant of but, rather, messily entwined with the culture of Ireland. And that's the kind of complex, often contradictory tale worth trying to tell in many other contexts.

Notes

Abbreviations

ADV	Advocate
BP	Boston Pilot
GA	Gaelic American
IA	Irish-American
IE	Irish Echo
IN	Irish Nation
IW	Irish World and American Industrial Liberator
SU	Sunday Union

Introduction: An Audience of Some Importance

1. Ta-Nehisi Coates, "The Black Family in the Age of Mass Incarceration," *The Atlantic*, October 2015.

2. See, for instance, Jane Perlez, "Beyond 'Beyond the Melting Pot,' Moynihan and Glazer Feel Vindicated," *New York Times*, December 3, 1983.

3. Moynihan's essay is included, for instance, in *Making the Irish American: History and Heritage of the Irish in the United States*, ed. J. J. Lee and Marion R. Casey (New York: NYU Press, 2007), 475–525.

4. Kevin Kenny, *The American Irish: A History* (New York: Longman, 2000), 1.

5. Daniel P. Moynihan, "The Irish," in *Beyond the Melting Pot: The Negroes, Puerto Ricans, Jews, Italians, and Irish of New York City*, 2nd ed. (Cambridge: MIT Press, 1970), 251.

6. Moynihan was not alone in his premature eulogizing. Fellow sociologist Father Andrew Greeley memorably administered the last rites in "The Last of the American Irish Fade Away," *New York Times Magazine*, March 14, 1971.

7. See, for instance, Pete Hamill, "Notes on the New Irish: A Guide for the Goyim," *New York Magazine*, March 13, 1972.

8. See, for instance, Linda Dowling Almeida, "Irish America, 1940–2000," in Lee and Casey, *Making the Irish American*, 548–73.

9. See, for instance, Niall O'Dowd, "Capture the Moment," *Irish America*, December 31, 1996.

10. Moynihan, "The Irish," 247–48.

11. Ibid., 253–54.

12. Perhaps the failure of Moynihan's prophecy about the fate of the Irish writers in Irish America corresponds somehow to his inaccurate prognostication about the disappearance of the "most visible Irish contribution to the New York scene, the Irish saloon"—which Moynihan believed had been "decimated by prohibition" and, he imagined, would be "unable to compete with the attractions of television and the fact that Italians can cook" (ibid., 252). The Irish pub as an American social construct is surely worth scholars' time and consideration.

13. The Irish Writers poster also includes Jonathan Swift, Oliver Goldsmith, Samuel Beckett, Flann O'Brien, and Patrick Kavanagh. There is another poster often sold in Irish gift shops and seen in Irish American homes and pubs titled "Ireland's Writers." Its twelve-person pantheon is slightly different, adding Thomas Moore and Bram Stoker, while deleting Goldsmith and Flann O'Brien. Another difference is that the images of the writers are drawings rather than photographs. A comparative analysis of these posters by a talented cultural critic would be a worthy project.

14. James Silas Rogers, introduction to *Extended Family: Essays on Being Irish American from New Hibernia Review* (Chester Springs, Pa.: Dufour Editions, 2013), 19.

15. John Boyne, "Twelve Irish Writers, Supposedly Our Greatest, and Not a Vagina between Them," *Irish Times*, December 12, 2017.

16. Alison Flood, "'A Tipping Point': Women Writers Pledge to Boycott Gender Biased Books after Very Male Anthology," *The Guardian*, January 12, 2018.

17. Seamus Deane, *Celtic Revivals: Essays in Modern Irish Literature, 1880–1980* (Winston-Salem: Wake Forest University Press, 1985), 11.

18. Hugh Kenner, *A Colder Eye: The Modern Irish Writers* (Baltimore: Johns Hopkins University Press, 1989), xi.

19. Peter Quinn, *Looking for Jimmy: A Search for Irish America* (Woodstock, N.Y.: Overlook Press, 2007), 43.

20. Maureen Dezell, *Irish America: Coming into Clover; The Evolution of a People and a Culture* (New York: Doubleday, 2000), 3.

21. Timothy Meagher, *The Columbia Guide to Irish American History* (New York: Columbia University Press, 2005), 130.

22. Despite my quibbles with his word choice in the passage quoted in the text, Meagher, in works such as his introduction to *From Paddy to Studs: Irish American Communities in the Turn of the Century Era, 1880–1920* (New York: Greenwood Press, 1986) and *Inventing Irish America: Generation, Class, and Ethnic Identity in a New England City, 1880–1928* (Notre Dame: University of Notre Dame Press, 2001), has been one of the leading advocates for a sophisticated historiography of the American Irish as a multigenerational ethnic group, a historiography that rejects an outdated assimilationist model of ethnic group adjustment which uses a linear conception to try to pinpoint some exact moment when immigrants supposedly become integrated into the host society. Instead, Meagher has called for a more dynamic model that allows for the malleability of ethnic identity based on historical and demographic circumstances. The purpose and goals of this

book were no doubt underpinned by this dynamic understanding of ethnicity.

23. Moynihan, "The Irish," 253.

24. Jonathan E. Rose, "A Preface to a History of Audiences," in *The Intellectual Life of the British Working Classes* (New Haven: Yale University Press, 2002), 4.

25. John P. Harrington, *The Irish Play on the New York Stage, 1874–1966* (Lexington: University Press of Kentucky, 1997), 4 and 6.

26. Lawrence Rainey, *Institutions of Modernism: Literary Elites and Public Culture* (New Haven: Yale University Press, 1998), 106.

27. Ibid., 8–9.

Chapter 1: "Speranza's Son"

1. Thomas Beer, *The Mauve Decade* (New York: Vintage Books, 1961), 3.

2. William V. Shannon, *The American Irish: A Political and Social Portrait* (New York: Macmillan, 1963), 97.

3. "Oscar Wilde's Arrival," *New York World*, January 3, 1882.

4. Richard Ellmann, *Oscar Wilde* (New York: Knopf, 1988), 151.

5. "Oscar's Arrival," *IN*, January 7, 1882.

6. Quoted in Ellmann, *Oscar Wilde*, 5.

7. "Speranza's Son," *IN*, January 14, 1882.

8. Thomas N. Brown, *Irish-American Nationalism, 1870–1890* (Philadelphia: Lippincott, 1966), 118.

9. "Additional Description/Biographical Note," finding aid to the Thomas F. Meehan Papers, Georgetown University Libraries, https://findingaids.library.georgetown.edu/repositories/15/resources/10116.

10. David Brundage, "'In Time of Peace, Prepare for War': Key Themes in the Social Thought of New York's Irish Nationalists, 1890–1916," in *The New York Irish*, ed. Ronald H. Bayor and Timothy J. Meagher (Baltimore: Johns Hopkins University Press, 1997), 323.

11. "Wilde" *IA*, January 21, 1882.

12. Untitled notice, *IA*, January 21, 1882.

13. "Personal," *IA*, February 4, 1882.

14. Untitled notice, *IA*, February 18, 1882.

15. "Fireside Sparks," *IA*, March 25, 1882.

16. J. Ryan, "To Oscar Wilde," *SU*, January 29, 1882.

17. Oscar Wilde, "O, Roma, Roma!," *SU*, February 12, 1882.

18. "Quite," *SU*, March 12, 1882.

19. "Incident and Anecdote," *SU*, March 6, 1882.

20. Quoted in Ellmann, *Oscar Wilde*, 196.

21. Kevin O'Brien, *Oscar Wilde in Canada: An Apostle for the Arts* (Toronto: J. Wiley, 1982), 97.

22. This period of John Boyle O'Reilly's life is chronicled in Thomas Keneally, *The Great Shame and the Triumph of the Irish in the English-Speaking World* (New York: Doubleday, 1999), 423–28. This period of John Devoy's life is chronicled in Terry Golway, *Irish Rebel: John Devoy and America's Fight for Ireland's Freedom* (New York: St. Martin's Press, 1999), 65–69.

23. Keneally, *Great Shame*, 461–70.

24. Ibid., 480–89.

25. Lady Wilde [Jane Francessa Elgee], *The American Irish*, undated pamphlet appended to *Speranza: A Biography of Lady Wilde* by Horace Wyndham (New York: Philosophical Library, 1951), 216.

26. Lloyd Lewis and Henry Justin Smith, *Oscar Wilde Discovers America, 1882* (New York: Harcourt, Brace and Company, 1936; reissued by B. Blom, 1967), 116.

27. *The Complete Letters of Oscar Wilde*, ed. Merlin Holland and Rupert Hart-Davis (New York: Henry Holt, 2000), 33.

28. Oscar Wilde, "Rome Unvisited," *BP*, February 2, 1882.

29. Lady Wilde, "The Future Opportunities for Woman," *BP*, February 2, 1882.

30. *Complete Letters of Oscar Wilde*, 182.

31. Ibid., 192.

32. "Oscar Wilde: Something about His Parents and His Poems," *BP*, January 14, 1882.

33. Untitled editorial, *BP*, January 14, 1882.

34. "Oscar Wilde on the School of Aesthetics," *BP*, January 21, 1882.

35. Untitled editorial, *BP*, January 21, 1882.

36. Davis Coakley, *Oscar Wilde: The Importance of Being Irish* (Dublin: Town House, 1994), 183.

37. Ellmann, *Oscar Wilde*, 195.

38. "Oscar's Opinions," *IN*, March 18, 1882.

39. Oscar Wilde, *Irish Poets and Poetry of the Nineteenth Century: A Lecture Delivered in Platt's Hall, San Francisco, on Wednesday, April 5th, 1882*, ed. Robert D. Pepper (San Francisco: Book Club of California, 1972), 29–34.

40. Robert D. Pepper, introduction, ibid., 14.

41. Ibid., 6–7.

42. Ibid., 21–22. Had Wilde been publicly accused of plagiarism when he delivered his "Irish Poets" lecture, it would not have been the first time. Ellmann describes how Wilde's debut volume of poetry was rejected by the library of the Oxford Union after Oliver Elton and Henry Newbolt "compiled a list of supposed borrowing from other poets" including Shakespeare, Donne, Byron, and Swinburne (*Oscar Wilde*, 146).

43. Pepper, introduction, 18–19.

44. Josephine M. Guy and Ian Small, *Oscar Wilde's Profession: Writing and the Culture Industry in the Late Nineteenth Century* (Oxford: Oxford University Press, 2000), 35.

45. Coakley, *Oscar Wilde*, 183–84.

46. Pepper, introduction, 17–18.

47. Quoted in E. H. Mikhail, *Oscar Wilde: Interviews and Recollections*, vol. 1 (New York: Harper & Row, 1979), 95. Wilde's sentiments linking the cause of Ireland to that of the South are consistent with the view of John Mitchel, prominent Young Irelander and, later, Confederate propagandist. But perhaps Oscar's surprising empathy with the struggles of the Confederacy can be better explained by family ties described in an item in the *Irish-American*, March 25, 1882, which revealed how Wilde's maternal uncle John K. Elgee participated in the convention that passed Louisiana's ordinance of secession. The article also explained how Elgee had designed a new state banner for Louisiana—"an extraordinary production, consisting of red, white, blue and orange stripes, with a flaming gold star on a fierce red ground." The piece closed with this facetious comment: "These facts are revived to show the operation of the principle of heredity in the family of the Apostle of Aestheticism and to support the suggestion that Elgee's banner was the germ of Oscar Wilde's combination of the lily and the sunflower."

48. Quoted in Ellmann, *Oscar Wilde,* 196.
49. In 1894 Wilde would engage T. P. O'Connor, the Nationalist Party politician and successful editor of the *Weekly Sun,* in a somewhat bizarre public imbroglio regarding a patriotic poem titled "The Shamrock" which O'Connor printed under Wilde's name but subsequently accused Wilde of plagiarizing. Wilde harangued O'Connor and denied any authorship of the "doggerel verses" in a letter to the *Pall Mall Gazette.* Eventually it was discovered that the poem had actually been written by an inmate of the Cork Blind Asylum named Helena Callanan (see *Complete Letters of Oscar Wilde,* 611–15).
50. "In Memoriam Speranza," *SU,* May 7, 1882.
51. Lady Wilde, "The War of Nations," *IN,* September 9, 1882.
52. Speranza, "The Shorn Sheep," *IW,* December 30, 1882.
53. James Paul Rodechko, "An Irish-American Journalist and Catholicism: Patrick Ford of the *Irish World,*" *Church History* 39, no. 4 (December 1970): 525n4.
54. Hamil Grant, *Two Sides of the Atlantic: Notes of an Anglo-American Newspaperman* (London: Grant Richards, 1917), 76.
55. Lady Wilde, *American Irish,* 216.
56. "To Speranza," *IW,* December 30, 1882.
57. Coincidentally, shortly before his death Wilde expressed the hope that his former adversary O'Connor would publish the "Ballad of Reading Gaol" in his paper, the *Weekly Sun,* with a preface to the work advocating prison reform; Wilde also considered asking Davitt to write the preface (see *Complete Letters of Oscar Wilde,* 966–72 and 1058–60).
58. "Oscar Going Home," *IN,* December 30, 1882.
59. Ellmann, *Oscar Wilde,* 438.
60. Brown, *Irish-American Nationalism,* 181.
61. Rodechko, "An Irish-American Journalist," 535–36.
62. For the discussion that follows, see "Wilde as We Knew Him," *IW,* April 13, 1895.

Chapter 2: The Celt in Irish America

1. Oscar Wilde, "Yeats's *The Wanderings of Oisin,*" in *The Artist as Critic: Critical Writings of Oscar Wilde,* ed. Richard Ellmann (Chicago: University of Chicago Press, 1982), 150.
2. George Moore, *Hail and Farewell: Ave,* pt. 1 (New York: D. Appleton and Company, 1912), 251.
3. Quoted in *The Collected Letters of W. B. Yeats,* vol. 4, *1905–1907,* ed. John Kelly and Ronald Schuhard (Oxford: Oxford University Press, 2005), 79n1.
4. *The Collected Works of W. B. Yeats,* vol. 3, *Autobiographies,* ed. William H. O'Donnell and Douglas N. Archibald (New York: Scribner, 1995), 41–53.
5. Ibid., 46.
6. Ibid., 47.
7. Declan Kiberd, *Inventing Ireland: The Literature of a Modern Nation* (Cambridge: Harvard University Press, 1995), 32.
8. Ibid., 99.
9. W. B. Yeats, "How Ferencz Renyi Kept Silent," *BP,* August 6, 1887.
10. *The Collected Works of W. B. Yeats,* vol. 7, *Letters to the New Island,* ed. George Bornstein and Hugh Witemeyer (New York: Macmillan, 1989), 160.

11. Ibid., xv.

12. Ibid., 162.

13. Ibid., 32. Though I examined the *Pilot* articles on microfilm, I have chosen to cite the article as reproduced in *The Collected Works of W. B. Yeats,* vol. 7, *Letters to the New Island,* a text that is much more easily accessible to scholars than copies of the newspaper.

14. Ibid., 112.

15. Ibid., 113.

16. Terence Brown, *The Life of W. B. Yeats: A Critical Biography* (Oxford: Blackwell Publishers, 1999), 47–48.

17. *Collected Works of W. B. Yeats,* 7:63.

18. *The Collected Letters of W. B. Yeats,* vol. 1, *1865–1895,* ed. John Kelly (Oxford: Clarendon Press, 1986), 145.

19. Roy Foster, *W. B. Yeats: A Life,* vol. 1, *The Apprentice Mage, 1865–1914* (Oxford: Oxford University Press, 1997), 97.

20. *Collected Works of W. B. Yeats,* 7:63.

21. Ibid., 64–66.

22. Ibid., 66–67.

23. *Collected Works of W. B. Yeats,* 3:169.

24. Ibid., 173.

25. Ibid., 174.

26. Ibid., 173.

27. William Butler Yeats, "The Literary Movement in Ireland," *North American Review* 169, no. 517 (December 1899): 855.

28. Ibid., 857.

29. Ibid.

30. Ibid., 856–57.

31. *The Collected Letters of W. B. Yeats,* vol. 2, *1896–1900,* ed. Warwick Gould, John Kelly, and Deirdre Toomey (Oxford: Clarendon Press, 1997), 712.

32. Ibid., 674.

33. Ibid., 669.

34. Ibid., 673.

35. James Joyce, *A Portrait of the Artist as a Young Man* (New York: Viking Press, 1962), 226–27.

36. The letter is reproduced almost entirely in Richard Ellmann, *James Joyce,* new and rev. ed. (New York: Oxford University Press, 1982), 753–54.

37. Brown, *The Life of W. B. Yeats,* 129.

38. B. L. Reid, *The Man from New York: John Quinn and His Friends* (New York: Oxford University Press, 1968), 8.

39. Ibid., 3.

40. "Three Irish Plays," *IA,* May 29, 1903.

41. "The Irish Literary Plays," *IA,* June 6, 1903.

42. *The Letters of John Quinn to William Butler Yeats,* ed. Alan Himber (Ann Arbor: University of Michigan Research Press, 1983), 48–49.

43. Ibid., 51.

44. Ibid.

45. *The Collected Letters of W. B. Yeats,* vol. 3, *1901–1904,* ed. John Kelly and Ronald Schuhard (Oxford: Clarendon Press, 1994), 398.

46. Declan Kiely, "Yeats in America," *The Recorder* 15, no. 1 (Spring 2002): 44.

47. Quoted ibid., 44–45.

48. "The Irish Literary Revival," *IA*, November 14, 1903.

49. "William Butler Yeats: The Famous Irish Poet and Dramatist Lecturing before American Colleges," *GA*, November 21, 1903.

50. "Gaelic Notes," *IW*, November 28, 1903.

51. "Ireland's Intellectual Revival," *IW*, January 16, 1904.

52. "The Intellectual Revival in Ireland," *IA*, November 28, 1904.

53. "Gaelic Notes," *IW*, December 5, 1904.

54. "Yeats on Gaelic Ireland," *IW*, December 12, 1903.

55. "Mr. Yeats's Answer," *IW*, December 12, 1903.

56. "Ireland's Intellectual Revival," *IA*, December 19, 1903.

57. "William Butler Yeats Lectures," *IW*, December 19, 1903.

58. "Yeats' Patriotic Mission: Using the Irish Theatre as a Means to Help Along the National Revival Movement," *IW*, December 19, 1903.

59. "William Butler Yeats: Will Lecture at Carnegie Hall," *GA*, December 19, 1903.

60. "W. B. Yeats Honored: County Sligo Men Give a Dinner to the Irish Poet and Dramatist," *IW*, December 26, 1903.

61. Foster, *W. B. Yeats,* 1:306.

62. *Collected Letters of W. B. Yeats,* 3:496.

63. Ibid., 540.

64. *Letters of John Quinn,* 86.

65. "The Irish Literary Revival: Splendid Lecture by William Butler Yeats at Carnegie Hall," *GA*, January 9, 1904.

66. "Yeats at Indianapolis: Nationalists Give Him a Banquet and Applaud His Strongly Nationalist Speech," *GA*, January 23, 1904.

67. "Indiana Irishmen Enthusiastically Welcome the Irish Poet and Dramatist," *IW*, January 23, 1904.

68. J. P. O'Mahony, "To Erin's Bard," *IW*, January 23, 1904.

69. *Collected Letters of W. B. Yeats,* 3:522.

70. Ibid., 520.

71. Ibid., 534.

72. "Yeats Captures California," *GA*, February 13, 1904.

73. Quoted ibid.

74. Kiely, "Yeats in America," 50–51.

75. *Collected Letters of W. B. Yeats,* 3:552.

76. "Emmet the Apostle of Irish Liberty: W. B. Yeats Delivers a Great Speech on the Patriot and His Legacy," *GA*, March 5, 1904.

77. Foster, *W. B. Yeats: A Life,* 1:313.

78. Brown, *The Life of W. B. Yeats,* 157.

79. Patrick McCartan, "William Butler Yeats: The Fenian," *Ireland American Review,* November 1940, 413.

80. Foster, *W. B. Yeats,* 1:306.

Chapter 3: "No End of a Row"

1. *The Collected Letters of W. B. Yeats,* vol. 3, *1901–1904,* ed. John Kelly and Ronald Schuhard (Oxford: Clarendon Press, 1994), 442.

2. Ibid., 442n1.

3. *The Collected Works of W. B. Yeats,* vol. 8, *The Irish Dramatic Movement,* ed. Mary Fitzgerald and Richard J. Finneran (New York: Scribner, 2003), 32.

4. Quoted in *Collected Letters of W. B. Yeats,* 3:442n1.

5. Quoted in *Collected Works of W. B. Yeats,* 8:243n1.

6. *Collected Letters of W. B. Yeats,* 3:443.

7. *Collected Works of W. B. Yeats,* 8:33.

8. Ibid., 33–34.

9. *The Collected Works of W. B. Yeats,* vol. 7, *Letters to the New Island,* ed. George Bornstein and Hugh Witemeyer (New York: Macmillan, 1989), 113.

10. Joseph Holloway, *Joseph Holloway's Abbey Theatre: A Selection from His Unpublished Journal Impressions of a Dublin Playgoer,* ed. Robert Hogan and Michael J. O'Neill (Carbondale: Southern Illinois University Press, 1967), 81.

11. Quoted in B. L. Reid, *The Man from New York: John Quinn and His Friends* (New York: Oxford University Press, 1968), 48.

12. Quoted in Holloway, *Joseph Holloway's Abbey Theatre,* 87.

13. *The Collected Letters of W. B. Yeats,* vol. 4, *1905–1907,* ed. John Kelly and Ronald Schuhard (Oxford: Oxford University Press, 2005), 628.

14. William Butler Yeats, "Beautiful Lofty Things," in *Selected Poems and Four Plays,* ed. M. L. Rosenthal (New York: Scribner, 1996), 187.

15. *Collected Letters of W. B. Yeats,* 4:627.

16. Ibid., 627.

17. Ibid.

18. Ibid., 628.

19. Ibid.

20. Ibid., 84–87.

21. *The Letters of John Quinn to William Butler Yeats,* ed. Alan Himber (Ann Arbor: University of Michigan Research Press, 1983), 83.

22. Ibid., 83–84.

23. Ibid., 84

24. Ibid., 85.

25. John C. O'Connor was the grandfather of Carroll O'Connor, the actor who famously portrayed the reactionary crank Archie Bunker on the long-running television sitcom *All in the Family.* Carroll O'Connor financed the preservation of the family newspaper on microfilm, but unfortunately, the first eleven years of the publication are lost to history.

26. "The Neo-Celtic Drama," *ADV,* February 8, 1908.

27. "Irish Plays for New York," *IA,* February 15, 1908.

28. "The Irish Play," *IA,* February 22, 1908.

29. "An Unwise Ally," *IA,* February 22, 1908.

30. "The Irish Industrial Movement," *IA,* January 4, 1908.

31. *Letters of John Quinn,* 100–103.

32. Ibid., 115.

33. Ibid., 130.

34. "J. M. Synge Dead," *GA,* April 10, 1909.

35. *Letters of John Quinn,* 134.

36. Untitled notice, *America,* May 1, 1909.

Chapter 4: "Weary of Misrepresentation"

1. Lady Augusta Gregory, *Our Irish Theatre: A Chapter of Autobiography by Lady Gregory* (Oxford: Oxford University Press, 1972), 97–98.
2. Adele Dalsimer, "Players in the Western World: The Abbey Theatre's American Tours," *Eire-Ireland* 16, no. 4 (Winter 1981): 77.
3. Gregory, *Our Irish Theatre,* 138.
4. John P. Harrington, *The Irish Play on the New York Stage, 1874–1966* (Lexington: University Press of Kentucky, 1997), 74.
5. Quoted ibid., 56.
6. Scholars whose analyses echo Lady Gregory's interpretation include Edward Abood, "The Reception of the Abbey Theatre in America, 1911–1914" (PhD diss., University of Chicago, 1962); Neil Blackadder, "'This is Not Irish Life!' Defending National Identity: Synge's *The Playboy of the Western World*," in *Performing Opposition: Modern Theatre and the Scandalized Audience* (London: Praeger, 2003), 69–108; Kenneth Cox Lyman, "Critical Reaction to Irish Drama on the New York Stage, 1900–1958" (PhD diss., University of Wisconsin, 1960); Daniel J. Murphy, "The Reception of Synge's *Playboy* in Ireland and America, 1907–1912," *Bulletin of the New York Public Library* 64, no. 10 (October 1960): 515–33; Genevieve Lucille Oppen, "The Irish Players in America" (MA thesis, University of Washington, 1943).
7. Murphy, "The Reception of Synge's *Playboy,*" 533.
8. Harrington, *The Irish Play,* 62.
9. Terry Golway, *Irish Rebel: John Devoy and America's Fight for Ireland's Freedom* (New York: St. Martin's Press, 1999), 182–83.
10. Kevin Kenny, *The American Irish: A History* (New York: Longman, 2000), 193.
11. Francis Robert Walsh, "'The 'Boston Pilot': A Newspaper for the Irish Immigrant, 1829–1908" (PhD diss., Boston University, 1968), 278.
12. Blackadder ("This is Not Irish Life!"), Dalsimer ("Players in the Western World"), Murphy ("The Reception of Synge's *Playboy*"), and Oppen ("The Irish Players in America") have followed Lady Gregory's lead in refraining from consulting these other sources, while Lyman ("Critical Reaction to Irish Drama") considers just the *Gaelic American* and the *Irish-American*, and Abood ("Reception of the Abbey Theatre") consults only the *Gaelic American* and the *Irish World.* What's worse, though, is that neither Oppen, writing in 1943, nor Blackadder, writing in 2003, consulted the *Gaelic American* as a primary source; instead, they relied on the quotations in *Our Irish Theatre* or in other secondary sources. Clearly the practice of overrelying on Lady Gregory's version of events enjoyed a long tradition among commentators.
13. Blackadder, "This is Not Irish Life!," 104.
14. Abood, "Reception of the Abbey Theatre," 9.
15. Dalsimer, "Players in the Western World," 80.
16. Oppen, "The Irish Players in America," 11.
17. Untitled notice, *GA,* August 5, 1911.
18. "Shaemas O'Sheel's Poems," *GA,* August 19, 1911.
19. "Ancient Irish Poetry: Selected Translations by Professor Kuno Meyer," *GA,* September 2, 1911.
20. "Irish Folk Tales," *GA,* September 2, 1911.
21. *Devoy's Post Bag,* vol. 2, ed. William O'Brien and Desmond Ryan (Dublin: CJ Fallon, 1953), 365.

22. "So-Called Irish Players on the Wrong Track," *IW,* September 2, 1911.
23. Paula M. Kane, "'Staging a Lie': Boston Irish-Catholicism and the New Irish Drama," in *Religion and Identity,* ed. Patrick O'Sullivan, Irish World Wide Series 5 (Leicester and New York: Leicester University Press and St. Martin's Press, 1996), 114.
24. "So-Called Irish Players on the Wrong Track," *IW,* September 2, 1911.
25. Kane, "Staging a Lie," 128.
26. M. Kenny, S.J., "The 'Irish' Players and Playwrights," *America,* September 30, 1911.
27. Ibid.
28. "Irish Opinion on 'The Irish Players,'" *America,* October 7, 1911.
29. "The Plays of the 'Irish' Players," *America,* November 4, 1911.
30. "An Un-Irish Play," *GA,* September 23, 1911.
31. Murphy, "The Reception of Synge's *Playboy*," 528.
32. "An Un-Irish Play," *GA,* September 23, 1911.
33. Quoted in Terence Brown, *The Life of W. B. Yeats: A Critical Biography* (Oxford: Blackwell Publishers, 1999), 120.
34. "Irishmen Will Stamp Out the Playboy," *GA,* October 14, 1911.
35. Murphy, "The Reception of Synge's *Playboy*," 528.
36. Lady Gregory, *Our Irish Theatre,* 222.
37. "Irish Players Well Received in Boston," *GA,* September 30, 1911.
38. "The Irish Players," *BP,* September 30, 1911.
39. "Careless Editing," *America,* November 4, 1911
40. "The Irish Players," *BP,* September 30, 1911.
41. Quoted in Gregory, *Our Irish Theatre,* 254.
42. See Gregory, *Our Irish Theatre,* 101; Blackadder, "This is Not Irish Life!," 103; and Dalsimer, "Players in the Western World," 77.
43. "Dr. J. T. Gallagher Denounces Irish Plays, Says They Are Vulgar, Unnatural, Anti-National and Anti-Christian," *Boston Post,* October 4, 1911.
44. "The Plymouth Players," *BP* October 14, 1911.
45. "The Irish Players," *BP,* October 21, 1911.
46. Rev. M. P. Mahon, "A Critique," *BP,* October 21, 1911.
47. "Currai an tSaogail," *IW*, October 28, 1911.
48. Ibid.
49. "Irish Players Well Received in Boston," *GA,* September 30, 1911.
50. Lyman, "Critical Reaction to Irish Drama," 372–73.
51. William Butler Yeats, "J. M. Synge and the Ireland of His Time," *The Forum,* August 1911.
52. "Irish Players Well Received in Boston," *GA,* September 30, 1911.
53. George Bernard Shaw, *John Bull's Other Island,* in *Modern Irish Drama,* ed. John P. Harrington (New York: W. W. Norton, 1991), 147.
54. Whether the story of the sheltered parricide was told to Synge in jest or in truth, John Harrington points out that Synge nevertheless revised the outcome significantly: "In the source story the people are incorruptible in solidarity, in hiding the fugitive from the police . . . However, the success of the community was precisely what he wrote out of the tale in adaptation" (*The Irish Play,* 56–57). In his influential study *Synge and Anglo-Irish Literature* (Cork: Cork University Press, 1947), Daniel Corkery takes Synge's claims for veracity at face value but writes of the incident, "The curious thought strikes one that the man himself who, having killed his father, found refuge among the people until he escaped, may have looked on

Synge's drama with his own eyes, when the Abbey company took it to America"
(191).

55. Edward Hirsch, "The Gallous Story and the Dirty Deed: The Two *Playboys,*" *Modern Drama* 26 (March 1983): 86.

56. Quoted in B. L. Reid, *The Man from New York: John Quinn and His Friends* (New York: Oxford University Press, 1968), 115.

57. Ibid.

58. Lyman, "Critical Reaction to Irish Drama," 370.

59. Ibid., 372.

60. Abood, "Reception of the Abbey Theatre," 8.

61. J. B. Yeats, "Synge and the Irish," *Harper's Weekly,* November 25, 1911.

62. Quoted in Colm Toibin, *Lady Gregory's Toothbrush* (Madison: University of Wisconsin Press, 2002), 65.

63. "Bernard Shaw's Views on the Irish Players and Clan-Na-Gael," *ADV,* December 16, 1911.

64. Hirsch, "The Gallous Story and the Dirty Deed," 90–91.

65. John M. Synge, *The Complete Plays* (New York: Vintage, 1960), 3–4.

66. Shaun Richards and David Cairns, "Reading a Riot: The 'Reading Formation' of Synge's Abbey Audience," *Literature and History* 13, no. 2 (1987): 229.

67. Harrington, *The Irish Play,* 64–65.

68. William Butler Yeats, *The Collected Works of W. B. Yeats,* vol. 3, *Autobiographies,* ed. William H. O'Donnell and Douglas N. Archibald (New York: Scribner, 1995), 347.

69. Oscar Wilde, "The Decay of Lying," in *The Artist as Critic: Critical Writings of Oscar Wilde,* ed. Richard Ellmann (Chicago: University of Chicago Press, 1982), 307.

70. Ibid., 297.

71. Arthur Power, *Conversations with Joyce,* ed. Clive Hart (London: Millington, 1974), 33.

72. Richard Seaver, *The Tender Hour of Twilight: Paris in the '50s, New York in the '60s; A Memoir of Publishing's Golden Age,* ed. Jeanette Seaver (New York: Farrar, Straus and Giroux), 144.

73. Kane, "Staging a Lie," 115.

74. Quoted in Gregory, *Our Irish Theatre,* 102–3.

75. Doris Kearns Goodwin, *The Fitzgeralds and the Kennedys: An American Saga* (New York: St. Martin's Press, 1991), 204–7.

76. Reid, *The Man from New York,* 13.

77. J. D. Hackett, letter to the editor, *Advocate,* October 7, 1911.

78. James P. Conway, "A Justification of Synge's Study of One Side of the Irish Character," *New York Sun,* November 25, 1911.

79. "Seamus M'Manus Raps 'The Playboy'" *New York Times,* November 27, 1911.

80. "MacManus Raps the Play," *GA,* December 9, 1911.

81. "An Honest American View," *GA,* December 9, 1911.

82. Ibid.

83. Perhaps not surprisingly, a James Reidy is described in Golway's biography of John Devoy as an "assistant at the *Gaelic American* . . . a young redhead with a large and rambunctious family" (*Irish Rebel,* 190).

84. Quoted in Lyman, "Critical Reaction to Irish Drama," 360.

85. Patrick L. Quinlan, "Warm Words from 'a Real Irishman,'" *New York Sun,* November 29, 1911.

86. Pat Bell, "The Irish Players," *ADV*, December 9, 1911.

87. George O'Neill, "Irish Drama and Irish Views," *American Catholic Quarterly*, April 1912, 323.

88. Ibid., 325.

89. Ibid., 327–28.

90. Wilde, "The Decay of Lying," 297.

91. "An Impartial Committee's Report," *IW*, November 4, 1911.

92. "Bernard Shaw's Views on the Irish Players and Clan-Na-Gael," *ADV*, December 16, 1911.

93. "Shaw Scores Philadelphia," *New York Times*, January 20, 1912.

94. Murphy, "The Reception of Synge's *Playboy*," 532.

95. See Gregory, *Our Irish Theatre*, 236–39.

96. "Bernard Shaw's Greatest Masterpiece," *GA*, December 16, 1911.

97. "Shaw Gives Himself Away," *GA*, December 16, 1911.

98. Harrington, *The Irish Play*, 64.

99. Stephen M. Faherty, "Pshaw," *ADV*, December 16, 1911.

100. "A Letter from the Playboy Himself," *IA*, February 17, 1911.

101. "Jew Papers and Irish Readers," *GA*, December 9, 1911.

102. "Yeats's Anti- Irish Campaign," *GA*, November 18, 1911.

103. Gearoid MacCarthaig, "A Shameless and Mercenary Crew," *Irish World*, November 11, 1911.

104. Gregory, *Our Irish Theatre*, 112.

105. Ibid., 121.

106. Reid, *The Man from New York*, 117.

107. On McGarrity's historical importance, see Kenny, *The American Irish*, 194–95; and Golway, *Irish Rebel*, 194–295. The Falvey Memorial Library at Villanova University also houses a Joseph McGarrity Collection, much of which has been digitized.

108. Joseph McGarrity, "On Verses by Yeats in 'The Smart Set,'" typescript: "Poems of Joseph McGarrity," n.d., Joseph McGaritty Papers, Joseph McGaritty Collection, Falvey Memorial Digital Library, Villanova University, https://digital.library.villanova.edu/Record/vudl:140708.

109. Quoted in Gregory, *Our Irish Theatre*, 235.

110. "New York's Protest against a Vile Play," *GA*, December 2, 1911.

111. "Playboy Dead as a Nail in the Door," *GA*, December 9, 1911.

112. "Denial from Irish Girls," *GA*, December 30, 1911.

113. "Protests of No Avail," *GA*, November 11, 1911. It is not clear if the *Gaelic American* used the term "wasps" as in the modern demographic shorthand, WASPs, for "white Anglo-Saxon Protestants" or simply as part of a derogatory phrase describing certain journalists, that is, "editorial wasps." If it was the former, though, then this use of the term would predate the *Oxford English Dictionary*'s first recorded use by a remarkable fifty-one years. But in either case, the "wasps" are unequivocally presented as harboring nativist, anti-Irish sentiment.

114. "Jew Papers and Irish Readers," *GA*, December 9, 1911.

115. Ibid.

116. Iveragh, "Protestors Were Right," *GA*, December 16, 1911.

117. "Jew Papers and Irish Readers," *GA*, December 9, 1911.

118. Thomas N. Brown, *Irish-American Nationalism, 1870–1890* (Philadelphia: Lippincott, 1966), 182.

119. "Deserved Rebuke to Irish Players," *ADV,* December 2, 1911.
120. Harrington, *Irish Play,* 69.
121. Corrig O'Sheen, "W. B. Yeats and His Work," *ADV,* November 4, 1911.
122. Gregory, *Our Irish Theatre,* 105.
123. Louis Sherwin, "Applause for Irish Players Quickly Drowns All the Hisses," *Globe and Commercial Advertiser,* November 21, 1911.
124. Mary F. McWhorter, "The Abbey Players and Their Plays," *National Hibernian,* March 15, 1913.
125. Ibid.
126. Ibid.
127. Wilde, "The Decay of Lying," 306.

Chapter 5: Meet The New Gossoon, *Same as the Old Gossoon*

1. Maureen Murphy, "Irish-American Theatre," in *Ethnic Theatre in the United States,* ed. Maxine Schwartz Seller (Westport, Conn.: Greenwood Press, 1983), 226.
2. Quoted in Terence Brown, *The Life of W. B. Yeats: A Critical Biography* (Oxford: Blackwell Publishers, 1999), 120.
3. Adele Dalsimer, "Players in the Western World: The Abbey Theatre's American Tours," *Eire-Ireland* 16, no. 4 (Winter 1981): 87–91. Dalsimer identifies a total of seven American tours made by the Abbey Theatre between 1911 and 1938. But other scholars list a total of nine tours during this period: (1) 1911–12, (2) 1913, (3) 1914, (4) 1921–22, (5) 1927–28, (6) 1931, (7) 1932–33, (8) 1934–35, (9) 1937–38. Dalsimer appears to have omitted the 1921–22 and 1927–28 tours from her list, probably because these tours each featured extremely limited repertoires, the former offering only Robinson's *Whiteheaded Boy* and the latter only O'Casey's *Juno and the Paycock* and *The Plough and the Stars.*
4. Ibid., 92.
5. George Jean Nathan, "Erin Go Blah," *Newsweek,* December 27, 1937
6. Dalsimer, "Players in the Western World," 92.
7. Adrian Frazier, "Barry Fitzgerald: From Abbey Tours to Hollywood Films," in *Irish Theatre on Tour,* ed. Nicholas Grene and Chris Morash (Dublin: Carysfort Press, 2005), 89–93.
8. These lines are from the infamous *Silver Tassie* letter which is quoted in Roy Foster, *W. B. Yeats: A Life,* vol. 2, *The Arch-Poet* (Oxford: Oxford University Press, 2003), 367.
9. Quoted in Robert Lowery, *A Whirlwind in Dublin: The Plough and the Stars Riots* (Westport, Conn.: Greenwood Press, 1984), 31.
10. Dalsimer, "Players in the Western World," 90. See also "Irish Groups Here Fight Abbey Plays," *New York Times,* January 27, 1933.
11. "Ireland in New York," *Time,* December 21, 1931.
12. Brooks Atkinson, "Making or Breaking O'Casey," *New York Times,* November 10, 1929.
13. For an insightful discussion of Farrell's brief but consequential career as a promoter of Irish art in New York, see Eimar O'Connor, "America Called: The Helen Hackett Gallery and the Irish Art Rooms, 1924–1934," *New Hibernia Review* 15, no. 4 (Winter 2011): 16–33. In his zeal for Irish art and literature, as well as in his talent for promoting Irish artists, Farrell in the 1930s seems like something of a spiritual descendant of John Quinn, who had passed away in 1924.

Interestingly enough, Farrell's *Times* obituary (August 1, 1992) explains how in 1959 Farrell became involved in a legal imbroglio concerning the publication by Peter Kavanagh Hand-Press of material from the John Quinn papers owned by the New York Public Library.

14. "Replies to Attack on Abbey Players," *New York Times*, January 28, 1933.

15. "New Attack Made on Abbey Theatre," *New York Times*, May 10, 1934.

16. John P. Harrington, *The Irish Play on the New York Stage, 1874–1966* (Lexington: University Press of Kentucky, 1997), 114.

17. Grenville Vernon, "The Play and Screen," *The Commonweal*, November 9, 1934.

18. Elizabeth Jordan, "Sean O'Casey's Crawling World," *America*, November 24, 1934.

19. "Boston v. O'Casey," *Time*, January 28, 1935.

20. Terence L. Connolly, S.J., "O'Casey's Pen," *America*, February 2, 1935.

21. Terence L. Connolly, S.J., "Critics, Interviews and Sean O'Casey," *America*, January 19, 1935. Despite the vehemence of his opposition to O'Casey, Connolly was supportive of T. C. Murray's career; see Albert J. Degiacomo, "'Gloom without Sunshine': The Reception of T. C. Murray in America, 1911–1938," *Éire-Ireland* 30, no. 3 (Fall 1995): 163.

22. Harrington, *The Irish Play*, 120.

23. George Tyler, *Whatever Goes Up: The Hazardous Fortunes of a Natural Born Gambler* (Indianapolis: Bobbs-Merrill Company, 1934), 250.

24. Dalsimer, "Players in the Western World," 93.

25. Harrington, *The Irish Play*, 100.

26. Lennox Robinson, *Curtain Up: An Autobiography* (London: Michael Joseph, 1942), 41–42.

27. Thomas N. Brown, *Irish-American Nationalism, 1870–1890* (Philadelphia: Lippincott, 1966), 179.

28. Quoted in Terry Golway, *Irish Rebel: John Devoy and America's Fight for Ireland's Freedom* (New York: St. Martin's Press, 1999), 319.

29. Murphy, "Irish-American Theatre," 231.

30. For a fuller history of the TDIP, an organization that continued producing Irish plays until 1997, see Stephen Butler, "Remembering the Thomas Davis Irish Players: Importers of Ireland's National Drama, 1933–1997," *New York Irish History* 28 (2014): 40–49.

31. Eric Bentley, "Irish Theatre: Splendeurs et Miseres," *Poetry* 79, no. 4 (January 1952): 231.

32. Daniel P. Moynihan, *Beyond the Melting Pot: The Negroes, Puerto Ricans, Jews, Italians, and Irish of New York City*, 2nd ed. (Cambridge: MIT Press, 1970), 253.

33. For a full list of all the plays performed by the TDIP, see Butler, "Remembering the Thomas Davis Irish Players."

34. William Butler Yeats, *The Collected Works of W. B. Yeats*, vol. 7, *Letters to the New Island*, ed. George Bornstein and Hugh Witemeyer (New York: Macmillan, 1989), 3.

35. William Butler Yeats, *Theatre and Nationalism in Twentieth-Century Ireland*, ed. Robert O'Driscoll (Toronto: University of Toronto Press, 1971), 85–86.

36. "William Butler Yeats Ireland's Greatest Poet, World Renowned in Literary Realm, Dies in France," *Gaelic American*, February 4, 1939.

37. "'Stage Irishman' Struts at the Lyceum Theatre," *Gaelic American*, February 18, 1939.

38. Oscar Wilde, "The Decay of Lying," in *The Artist as Critic: Critical Writings of Oscar Wilde*, ed. Richard Ellmann (Chicago: University of Chicago Press, 1982), 308–9.

Chapter 6: Through a Bowl of Bitter Tears, Darkly

1. Quoted in *James Joyce: A Literary Reference*, ed. A. Nicholas Fargnoli (New York: Carroll & Graf Publishers, 2003), 95.
2. Thomas Beer, *The Mauve Decade* (1926; New York: Vintage Books, 1961), 114.
3. This play on words is borrowed from Maurizia Boscagli and Enda Duffy, "Joyce's Face," in *Marketing Modernisms: Self-Promotion, Canonization, and Rereading*, ed. Kevin Dettmar and Stephen Watt (Ann Arbor: University of Michigan Press, 1996), 133–60.
4. Ann McCullough, O.P., "Joyce's Early Publishing History in America," in *James Joyce: The Centennial Symposium*, ed. Morris Beja (Urbana: University of Illinois Press, 1986), 187–88.
5. For an interesting contextualization of the production, see John P. Harrington, "James Joyce Downtown," in *The Irish Play on the New York Stage, 1874–1966* (Lexington: University Press of Kentucky, 1997), 75–98.
6. Quoted in Paul Vanderham, *James Joyce and Censorship: The Trials of Ulysses* (New York: New York University Press, 1998), 89.
7. Untitled review, *America*, February 3, 1917.
8. Francis Hackett, "Green Sickness," *New Republic*, March 3, 1917, 139.
9. John Quinn, "James Joyce, A New Irish Novelist," *Vanity Fair*, May 1917, 48, 128.
10. Padraic Colum, "James Joyce," *Pearson's Magazine*, May 1918, 40–41.
11. Francis Hackett, Review of *Exiles*, *The New Republic*, October 12, 1918, 318.
12. Padraic Colum, "James Joyce as a Dramatist," *The Nation*, October 12, 1918, 430.
13. Stephen J. Brown, S.J., *Ireland in Fiction: A Guide to Irish Novels, Tales, Romances, and Folk-Lore* (Dublin: Maunsel and Company, 1919).
14. Stephen J. Brown, S.J., *A Readers' Guide to Irish Fiction* (London: Longmans, Green and Co., 1910), and *A Guide to Books on Ireland*, pt. 1, *Prose Literature, Poetry, Music and Plays* (London: Longmans, Green and Co., 1912).
15. Brown, *Ireland in Fiction*, 149.
16. Ibid.
17. William S. Brockman, "American Librarians and Early Censorship of *Ulysses*: 'Aiding the Cause of Free Expression'?," *Joyce Studies Annual* 5 (Summer 1994): 57.
18. Timothy Meagher, *The Columbia Guide to Irish American History* (New York: Columbia University Press, 2005), 256.
19. Stephen J. Brown, S.J., "The National Idea in Novels," *IW*, June 26, 1920.
20. Advertisement for "Gems of Irish Propaganda," *IW*, June 26, 1920.
21. Untitled notice, *IW*, June 26, 1920. Apparently the colonel shared an interest with James Joyce not just in autobiographical writing but in the Bard. See "A Comic Shakespeare," *New York Times*, May 7, 1904, which reviews Colonel Joyce's curious-sounding book *Shakespeare: Personal Recollections*. Another connection: like Joyce's father, John, this John Joyce was a revenue agent accused of impropriety. Colonel Joyce was convicted for participating in the Whiskey Ring scandal in St. Louis but was later pardoned by President Hayes.
22. William V. Shannon, *The American Irish: A Political and Social Portrait* (New York: Macmillan, 1963), 167.
23. Jackson R. Breyer, "Joyce, *Ulysses*, and the *Little Review*," *South Atlantic Quarterly* 66, no. 2 (Spring 1967):149.

24. Ibid., 153–55.
25. Vanderham, *James Joyce and Censorship*, 6.
26. Ibid., 2.
27. Quoted in Breyer, "Joyce, *Ulysses*, and the *Little Review*," 155–56.
28. Quoted in B. L. Reid, *The Man from New York: John Quinn and His Friends* (New York: Oxford University Press, 1968), 447.
29. Quoted ibid., 446–47.
30. Ibid., 448.
31. Quoted ibid., 449.
32. Quoted in Breyer, "Joyce, *Ulysses*, and the *Little Review*," 158.
33. Ibid., 160.
34. Quoted in Reid, *The Man from New York*, 454.
35. Margaret Anderson, *My Thirty Years' War* (New York: Horizon Press, 1970), 219.
36. Ibid., 221.
37. Quoted in Reid, *The Man from New York*, 455.
38. Quoted ibid.
39. Lawrence Rainey, *Institutions of Modernism: Literary Elites and Public Culture* (New Haven: Yale University Press, 1998), 47–50.
40. Mary Colum, "The Confessions of James Joyce," *Freeman*, July 19, 1922, 450–52.
41. Ibid.
42. Joseph Kelly, *Our Joyce: From Outcast to Icon* (Austin: University of Texas Press, 1998), 9.
43. Joseph Brooker, *Joyce's Critics: Transitions in Reading and Culture* (Madison: University of Wisconsin Press, 2004).
44. Ernest Boyd, *Ireland's Literary Renaissance* (New York: Alfred A. Knopf, 1922), 404.
45. Harrington, *The Irish Play*, 89.
46. Boyd, *Ireland's Literary Renaissance*, 405.
47. Ernest Boyd, "Order Established in the Literary Choas [*sic*] of James Joyce; A Guide to 'Ulysses' and Its Author," *New York Times Book Review*, March 2, 1924; Ernest Boyd, "Concerning James Joyce," *New York World*, January 25, 1925; Ernest Boyd, "James Joyce," *Neighborhood Playbill* 3 (1924–25): 1–2.
48. Reid, *The Man from New York*, 530.
49. Quoted ibid., 457.
50. Lawrence Weschler, "Vermeer in Bosnia," in *Occasions for Writing: Evidence, Idea, Essay*, ed. Pat C. Hoy II and Robert DiYanni (Boston: Wadsworth, Cenage Learning, 2008), 780. Joyce is actually a felt presence in the latter part of Weschler's essay. Weschler describes the interethnic violence that followed the breakup of Yugoslavia as a return to a nightmarish cycle of history driven by "the relentless maw of vengeance," a cycle of history he connects to "the moral universe of epic poetry: the Iliad, Beowulf, the Chanson de Roland, the Mahabharata, and of course, *Finnegans Wake*" (784).
51. Quoted in Reid, *The Man from New York*, 530.
52. "Notes of the Week," *ADV*, March 5, 1927.
53. Leo Hamalian, "Nobody Knows My Names: Samuel Roth and the Underside of Modern Letters," *Journal of Modern Literature 3, no. 4* (April 1974): 894–95.
54. "Notes of the Week," *ADV*, March 5, 1927.
55. "Review of Irish and Catholic Books and Authors," *ADV*, June 3, 1939.
56. R. D. Joyce, "The Boys of Wexford," *IW*, November 18, 1933.

57. P. W. Joyce, "How Ancient Irish Built and Arranged Their Houses," *GA*, January 6, 1934.

58. "A Hurler's Viewpoint on the Galway-Kerry Game," *IW*, May 20, 1939.

59. "Death of Michael Joyce," *GA*, February 1, 1941.

60. Francis Talbot, S.J., "Ulysses the Dirty," *America*, September 1, 1934.

61. Vanderham, *James Joyce and Censorship*, 130.

62. Morris L. Ernst, "Reflections on the 'Ulysses' Trial and Censorship," *James Joyce Quarterly* 3, no. 1 (Fall 1965): 4.

63. Vanderham, *James Joyce and Censorship*, 131.

64. Ibid., 144.

65. "Conboy Recites from *Ulysses* and Girl Flees," *New York Daily News*, May 18, 1934.

66. Ernst, "Reflections," 5.

67. Quoted in Richard Ellmann, *James Joyce*, new and rev. ed. (Oxford: Oxford University Press, 1982), 726n.

68. *Letters of James Joyce*, vol. 3, ed. Richard Ellmann (New York: Viking Press, 1966), 444.

69. Ibid., 403.

70. Michael J. Lennon, "James Joyce," *Catholic World*, March 1931.

71. Oliver St. John Gogarty, "The Joyce I Knew," *Saturday Review of Literature*, January 25, 1941.

72. Padraic Colum, "Oliver Gogarty on James Joyce," *Saturday Review of Literature*, February 22, 1941.

73. "Notes and Comment," *ADV*, January 18, 1941.

74. John J. Doyle, "James Joyce," *ADV*, January 25, 1941.

75. "Mr. Martin Conboy to Address the American Fraternity Sons of Erin," *ADV*, January 25, 1941.

76. "Notes and Comment," *ADV*, February 1, 1941.

77. Mary Colum, *Life and the Dream* (Garden City, N.Y.: Doubleday, 1947), 381.

78. Stephen J. Brown, S.J., and Thomas McDermott, *A Survey of Catholic Literature* (Milwaukee: Bruce Publishing Company, 1949), 203.

79. Ibid., 203–4.

80. Ibid., 202.

81. L. A. G. Strong, *The Sacred River: An Approach to James Joyce* (New York: Pellegrini & Cudahy, 1951), 161.

82. Sam Hynes, "The Catholicism of James Joyce: The Artist as Apostate," *The Commonweal*, February 1952, 487–89.

83. Arland Ussher, "James Joyce: Doubting Thomist and Joking Jesuit," in *Three Great Irishmen: Shaw, Yeats, Joyce* (New York: Devin-Adair Company, 1953), 115–60.

84. William T. Noon, S.J., *Joyce and Aquinas* (New Haven: Yale University Press, 1957).

85. Kevin Sullivan, *Joyce among the Jesuits* (New York: Columbia University Press, 1958).

86. J. Mitchell Morse, *The Sympathetic Alien: James Joyce and Catholicism* (New York: New York University Press, 1959).

87. Mary and Padraic Colum, *Our Friend James Joyce* (Garden City, N.Y.: Doubleday, 1958).

88. Jeffrey Segall, *Joyce in America: Cultural Politics and the Trials of Ulysses* (Berkeley: University of California Press, 1993), 9.

89. Ibid., 168.

90. Ibid., 140–41.

91. I recently tried to verify this memory by tracking down the book with the annotation, but unfortunately, the library at Cathedral Prep is no longer a space housing books but rather a "digital media center."

92. Hugh Kenner, *Dublin's Joyce* (London: Chatto & Windus, 1955).

93. Richard Ellmann, *James Joyce* (New York: Oxford University Press, 1959).

94. Herbert Howarth, *The Irish Writers, 1880–1940* (New York: Hill and Wang, 1958), 288.

95. Iona College Libraries, New Rochelle, N.Y., Ryan Library Irish Collection, I 820.9 H 853i.

96. John Fitzgerald Kennedy, *Joint Sitting of the Dáil Éireann and Seanad Éireann on the Occasion of the Visit of John Fitzgerald Kennedy President of the United States* (Dublin: Stationery Office, Cahill & Co., 1963), 11.

97. James Joyce, *Ulysses,* ed. Hans Walter Gabler (New York: Vintage, 1986), 1. 249.

Chapter 7: Receptions of an Irish Rebel

1. Michael O'Sullivan, *Brendan Behan: A Life* (Boulder: Roberts Rinehart, 1999), 263.

2. Thomas Maier, *The Kennedys: America's Emerald Kings* (New York: Basic Books, 2003), 363.

3. Thomas Kinsella, *Davis, Mangan, Ferguson? Tradition and the Irish Writer* (Dublin: Dolman Press, 1970), 64–65.

4. Daniel P. Moynihan, "The Irish," in *Beyond the Melting Pot: The Negroes, Puerto Ricans, Jews, Italians, and Irish of New York City,* 2nd ed. (Cambridge: MIT Press, 1970), 253.

5. Ibid., 254.

6. Henry Lee, "Behan Nixed, but He Marches On," *New York Daily News,* March 15, 1961.

7. O'Sullivan, *Brendan Behan,* 12–13. Koch's quip is recounted in Tim Russert, *Big Russ & Me* (New York: Miramax Books, 2004), 262.

8. Henry Lee, "Jersey City Irishmen Get You Know Who," *New York Daily News,* March 16, 1961.

9. Quoted in Ulick O'Connor, *Brendan* (Englewood Cliffs, N.J.: Prentice Hall, 1970), 279.

10. Ibid., 267.

11. Brendan Gill, "The Borstal Boy in New York," *Grand Street* 8, no. 4 (Summer 1989): 106.

12. Historical/biographical note, "Guide to the James J. Comerford Papers AIA.010," Tamiment Library & Robert F. Wagner Labor Archives, New York University, http://dlib.nyu.edu/findingaids/html/tamwag/aia_010/.

13. Ann M. Shea and Marion Casey, *The Irish Experience in New York: A Select Bibliography* (New York: New York Irish History Roundtable, 1995), 10.

14. Quoted in O'Connor, *Brendan,* 183.

15. Kenneth Cox Lyman, "Critical Reaction to Irish Drama on the New York Stage, 1900–1958" (PhD diss., University of Wisconsin, 1960), 684.

16. Quoted in O'Connor, *Brendan,* 231.

17. Euphemia Van Rensselaer Wyatt, "Theater," *Catholic World,* February 1959.

18. Richard Hayes, "The Irish Presence," *Commonweal,* January 23, 1959, 438–39.

19. Sam Hynes, "An Irish Success," *Commonweal,* March 4, 1960, 627–29.

20. Advertisement for *Broth of a Boy, ADV,* January 2, 1960.

21. Edmund F. O'Rourke, letter to the editor, *ADV,* March 12, 1960.
22. Daniel Patrick Moynihan credits this moniker to the journalist Heywood Broun but does not reveal the context in which the label was applied. See Moynihan, *Beyond the Melting Pot,* 282.
23. Claire Grimes, "History of the *Irish Echo,*" *New York Irish History* 8 (1993–94): 5.
24. Ray O'Hanlon, *The New Irish Americans* (Boulder: Roberts Rinehart, 1998), 155–56.
25. Robert C. Roman, "Sean O'Casey and His Writings Closely Studied in New Biography," review of David Krause's *Sean O'Casey: The Man and His Work, IE,* August 20, 1960.
26. Frank O'Connor, "Behan the Terrible," *IE,* August 20, 1960.
27. John J. Reagan, "Beahan [*sic*] and O'Casey," *IE,* September 24, 1960.
28. "'The Hostage' First Was Written, Played in Irish," *IE,* September 10, 1960.
29. "Irish Actress for Broadway," *IE,* August 27, 1960.
30. Sean Maxwell, "Behan's 'Agro-Phobia,'" *IE,* August 27, 1960.
31. Michael Sheehan, "Brendan Behan," *IW,* September 17, 1960.
32. Michael Sheehan, "Brendan Behan," *IW,* September 24, 1960.
33. Pete Lee, "Pete Lee Says," *ADV,* September 17, 1960.
34. Pete Lee, "Pete Lee Says," *ADV,* October 1, 1960.
35. Beatrice Behan, with Des Hickey and Gus Smith, *My Life with Brendan* (London: Leslie Frewin, 1973), 26.
36. Gill, "The Borstal Boy in New York," 111.
37. "Irish Not Heavy Drinkers Says Le Mass," *ADV,* September 3, 1960.
38. "Explode a Damaging Myth," *ADV,* September 3, 1960.
39. "Not Behan's Business," *ADV,* September 3, 1960.
40. Untitled editorial, *ADV,* September 10, 1960.
41. Quoted in O'Connor, *Brendan,* 267.
42. Mary Jane Grimes, "They Can Keep 'The Hostage,'" *IE,* October, 1 1960.
43. Frank O'Connor, "The Borstal Bostoon," *IE,* October 22, 1960.
44. "Walk-out Protest at Behan Play," *IE,* November 26, 1960.
45. Stephen P. Ryan, "Play of the Month," *Catholic World,* November 1960.
46. Paul Vanderham, *James Joyce and Censorship: The Trials of Ulysses* (New York: New York University Press, 1998), 152.
47. Stephen P. Ryan, "Play of the Month," *Catholic World,* November 1960.
48. Brendan Behan, letter to the editor, *ADV,* October 29, 1960.
49. Brendan Behan, letter to the editor, *IW,* November 5, 1960.
50. Theophilus Lewis, "Theatre," *America,* October 22, 1960.
51. Pete Lee, "Pete Lee Says: The Hostage Is on the Move," *ADV,* November 19, 1960.
52. Edward F. X. Hughes, letter to the editor, *ADV*, December 3, 1960.
53. P. O Murcada, letter to the editor, *ADV*, November 12, 1960.
54. Sean Maxwell: "Behan's Trail of Glory," *IE,* September 24, 1960.
55. Brendan Behan, *The Hostage,* in *The Complete Plays* (New York: Grove Press, 1978), 203–4.
56. Rae Jeffs, *Brendan Behan: Man and Showman* (London: Corgi Books, 1968), 143.
57. Frank O'Connor, "Buttermilk on Broadway," *IE,* December 17, 1960.
58. Declan Kiberd, *Inventing Ireland: The Literature of a Modern Nation* (Cambridge: Harvard University Press, 1995), 525.
59. Advertisement for *The Country Boy, IW,* November 19, 1960.
60. Advertisement for *The Country Boy, ADV,* February 25, 1961.

61. C.B.Q., "The Country Boy," *ADV,* December 17, 1960.
62. "'The Country Boy' Opens on November 19," *ADV,* October 29, 1960.
63. Quoted in John B. Duff, *The Irish in the United States* (Belmont, Calif.: Wadsworth, 1971), 87.
64. John Fitzgerald Kennedy, *Joint Sitting of the Dáil Éireann and Seanad Éireann on the Occasion of the Visit of John Fitzgerald Kennedy President of the United States* (Dublin: Stationery Office, Cahill & Co., 1963), 15.
65. Hugh Hardy, "What's New . . . with Hugh," *IE,* March 28, 1964.
66. "Carbery Calling," *IE,* April 4, 1964.
67. Sean Maxwell, "In Memoriam," *IE,* April 11, 1964.
68. Pete Lee, "Pete Lee Says: A Man Called Behan," *ADV,* March 28, 1964.
69. Notice for Brendan Behan memorial mass, *ADV,* April 4, 1964.
70. Maureen Patricia Ford, "Brendan Behan—The Rebel," *IW,* April 4, 1964.
71. "Borstal Governor Calls Brendan Behan Intensely Religious," *IW,* April 18, 1964.
72. "News and Notes," *IW,* April 4, 1964.
73. Calvin Trillin, "Democracy in Action," in *Making the Irish American: History and Heritage of the Irish in the United States,* ed. J. J. Lee and Marion R. Casey (New York: New York University Press, 2007), 535.
74. Ibid.
75. Ibid., 539.
76. Maureen Dezell, *Irish America: Coming into Clover: The Evolution of a People and a Culture* (New York, Doubleday, 2000), 216.

Conclusions

1. Michael Fitzgerald, letter to the editor, *ADV,* March 21, 1964.
2. See, for instance, Gearoid MacCarthaig, "A Shameless and Mercenary Crew," *Irish World,* November 11, 1911.
3. Thomas J. Fogarty, letter to the editor, *ADV,* March 28, 1964.
4. Daniel P. Moynihan, "The Irish," in *Beyond the Melting Pot: The Negroes, Puerto Ricans, Jews, Italians, and Irish of New York City,* 2nd ed. (Cambridge: MIT Press, 1970), 247–48.
5. John V. Kelleher, "The Perceptions of James Joyce," *Atlantic Monthly,* March 1958; Kevin Sullivan, *Joyce among the Jesuits* (New York: Columbia University Press, 1958).
6. Moynihan, "The Irish," 248.
7. See James McKillop's essay "The Unauthorized History of the American Conference for Irish Studies," unpublished but available to download on his website, http://www.jamesmackillop.com/Books.htm. See also Lawrence J. McCaffrey, "The American Committee for Irish Studies," *Irish Historical Studies* 15, no. 60 (September 1967): 446–49.
8. See the "About Us" section on the website of the Irish American Cultural Institute, http://www.iaci-usa.org/aboutus.html.
9. Joan FitzPatrick Dean, "MacLiammoir's *The Importance of Being Oscar* in America," in *Irish Theatre in America: Essays on Irish Theatrical Diaspora* (Syracuse: Syracuse University Press, 2009), 113.
10. See, for instance, Seamus Deane, introduction to *Selected Plays of Brian Friel* (Washington, D.C.: Catholic University of America Press, 1986), 16.
11. In George O'Brien, "'Meet Brian Friel': The 'Irish Press' Columns," *Irish University Review* 29, no 1 (Spring–Summer 1999): 30–41, the author analyzes the sixty col-

umns Friel wrote for the *Irish Press*, including the "American Diary" series. O'Brien does not mention that the "American Diary" columns appeared in the *Irish Echo*. When the series began, the *Echo* promised readers eleven articles from Friel, but the *Echo*'s readers did not get to see the last three columns noted by O'Brien.

12. Brian Friel, "Arrival in New York City," *IE,* October 19, 1963; "Sight-Seeing," *IE,* October 26, 1963; "History Lesson," *IE,* November 2, 1963; "On Speaking the Language," *IE,* November 9, 1963; "Lofty Debate," *IE,* November 16, 1963; "The Checking Account," *IE,* November 23, 1963; "Nostalgia," *IE,* December 7, 1963; "It's a Dog's Life," *IE,* December 14, 1963.

13. Dean, "MacLiammoir's *The Importance of Being Oscar,*" 113.

14. Davis Coakley, *Oscar Wilde: The Importance of Being Irish* (Dublin: Town House, 1994); Richard Pine, *The Thief of Reason: Oscar Wilde and Modern Ireland* (New York: St. Martin's Press, 1995); Declan Kiberd, *Inventing Ireland: The Literature of a Modern Nation* (Cambridge: Harvard University Press, 1995); Jerusha McCormack, ed., *Wilde the Irishman* (New Haven: Yale University Press, 1998).

15. Of course there are some critics who take issue with this so-called greening of Wilde. See Josephine M. Guy and Ian Small, *Oscar Wilde's Profession: Writing and the Culture Industry in the Late Nineteenth Century* (Oxford: Oxford University Press, 2000). Guy and Small are unconvinced that Wilde was driven by a sense of oppositional politics, and they highlight a number of flaws, or at least ambiguities, in this Irish nationalist thesis: Wilde's position as a Protestant landowner, the voluntary nature of his exile from Ireland, his desire to seek a position in the British civil service, and the lack of any sustained Celtic discourse in his work. See also Geoffrey Wheatcroft, "Not Green, Not Red, Not Pink," *Atlantic Monthly,* May 2003. Wheatcroft argues that Wilde has "become an object of literary graverobbing, with interested parties trying to appropriate his shroud—and forever projecting their own interests and obsessions on him."

16. William Butler Yeats, *A Book of Irish Verse: Selected from Modern Writers with an Introduction and Notes by W. B. Yeats* (London: Methuen, 1900), xxvi–xxvii.

17. Augustine Martin, "That Childhood Country: Extracts from a Biography of Patrick Kavanagh," *Irish University Review* 22, no. 1 (Spring–Summer 1992): 111–12.

18. Descriptive language quoted from the "About this Journal" section of the website of the *Irish University Review,* https://www.euppublishing.com/loi/iur. A search for John Boyle O'Reilly in Project Muse's *Éire-Ireland* holdings, which begin with vol. 29, no. 4 (1994), also turns up just one hit: an article about Justin McCarthy that mentions O'Reilly in a footnote. Ford and Devoy are much better represented in this journal (nine articles mention Ford, and twenty-one mention Devoy). As I type these sentences at my dining room table, I see in the distance a bottle of blended Australian red on whose label John Boyle O'Reilly's mug shot has been affixed. If nothing else, perhaps the integrated marketing campaign for 19 Crimes brand wine will draw the scrutiny of cultural critics interested in Irish studies.

19. Lady Wilde [Jane Francessa Elgee], *The American Irish,* undated pamphlet appended to Horace Wyndham, *Speranza: A Biography of Lady Wilde* (New York: Philosophical Library, 1951), 209–10.

20. Oscar Wilde, "Mr. Froude's Blue Book [on Ireland]," in *The Artist as Critic: Critical Writings of Oscar Wilde,* ed. Richard Ellmann (Chicago: University of Chicago Press, 1982), 136.

21. Though the controversy is well beyond the scope of this book, it is worth noting that Irish Voice, Inc., through the posting of an article titled "Forgotten White

Slaves" on the IrishCentral Facebook page on March 28, 2015, played a major role in helping to popularize a white slavery meme embraced by white supremacists. Liam Hogan of the University of Limerick wrote an open letter to the editors asking them to remove the disinformation, and Hogan has led the effort to explain the significant difference between the chattel slavery system under which African Americans suffered and the system of indentured servitude under which some Irish toiled. Hogan has posted all his work tracking the meme and debunking the myth of white slavery on the website Medium.

22. Cahir O'Doherty, "Remembering James Joyces' [*sic*] 'Ulysses' on Trial," Irish-Central, June 10, 2017, https://www.irishcentral.com/news/irishvoice/remembering-ulysses -on-trial.

23. B. L. Reid, *The Man from New York: John Quinn and His Friends* (Oxford: Oxford University Press, 1968), 441–58.

24. While trying to compose this conclusion, I learned that Hassett had presented his insights into the *Ulysses* trials in a new context; see Joseph M. Hassett, "Trump Can't Ban 'Fire and Fury.' Thank James Joyce's 100-Year-Old 'Ulysses' for That," *Washington Post*, January 11, 2018.

25. Tom Deignan, "The Battle over *Ulysses:* Joyce's Irish-American Ally," *Irish America*, October–November 2008, 41.

26. Peter Quinn, *Looking for Jimmy: A Search for Irish America* (Woodstock, N.Y.: Overlook Press, 2007), 274–75.

27. That version of radical countercultural Irishness can also be found in recent political commentary written for the mainstream press by a non-Irish-identifying academic. See Van Gosse, "Why Are All the Conservative Loudmouths Irish-Americans?" *Newsweek*, October 24, 2017, which concludes with these reflections: "When I think of [Tom] Hayden and [Elizabeth Gurley] Flynn and the Berrigans [i.e., Daniel and Phillip], that's an Irish America I can embrace, warts and all. To the devil with Bill O'Reilly and [Steve] Bannon. They're no more Irish than I am." Another example related to the larger problem I'm trying to identify is noted by the historian David M. Emmons in a sharp, insightful review of *The Immortal Irishman: The Irish Revolutionary Who Became an American Hero*, written by Timothy Egan, a *New York Times* columnist. Emmons predicted: "*Immortal Irishman* will be taken by Irish historical revisionists as further proof that Americans are incurable Irish nationalists (jingoes, really) and can't get their history straight. The revisionists will be wrong in that assessment, but that will not prevent them from dismissing Egan's book as little more than pandering." Timothy Egan, book review, *New York Irish History* 29 (2015): 61.

28. The famous aphorism comes from F. Scott Fitzgerald, "The Crack-Up," *Esquire*, February 1936, 41. The confusion about where Fitzgerald lived comes from his mention of "my drab room in the Bronx" in his nostalgic essay "My Lost City," in *The Crack-Up* (New York: New Directions, 1945), 25. One biographer states definitively that "there is no evidence that Fitzgerald lived in the Bronx"; see Matthew J. Bruccoli, *Some Sort of Grandeur: The Life of F. Scott Fitzgerald* (New York: Harcourt, Brace, Jovanovic, 1981), 99fn. But there is ample evidence that Fitzgerald lived at 200 Claremont Avenue in Morningside Heights.

29. Phillip Lopate, "How Do You End an Essay?," *Salmagundi*, no. 168/169 (Fall 2010–Winter 2011): 145.

Index

Abbey Theatre, 60–61; actors in, 110; American tour including *The Playboy*, 68–69; American tours, 109, 197n3; *The Big Birthday* (film), 153; criticism of, 117; Free State subsidy, 112–13; later American tour, success of, 115–16; saved from bankruptcy, 110; verbal attack, 74–75. *See also* Irish Players

Abood, Edward, 87

Act of Union (1801), 110

Advocate, 72; Behan letter and response, 161–63; Behan obituaries and memorials, 169; *Broth of a Boy*, advertisement, 153; comments on *The Playboy*, 91, 93; criticism of Synge, 64; "Irish Not Heavy Drinkers," 158; "Irish Plays for New York," 64; Joyce death notice, 140, 142; Lee on Behan's reputation, 156–57; Lee's defense of Behan, 162; letter denouncing *Juno and the Paycock*, 153–54; letter on Wilde, 173–74; name change, 72; review of *The Country Boy*, 166–67; review of *Finnegans Wake*, 135; review of *The Hostage*, 157; review of *The Importance of Being Oscar*, 175; review of *The Pot of Broth*, 64–66; *Roscommon Herald* reprint

on Joyce, 134; "The Wearing of the Green," 100

A.E. *See* Russell, George

Allingham, William, 36

America (Jesuit periodical), 113–14; criticism of Abbey Theatre, 76–78; criticism of Irish Players, 80; on Behan's plays, 162; "The 'Irish' Players and Playwrights," 75; review of *Portrait*, 122; Synge obituary, 66–67; "Ulysses the Dirty," 136

American Catholic Quarterly, 94

American Committee for Irish Studies, 175

An Claidheamh Soluis, 59

Anderson, Margaret, 127–30

anti-Semitism, 137; Jewish-nativist conspiracy, 104, 196n13

Arnold, Matthew, 34; *On the Study of Celtic Literature*, 25–26

Ascendancy Saxonism, 103

Atkinson, Brooks, 112–13

Atlanta Constitution, 27

audience response, 9–11

Baldwin, James, "Notes of a Native Son," 183

Beer, Thomas, 14, 121–22

Behan, Beatrice (née ffrench-Salkeld), 157

STEPHEN G. BUTLER was born and raised in Woodside, Queens, New York City. His parents, Matthew Butler of Culleens, Co. Sligo, and Anne O'Connell, of Duagh, Co. Kerry, fostered his interest in Irish culture. This interest was cultivated by teachers at PS 229, IS 73, Cathedral Prep, Iona College (BA 1999), the City College of New York (MA 2001), and Drew University (PhD 2011). During graduate school, Butler worked as a concierge; his union, Local 32BJ of the SEIU, generously supported his education through a Thomas Shortman Fund scholarship. Butler has taught courses in literature, humanities, and composition at Iona, Kean University, and New York University, where he holds an appointment as senior lecturer in the Expository Writing Program. He has published regularly in *New York Irish History,* a journal he helps edit. Butler currently lives in northern New Jersey, his exile made bearable by the company of his wife, Erin, and his daughters, Brigid, Lily, and Adare.